The
EVERYTHING®
Fundraising Book

Dear Reader:

In the twenty-first century, fundraising has emerged as a significant part of our American culture. The events of September 11, 2001, coupled with a struggling economy, have resulted in many individuals taking stock of what really matters most in life. People have turned to focusing on helping others in their community and in the world around them. The increase in fundraising efforts is seen at all levels from public schools to *Fortune* 500 corporations.

The Everything® Fundraising Book takes a look at the world of fundraising as it impacts us today, and we invite you to take on the challenge of raising funds for something you believe in. From a school bake sale to a golf tournament to e-fundraising efforts, there are so many ways in which you can raise money. The goal of reaching out and soliciting funds from donors is explored throughout the book from many perspectives. Various aspects of the fundraising process, including bookkeeping, accounting, taxes, communications, and computer equipment, are also included.

While there are many "how tos" involved in learning the best means of raising funds, the important element of FUNdraising is brought to the forefront on several occasions as a reminder that you can get great joy from, and take great pride in, your fundraising efforts.

Sincerely,

Rich Mintzer

D1444974

The EVERYTHING® Series

Editorial

Publishing Director	Gary M. Krebs
Managing Editor	Kate McBride
Copy Chief	Laura MacLaughlin
Acquisitions Editor	Eric M. Hall
Development Editor	Karen Johnson Jacot
Production Editor	Khrysti Nazzaro

Production

Production Director	Susan Beale
Production Manager	Michelle Roy Kelly
Series Designers	Daria Perreault
	Colleen Cunningham
Cover Design	Paul Beatrice
	Frank Rivera
Layout and Graphics	Colleen Cunningham
	Rachael Eiben
	Michelle Roy Kelly
	Daria Perreault
	Erin Ring
Series Cover Artist	Barry Littmann

Visit the entire Everything® Series at everything.com

THE
EVERYTHING
FUNDRAISING
BOOK

Create a strategy, plan events, increase visibility,
and raise the money you need

Rich Mintzer with Sam Friedman

Adams Media Corporation
Avon, Massachusetts

I dedicate this book to my parents, Muriel and Jerry, for their many years of inspirational and devoted fundraising work, from which I learned so much.

An Everything® Series Book.
Everything® and everything.com® are registered trademarks of F+W Publications, Inc.

Published by Adams Media, an F+W Publications Company
57 Littlefield Street, Avon, MA 02322 U.S.A.
www.adamsmedia.com

ISBN: 1-58062-953-9
Printed in the United States of America.

J I H G F E D C B

Library of Congress Cataloging-in-Publication Data
Mintzer, Richard.
The everything fundraising book / Rich Mintzer with Sam Friedman.
p.   cm.
(An everything series book)
ISBN 1-58062-953-9
1. Fund raising. I. Friedman, Sam. II. Title.
III. Series: Everything series.
HG177.M56   2003
658.15'224–dc21   2003007425

This book is available at quantity discounts for bulk purchases.
For information, call 1-800-872-5627.

SOC

Contents

Acknowledgments / ix
Top Ten Fundraising Tips You Will Learn from This Book / x
Introduction / xi

Fundraising Basics / 1
Why Have a Fundraiser? **2** • Setting a Goal **3** • Targeting an Audience **4** • Rallying Some Troops **6** • Formulating a Plan **8** • Honing and Presenting Your Plan **9**

Selecting the Fundraiser for You / 11
From Car Wash to Black-Tie Dinner **12** • Group Dynamics **12** • Establishing a Time Frame **15** • Costs to Consider **16** • Resources **17** • Quality and Customer Service **19** • Fundraising Options **19**

Getting Started / 27
Selecting or Electing a Leader **28** • Who Is on Board? **30** • Evaluating Your Personnel **32** • Who's on *the* Board? **34** • The First Meetings **36** • Motivation **38** • Fundraising Consultants **40**

Where and When? The Details of Your Fundraiser / 43
Location Selection **44** • The "Right" Date **46** • Organizing and Record Keeping **47** • Setting up a Schedule **47** • Tracking Your Progress **50** • Contingency Plans **51** • Inviting Special Guests **52** • Staging Repeat Performances **54**

Organizing the Troops / 57
Setting Guidelines **58** • Finding Volunteers **59** • Training Tips **61** • Creating Schedules **62** • Working by Committee **63** • Showing Appreciation to Volunteers **65** • Hiring Professionals **66**

The Big Bucks / 69

Assessing Your Costs **70** • Budgeting Expenses **71** • Finding Sources of Funding **73** • Individual Contributors **75** • Foundations **76** • Corporations **77** • Other Major Donors **78** • Tapping Your Sources **79** • Giving Something Back **81**

Honing Your Skills for Effective Fundraising / 83

Fancy Phone Techniques **84** • Direct Mail Campaigns **86** • Fundraising Letters **89** • Test Marketing **90** • Building Your Web Presence **90** • Public Speaking **92** • Annual Campaigns **93** • A Public Relations Primer **95**

A Lesson in Ethics / 99

Establishing a Code of Conduct **100** • Taking Gifts **102** • Conflicts of Interest **103** • Selling Mailing Lists **103** • Credibility **106** • Activities to Avoid **107**

Communications Tools and Practices / 111

Your Communications Infrastructure **112** • Knowing Who to Contact **113** • Information Storage **114** • Using a Web Page for Your Fundraiser **118** • The Future of E-Fundraising **120**

Spreading the Word! / 125

Internal Publicity **126** • Defining Your Advertising Needs **128** • Public Service Announcements **128** • Going on Air **129** • The Internet and E-Mail **130** • Online Newsletters **130** • The Print Media **131** • Signs, Flyers, and Posters **132** • Promotional Activities **133** • Printing **136** • Visual Effects **138**

11

Corporate Fundraising / 141

The Role of Corporations in Fundraising **142** • Approaching Corporations **144** • Developing Partnerships **148** • Employee Donations **149** • The United Way **151**

12

Community Fundraising / 153

Involving the Whole Community **154** • Establishing a Nucleus **154** • Identifying the Issues **157** • Making Things Happen **157** • Working with Your Community Board **158** • Finding Local Sponsors **159** • Laws and Ordinances **160** • Promoting Locally **161** • Becoming Established in the Community **162** • An Award-Winning Community Effort **164**

13

Grassroots Fundraising / 167

Small-Scale Efforts, Big Results **168** • Brainstorming **168** • Dividing up Responsibilities **170** • How Much Should You Do? **170** • Maintaining Focus **172** • Credibility **173** • Your Secret Weapon: The Warm Fuzzies **175**

14

Fundraising with Kids and Teens / 177

Getting Kids Started **178** • Teaching Kids the Ropes **179** • Kid-Friendly Possibilities **181** • School Fundraisers **183** • Selecting a Fundraising Company **184** • Rewarding a Job Well Done **187**

15

Political Fundraising / 189

The Campaign Fundraising Plan **190** • The Donor List **192** • Legal Issues **194** • The Fundraising Letter **195** • The House Party **196** • Personal Appearances **197** • Big-Name Support **198** • Image Is Everything **198** • Combating the Self-Funded Candidates **199**

16

Odds and Ends / 201
The Art of Collecting Money **202** • Ordering from Vendors **203** • Utilizing All Available Resources **204** • Shipping **205** • Baby-Sitting and Child Care **207** • Security Concerns **208** • Rehearsals or Walk-Throughs **208**

17

All about Grants / 209
Finding Grants **210** • The Application Process **213** • Timing and Follow-Up **216** • Corporate Grants **217** • Federal Grants **218**

18

Grant Writing 101 / 221
Overview of a Proposal **222** • The Project Summary **223** • About Your Organization **223** • The Problem Statement **224** • Goals and Objectives **224** • Your Plan of Action **225** • Evaluating the Program **226** • Your Budget **226** • And in the End **228** • Sample Grant Application **228**

19

Taxes and Accounting / 235
Your Tax Status **236** • Donor Contributions **238** • Deductions **240** • Filing with the IRS **240** • Bookkeeping Practices **241** • Reviewing Your Financial Picture **244** • Financial Accountability **246**

20

Measuring Success / 249
Evaluating Your Efforts **250** • Evaluation Standards **252** • Common Evaluation Errors **254** • Making Improvements **255** • Lasting Effects **257** • Wrapping up and Moving On **258** • Thank-Yous 260

Appendix A • Fundraising Resources / **261**
Appendix B • PBS: Thirty Years of Successful
Fundraising / **275**
Index / 281

Acknowledgments

A very special thank-you to some of the people who work in fundraising and helped provide valuable information for this book: Robert Altman, senior vice president for Development and Corporate Relations for Public Broadcasting Service, national headquarters in Alexandria, Virginia; June Badham, CEO and president of Corporate DevelopMint, a nonprofit consulting firm in Charleston, South Carolina; George C. Ruotolo, Jr., chairman and CEO of Ruotolo Associates Inc., professional fundraising consultants in Cresskill, New Jersey; Murray Brower, associate executive director of the Kidney & Urology Foundation of America, based in New York City; Felix Fornino, former president and current treasurer of the Adoptive Parents Committee, based in the New York–New Jersey–Connecticut region; Ed Federman of Federman Consulting, a New York City–based fundraising consulting firm.

I also want to thank Eric Hall and Nicole Faraguna of the *Borough News* magazine in Harrisburg, Pennsylvania, and journalist Rebecca Sultan. And, finally, I'd like to thank my family, whose hard work for the Kidney Foundation of New York was inspiring, and my wife, Carol, who has always shown great dedication and has worked hard for the Adoptive Parents Committee as a copresident, workshop leader, and more.

Top Ten Fundraising Tips
You Will Learn from This Book

1. Networking is important—have everyone in your group consider who they know who can donate goods and services to your fundraising activity.

2. Choose a locale for your fundraising activity that reflects the members of the organization and what the organization stands for.

3. Budget wisely—it is quite common for 50 percent of the income from a fundraiser to just cover expenses.

4. Highlight the accomplishments of your group in any grant proposal.

5. Provide proper lead time when trying to get media coverage. Magazines need greater lead time than newspapers and Web sites.

6. Take advantage of lower overhead—it costs almost nothing to send mass e-mails, including fundraising appeals, invitations, information on upcoming events, and thank-yous.

7. Raise money from corporations—studies have shown that over 80 percent of corporate employees feel a greater sense of pride and dedication to a company that is involved in philanthropic endeavors.

8. Build relationships—people are more likely to contribute if they believe in your dedication to the cause.

9. Learn where the money is centered in your town or region and understand the party demographics.

10. Use *Who's Who in America* or the *Standard & Poor Directory* to find information on potential high-profile donors.

Introduction

▶ LITTLE DID WE KNOW, as we pondered the so-called Y2K crisis, how much the world would change in the years to follow. Today, some three years later, global concerns for safety and security coupled with an unsteady economy have caused many people to reevaluate their priorities. People have been more willing than ever to focus on the needs of others in the community.

Money is fundamental to researching serious illnesses, fighting drug abuse and domestic violence, supplying urban schools with necessary computer equipment, sheltering the homeless, and helping those affected by violent crime and acts of terrorism. No matter what your cause, you will likely need to raise money at some point.

This book focuses not only on how the modern fundraiser goes about procuring money in a highly competitive world, but also on how he or she can best reach out and touch individuals in a manner that will get them to think, feel, and give.

There is an art to fundraising today, and it can become very complex, complete with software, advanced communications systems, marketing strategy, and corporate grant proposals, but at the root of it all is the same basic need—to raise money for your cause, whatever that may be. Keep in mind that the most comprehensive fundraising software program or Web sites still have not matched the success of eighty-plus years of Girl Scout cookie sales.

It is important, therefore, to take a simplified approach to raising funds, no matter how creative or complex your upcoming fundraising plan may be. We, therefore, take a practical, hands-on approach that can meet the needs of both the multimillion-dollar nonprofit organization and the local twenty-two-member PTO. After all, within the certain boundaries, there is no "right" or "wrong" means of fundraising, only the means by which you are successful at reaching your goal or goals.

The key to successful fundraising is not really whether you sell wrapping paper or scented candles, it's your inner desire to make a difference. If you have a passion and can convince others that you are working for a worthwhile cause, be it fighting domestic violence, finding a cure for Alzheimer's disease, or saving the whales, then other people will be touched and will step forward and pitch in with goods, supplies, volunteer hours, or good old money (funds!).

This book highlights examples of many small-scale fundraising efforts and builds on the theme that fundraising is doable at any level. The focus is at the local level, since fundraising really begins when a child asks his or her mom or dad if he or she will buy candy or wrapping paper to help raise money for the child's school, or when the church opens its doors for a bake sale one afternoon, or when the Cub Scouts offer car washes to the local community. Perhaps that's what is meant by the saying "charity begins at home." Ⓔ

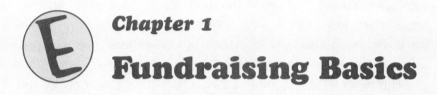

Chapter 1

Fundraising Basics

Whether it's to fix a leaky roof on an old church, buy new textbooks for the local high school, or help keep the homeless warm this winter, you have identified a need. But what next? How do you go about raising money to do the good deeds you want to do? This chapter introduces you to the world of fundraising.

Why Have a Fundraiser?

Fundraising can encompass a wide range of possibilities, from raising several million dollars for a new wing to be added to a local hospital, to raising a few hundred dollars for new sports equipment for an elementary school. The idea of fundraising, however, offers a community, school, or organization more than just a means of raising money. It can also provide camaraderie as you work together as a team, a place for individuals to use skills and talents they may not use in their everyday workplace, a lesson in responsibility for young people, and a sense of community.

Your fundraiser may be the starting point for members of your neighborhood to meet other likeminded individuals and start discussing various community issues. It may also be a way of generating support for a cause that you believe in.

Today, it is common to find schools encouraging students from grade school through college to engage in fundraising activities. While the parents could raise substantial amounts of money without the help of their children, these activities provide young people with a sense of teamwork and a lesson in responsibility.

And, of course, there is the personal satisfaction that you get from helping out a cause that you believe in.

Support and Involvement

When a group or organization, whether fraternal, charitable, or political, holds a fundraiser, they take some of the burden of financial support off of their membership and gain the support of a wider audience. This can help spur public involvement and promote public awareness.

For example, when individuals pledge money to PBS, they are becoming involved, in a small way, in the work of that organization, while also showing support. Not unlike showing up at a stockholders meeting, they can become a small part of something larger. Many people are involved in fundraising for the dual purposes of helping others and socialization. Helping to organize and run the annual carnival at your daughter's grade school not only raises money to help the school, but it's also a great way to meet other parents and get to know more people in the community.

To run a successful fundraising drive or event, you need to introduce your members, volunteers, and everyone involved in the activities to one another. You want to establish a team for a successful fundraising effort.

Good Public Relations

While raising money for a specific goal is the primary objective, be it fighting a disease or building a gymnasium, fundraising objectives also highlight and promote the work of your group or organization. You will find that while promoting a specific fundraising effort, you will also distribute literature and tell others by word of mouth about the goals and mission of your group and the cause behind your fundraiser.

For example, if representatives from the American Heart Association are collecting money at a street fair, they will very likely have fliers and data available to distribute so that the public can learn more about what they do. In addition they will probably provide important health-related news about how to keep your cholesterol levels down and similar information. Fundraising often provides a means of educating the public through providing pertinent information gathered by your organization.

Setting a Goal

Before you can set the wheels in motion, it is important that you, and everyone involved in the fundraising efforts, are clear regarding what the money will be used for. Determining your primary goal can often be the cause for great debate in groups or organizations looking to raise money. You must establish priorities for your organization—does the school need new textbooks more than it needs a new gymnasium?

Establishing priorities requires careful examination of the available data. For example, the purpose of your organization may be to fight the HIV/AIDS epidemic. There are many ways to support this cause—you must look at the data and determine what will allow you to be the most effective. Is there a greater need in your community to raise funds to help HIV/AIDS patients or to give to researchers at a medical facility who are seeking a cure for this dreaded disease?

Preliminary research, polls, and evaluations of existing solutions can help you determine which needs you want to prioritize. Studies in your community may show that money has been pouring in to support HIV/ AIDS research while little money has been donated to local housing for patients. Research may help you establish and then fine-tune your goals.

Even when the purpose seems obvious, such as raising money following the tragic events of September 11, 2001, make sure you are clear regarding how you see the funds being used. For example, many groups specifically raised funds for the families of the victims, while other groups sent money to help the relief workers at Ground Zero. Still other organizations raised money to help businesses that were affected by the tragedy.

Having a clear goal not only keeps your organization on track, but it also inspires confidence. The more clearly you have stated your goal, the more easily you will be able to convince others to spend their hard-earned money to help your cause. Do your homework. The best way to convince others to give money toward achieving a specific goal is to have the data to support your need for funding.

The benefits of setting a specific goal will help your organization structure its fundraising plans. A larger-scale goal such as building a new gymnasium will require a more detailed, larger-scale plan of action. Conversely, the goal of buying new cheerleading uniforms will take on a much smaller itinerary. Nonetheless, the goal needs to be clearly communicated to everyone involved directly and indirectly in the fundraising effort.

Targeting an Audience

It is important to establish, and look specifically at, your target audience even before planning the details of your fundraising events or activities.

Your goal is to raise money, but someone needs to be on the other end of that equation, writing out checks or handing over cash.

Can you profile potential donors? Do you know who will be interested in helping you meet your goal? Can you reach these people?

It is in your best interest to establish who will be donating money for your fundraising project to be a success. It will help you establish the magnitude of the project and determine whether your goal is feasible. If, for example, you are going to try to collect funds from the students at the local high school, it is highly unlikely that you are going to raise the cash needed to build a whole new gymnasium. You will need to either establish a fundraising plan that attracts the corporate leaders in your community or scale down your goal to converting the old auditorium into a part-time gymnasium, rather than having a new structure built from the ground up.

ALERT!

One of the biggest downfalls of local fundraisers is not knowing the community. Lofty goals and inappropriate fundraisers are a bad combination. Learn who comprises your target audience, what will attract it to your cause, and whom you may realistically tap for funding.

It is also presumptuous to expect everyone on campus or in the neighborhood to get involved and donate money. A large, high-profile organization such as the Red Cross has arms that can extend nationwide and even worldwide. They can expect a large return based on calculating the percentages and maintaining a database showing them how many people donate money annually. The majority of local fundraising efforts have neither such a database to work from nor such a far-reaching network. Therefore, you are well advised to do some preliminary research and look into the potential donor base for your project.

If, for example, you are raising money for a sports program for underprivileged kids, you might want to tap into the local athletes and sports enthusiasts in your area. Studies show that women will more readily donate to a school-based, education-related fundraiser than men will. College students have been known to have a greater passion for environmental and ecological concerns. Minorities have a greater concern for social and human rights issues. It is to your advantage to seek out such data prior to your fundraiser.

Rallying Some Troops

"I wish I could, but I'm just too busy." That's a phrase you will hear all too often when trying to rally troops to work on your fundraising efforts. Everyone feels pressed for time, and you may feel like it's hard to find people willing to carve out time in their schedules to work with you. But there *are* many people out there who will be ready to give some time and effort to support a good cause. You just have to find them.

Reasonable Goals

Set goals that you can reach. This may seem obvious, but it is important that you consider how much work can reasonably be accomplished by the number of volunteers you have. Trying to do too much with too few people will only frustrate everyone and may even drive away some volunteers.

It is also very important that you rally people behind the idea in a positive, but not pushy, manner. You need to gather prospective team members and promote the reasons behind the need for funding. In addition, you want to emphasize the idea of FUNdraising, or having a good time.

FACT

It is estimated that more than 75 percent of people involved in fundraising activities are in some manner touched personally by the cause or need to raise funds. From having a sister with kidney disease and joining the Kidney Foundation to simply enjoying the programming on PBS, most people donate time or money to a cause that they have a personal connection to.

Getting others involved in a fundraiser can be very easy if the cause, or need, is obvious and touches the members, students, or community personally. The less well informed your audience is about an issue, the more you need to be prepared. Gathering facts and figures isn't very difficult if you utilize the library, town records, and the Internet.

Show Them!

A simple example of winning over an audience with research and presentation comes from a young father of two young children, who went before a local town board in his New England community to propose a fundraiser for new and better playground facilities. Many of the people sitting before him were elders and had no idea what, if anything, was wrong with the current playground. His idea didn't get off the drawing board.

Nonetheless, this concerned father persevered, and at the next town meeting, he had documented proof of several injuries that had been sustained by youngsters as a result of the old equipment. To enhance his argument, he brought in visuals in the form of some photographs. In addition to a polished proposal with facts and figures to back up his request, he also brought with him a few of the local kids, including one whose arm was in a cast from a nasty fall off a wobbly set of monkey bars. Sure enough, the town was now behind him and offered their assistance for his fundraising efforts.

A more complex example might be when a "low profile," somewhat obscure illness needs research for funding. Putting together a fundraising dinner might mean presenting the need to raise funds for such an illness to a medical community that has been hard pressed to stretch their efforts for research to prevent other diseases. Your presentation will need to explain the importance of researching this illness.

You should prepare appropriate literature that supports your fundraising goal or goals. Such literature should clearly illustrate your mission to potential contributors and volunteers. It should also address the urgency behind your goal and the history or background of your group, association, organization, school, or other affiliation. Remember that the people collecting the money, which includes you and your volunteers, also need to present themselves in the most credible manner in your presentation.

Formulating a Plan

Many different elements factor into how you choose a fundraising event. Your fundraiser will become a project, and, not unlike starting a business, it will need to grow and incorporate the skills of various people whom you believe can help you reach the goal.

FACT

Individuals give over $150 billion per year, or 75 percent, of all contributions to charitable organizations, according to *Giving USA*, the publication for the American Association of Fundraising Counsel. Foundations, bequests, and corporations combined give the other 25 percent.

You will need to coordinate a time frame because an open-ended project is not really a project at all but a process. While established fundraising organizations will always be accepting donations, a specific fundraiser is just that—specific—with a time frame that indicates when sales or services end and totals are added up. Part of your goal will be to raise money to complete such a project by a desired date. The date may be selected for you by the nature of the project. For example, a fundraising drive to buy Christmas presents for underprivileged children will necessarily be time sensitive. Similarly, political fundraisers are planned around the calendar and with the election date in mind.

You will also find that, when starting the wheels in motion for a fundraising project, it is very likely that your school, group, association, organization, or company has done something before to raise funds for a project. Therefore, you need not reinvent the wheel. While you are planning something unique that will achieve this particular goal, you can get rough ideas from project outlines that may already be sitting in your files.

In the end, there are a lot of elements that you will need to consider in your plan. Ask yourself the following questions.

- What is the primary need for funding?
- How much money are you looking to raise?
- Who will be donating the funds? (Or what is your target audience?)
- Who can you rally around yourself to help put this plan together?
- What is your time frame?

Utilize project-planning software or simply get a notebook and start writing . . . and be prepared to cross out, erase, delete, or edit often, as even the simplest garage sale advertisement may require numerous revisions.

Honing and Presenting Your Plan

Your initial plan, or idea, will be shaped as you research the need for fundraising in greater detail. However, your idea won't become a full-fledged "plan" until you have gained support from your own organization, membership, student body, or association. Unless you can pull off a fundraising activity on your own, you will need to convince others to come on board with you, and listen to their input and suggestions.

Your idea needs to take shape and tell a short story. Remember, you need to rally internal support for the basic fundraising plan before you can start talking about the details and fleshing out the plan. It is essential that your cohorts, be they friends, fellow students, or club members, feel the same sense of passion for your cause as you do on a practical and emotional level. Sometimes this is very easy, as your organization is already dedicated to a specific cause, such as a foundation to fight diabetes.

Don't fill in all the blanks. Make your initial fundraising plan one that captivates and draws attention to your issue. However, you should leave room for other people to provide their ideas. It's much easier to get people to join a work in progress than to try to simply fit them into predetermined positions.

First, be ready to pitch or present your plan. This can be an informal pitch to a small group of fellow students or a prepared statement in front of the board of a long-standing 5,000-member nonprofit organization.

Second, be prepared to answer questions. How much money will we need to raise to build a new roof? Do we have a liaison to help us distribute the funds and any donated items to the local homeless population? Who will we hit up for funds? Your answers should be based on your research.

After you've presented the problem that exists, present your specific plan to solve it. Show the group what your organization will be able to do specifically to make a difference. Here's where you'll tell them what your project is—replacing old textbooks, donating money for medical research, or funding a soup kitchen.

You may need a show of hands to let you know how many people are with you, or a vote by the board to, say, move forward to the next step . . . which would likely answer the question, what type of fundraiser did you have in mind? We explore some of your answers to that pressing question in Chapter 2.

Chapter 2

Selecting the Fundraiser for You

One of the most significant aspects of the fundraising process will be the manner in which you choose to solicit funding. Deciding what your group will do is an exciting part of the process, but it also requires careful planning. This chapter focuses on a variety of fundraising events and activities and the considerations they entail.

From Car Wash to Black-Tie Dinner

Different fundraising approaches have long been enjoyed by various sectors of the fundraising population. For example, politicians often opt for the black-tie-and-tails fundraising dinner. Girl Scouts traditionally sell cookies, religious groups may hold a bazaar or sponsor a carnival or bingo game, and schoolchildren are very likely the reason why you have more rolls of wrapping paper in your closet than you will ever need. Established nonprofit organizations typically utilize a variety of fundraising methods, including telephone solicitation, direct mailings, and special events.

Your methods of fundraising should reflect a number of factors. By turning inward and examining your group and then looking at the potential donor base, you will be able to determine what type of activity will best help you reach your goals.

Then, you can narrow down your list of fundraising options to those that best suit your needs. You will want to determine which one generates the most enthusiasm from the members who will be working on the project.

Group Dynamics

The makeup of your organization, association, or other type of group will play a major factor in your selection of a means of fundraising. The age and sex of your members, their interests, lifestyles, and economic status will all factor into the type of project you are looking to undertake, along with their level of commitment. A group that is loosely formed without organizational ties or bylaws may choose to take on a less complicated project for fear of a loss of interest. After all, it's easier for one of several friends planning a project to just walk away if he or she is dissatisfied than it is for a board member of a long-standing nonprofit organization to do so.

In addition, finding the right fundraiser for a group to undertake is also determined by the resources of the group involved. Someone in your group may know retail sales, know how to run an auction, or be familiar with staging a local theater presentation. Take advantage of members' skills and talents as well as their connections. Who you know is often just as important as what you know.

FACT

Organizations that choose a fundraising effort together have a greater level of volunteerism than those that have one predetermined from previous members or an outside consultant or marketing firm. Studies show that volunteers work best when they have a sense of "ownership" stemming from being part of the decision-making process.

And, finally, the overall community standing of your group or organization and how you wish to be perceived by the community is a factor in your selection. The Hell's Angels could hold a biker rally and beer bash to raise funds and no one would blink an eye. If, however, a conservative neighborhood association held such an event, some people might question their credibility and standing in the community. Keep in mind the overall image you're presenting to the public.

Researching Your Target Audience

Who are the donors? Chapter 1 discussed learning about your potential audience of supporters. If you want to convince your audience to donate money, you'll need to find something that grabs their attention. Donations in the modern world of fundraising are driven by market research.

ALERT!

You've probably heard the expression "Give the people what they want." Take heed. One of the biggest failures of fundraising efforts is not taking the audience into consideration. Too often a group or organization gets caught up on a runaway train, going full speed ahead with an idea that it loves but that doesn't necessarily appeal to those whom it wants to be forking over contributions. Don't let this happen to you!

By doing preliminary research, you can characterize those individuals you expect to be donating funds. If, for example, you are doing a fundraising event for a public school, then you will know that students and their families are most likely to attend. What would interest the students and draw them and their parents back to the school in the evening or on a weekend?

The worthiness of your cause is the number one reason why people will donate. Others include:

- A personal involvement in the issue or cause.
- An enjoyment of the activity or a need for the services offered.
- Support of the group behind the fundraiser.
- Support for the community.
- The good feeling derived from giving.
- A tax write-off.

These are among the major reasons why people donate money to charities and other nonprofits.

Acting Locally

Although your first tendency may be to find an activity the entire town or city might attend, the reality is that fundraising efforts receive the bulk of their support from a nucleus that centers closely around the group running the activities. Initially, the people involved will reach out to those they know, and those people may then take it one step further and reach out to people they know. People within a small circle (three degrees of separation) will provide the bulk of your funds, unless you are able to build a large-scale marketing campaign. From kids selling magazine subscriptions to executives looking for players and supporters for a fundraising golf tournament, the first people members turn to are family, friends, neighbors, business associates, and social contacts (in no particular order).

The phrase "think globally, act locally" is appropriate when planning your activity. Sweeping changes in the environment may be your goals as you ponder rain forests being destroyed thousands of miles away. However, it is primarily the friends, family, and neighbors of your membership that will be showing up for your "clean up the environment" fundraising dinner on Friday night.

How far you branch out to the target audience will then depend largely on the other key factors, primarily including your cause, or the reason for the fundraiser; the activity you are planning; and how well you have promoted your need for money and for the fundraising activity.

Establishing a Time Frame

The three other integral factors influencing your decision regarding a fundraising activity will be time, money, and resources. An urgent need such as raising money to help the victims of a hurricane will present a time element that limits your ability to do much advance planning. In cases like that, you will be thinking, What can we do *tomorrow*?

In nonemergency situations, however, you will need to set your goals and plan your activities based on a variety of parameters. Some of these you will be able to control and others will be set for you by the nature of your organization, by the available resources (including a site), or by those individuals helping you plan the fundraiser. For example, the time frame for a new roof to be built on the library might be three months because the winter weather will delay construction. Therefore, you will need to plan your fundraising activities with enough preliminary time for contractors and builders to assess the situation and work on the problem at hand. The status of the current roof will also factor into your planning. Is it a potentially dangerous situation that needs to be addressed before a possible disaster occurs, or a matter of touch-up work and sealing to repair an old, but still sturdy, roof?

ALERT!

Consider every possible factor when determining how much time you will have to stage a fundraising event or activity. It's better to have too much time than too little. However, planning too far in advance may cause you to lose the momentum and support of many of your members.

You will build a time frame around that which warrants your attention. Often a fundraiser is held to provide funding to researchers working on the cure for a serious illness. The need is ongoing, so the time frame is, therefore, essentially open-ended. However, there is always a pressing need to move such research along more quickly. A sense of urgency makes people react and donate money more quickly.

Ultimately, you would like to plan a fundraising activity with enough time to rally your membership, handle all the details, make the necessary arrangements, and spread the word. The complexity and scale of the activity you are planning will factor into your time frame. No, it doesn't take months to launch an effective bake sale. On the other hand, a bike-a-thon through the city of Los Angeles will take more than a few days of planning and promoting.

Costs to Consider

There will be some expenses associated with most fundraising activities. Numerous online fundraising Web sites promote and sell all sorts of items from candles to jewelry in bulk quantity for you to resell as fundraising vehicles. Renting a hall to stage a banquet will incur a fee, not to mention the food and service involved. You will, therefore, need to carefully consider the costs before venturing into a fundraising activity.

Network! One of the best ways to eliminate unnecessary cost factors is to have everyone in your group consider who they know who might be willing to donate goods and services to your fundraising activity.

One of the most important aspects regarding the overall cost is determining what you can get for free. Donations of time, space, skills, and even tangible goods for sale or auction can make or break your profit margin. And, again, take advantage of what other members of your group can offer. One organization had a member whose business was dealing in sports collectibles. He had staged collectibles shows and auctions in various locations and had already established contacts in the field. Therefore, the organization was able to run a successful collectibles auction to raise money with little outlay of funds.

Resources

Another key factor, which goes hand in hand with money and your budget, is your resources. Remember, whatever you need (and do not have on hand) may cost you.

Materials

What can your group provide beyond the above-mentioned possibility of space and, in some cases, goods? Remember, there are resources needed behind the scenes beyond that which you are selling or auctioning off. For example, there always seems to be a need for tables and chairs, no matter what you are planning.

Behind the scenes, you may also need:

- Computers
- Vans or trucks
- Tables or display cases
- Ledgers and notebooks
- Paper goods
- A sound system
- A/V equipment
- Cleaning materials
- A cash register or cash box

The availability of larger items and those in the greatest need will factor into your planning. For example, if you need 300 chairs for a sit-down dinner and no one has access to inexpensive chairs, you might opt for a cocktail party where you can get away with having fewer seats for guests.

You should also consider what resources the group or organization already has. Many established clubs and associations have materials from meetings, parties, and other gatherings readily available for use. Review your inventory of items, some of which may be in the closets of your organization's offices or in storage.

Human Resources

Even after you've rallied the troops behind your pressing need for funding, you will still have to determine how many people are willing to roll up their sleeves and actually do the work to make your fundraising drive or activity a success. It does not take great numbers of people to launch and execute a successful fundraising activity. However, you will have to select an activity within the scope of the human resources available. Often, groups use a rough ten-to-one ratio when planning their events. Therefore, if you are holding an auction and expect 200 people to attend, you should probably have twenty people ready to handle the event.

You will need to consider the strengths and weaknesses of your membership and try to determine whether you, as a group, have the skills necessary for a particular undertaking. Often groups rally behind an idea and the assumption is that everyone will get involved. Think again. In a group as small as twenty members, if ten participate, or 50 percent, that's a marvelous percentage. The reality is that despite the best of intentions, active participation in your fundraiser will generally boil down to a small number of people doing a large amount of the work.

Be careful not to let one person take on too many tasks, as he or she may be overloaded and either unable to complete them all or simply suffer from burnout.

Look to bring a variety of individuals into your activity from the planning stages through executing and postactivity cleanup and/or evaluation. A wide range of individuals involved in the project can provide various skills, spawn a wealth of creative ideas, and even attract a greater diversity of the population to donate.

Quality and Customer Service

Goods and services auctions are a very popular method of fundraising in schools as well as for clubs and various organizations. People will bid on items donated by retailers and service providers. While people may bid more than an item is worth, they will still expect quality.

Therefore, before you stock up on 500 pairs of sunglasses from an online fundraising vendor or twenty-five signed lithographs from your neighbor's art shop, do your homework and make sure you are getting quality products. Simple common sense tells you not to plan a fundraising meal without tasting the food or at least hearing rave reviews from someone in your organization who has eaten at the location you have picked out. Likewise, you should not plan a fundraising picnic without checking that the location is not infested with yellow jackets. Always provide quality.

You will need to know what laws, regulations, and zoning ordinances allow in a given area before you select it as the site for your event. This includes county laws and restrictions regarding advertising, alcohol sale and consumption, crowd control, parking, noise levels, and the soliciting of funds. While nonprofits may get favorable treatment in some respects, rules and ordinances will dictate what you can and cannot provide at your fundraiser.

Good customer service means that, just like any good retailer or service provider, you need to be sensitive to the needs and concerns of your customers, or in this case your donors or contributors. Yes, you are all working for a good cause, and no, you are very likely not receiving any salary for your hard work. This does not excuse rudeness or inadequate service.Be prepared to deal promptly, and in a courteous manner, with any complaints people may have (hint: Be flexible).

Fundraising Options

So, what's it going to be—a barbeque, golf tournament, art auction? Or will you be selling candy, candles, magazines, or used cars? If you use your imagination, you can ponder all sorts of unique and interesting fundraising possibilities.

Among the most popular fundraising options today are auctions, walk- or bike-a-thons, carnivals, and the always-popular sale of magazines, candy, wrapping paper, or other easy-to-manage (and easy to transport and distribute) low-cost items. Benefit dinners, banquets, wine-tastings, and golf outings are more popular among the business and corporate crowd.

Auctions

In recent years, auctions have become a leading type of fundraiser for schools, associations, charitable groups, and religious organizations. The competitive nature of "winning" an item lends extra excitement to spending money. People are often willing to spend more than the value of the item, knowing it is for a worthy cause.

Auctions are a good choice for almost any type of group or organization because they can be run on so many different levels. By determining the economic level of your prospective attendees, you can get a feel for how "high-end" you want to go. Usually a cross section of reasonable goods and services works well for a club, association, school, or community/neighborhood group.

Types of Auctions

Traditional auctions need to be carefully planned so that the pace maintains a level of excitement. Items need to be displayed before the auction begins, and methods of bidding must be clearly explained. It is important (no matter how informally it is done) that there are written rules and guidelines regarding how the auction is run so that final sales are not contested later. A program listing the items also needs to be carefully prepared in advance and distributed to everyone in attendance.

FACT

School boards report that the fastest-growing trend in fund-raising for their PTA or directly for the school is the auction. The number of silent auctions, in particular, as a means of raising funds for schools has more than doubled in the past few years.

Silent auctions can be handled in one of two manners. Bids can be written down and placed in a bowl next to the item. The highest bidder then wins the item. Another way to run a silent auction is to have everyone purchase tickets at the door for a set amount and place the tickets in bowls next to the items they are interested in bidding on. Then a lottery-style drawing occurs for each item. This is called a "Chinese Auction."

Planning an Auction

An auction committee of about fifteen people running the show is ideal. Members of the committee will handle such areas as securing donations of goods and services (most important), cataloging or listing all donated items or services, picking up and storing auction items, transporting items to and from the auction site, preparing and printing up the list of items, publicizing the event, and manning the auction (which includes setting up, collecting and recording money transactions, and cleaning up).

While traditional auctions provide more excitement and can run the bidding up higher on popular items, a silent auction can allow the shy attendees to get involved, which is likely to increase the number of participants. Many people still think of auctions as a means of buying valuable paintings or antiques at a ritzy auction house and are intimidated by the idea of bidding. Nonetheless, either type of auction, or a combination of both, can prove highly successful, as evidenced by the recent surge in fundraising auctions.

Soliciting Donations

The key to a successful auction, of any kind, is having the goods and services of value to auction off. Parameters need to be set up regarding what range of items you are looking for. In some cases, auctions have a theme such as sports or food/cooking, but most often, schools, charities, and community groups auction off a wide range of items that are of reasonable value.

It is up to those staging the auction to tap into the community donations of items or free services to be provided. A letter, brochure, and/or flier describing the specific need for funding, such as buying new textbooks, will be necessary to attract donors. Also, the mission and background of your group or organization must be clearly explained in print and in your sales pitch. Credibility on the part of those handling the auction will make or break your number of donations.

ALERT!

Coordinate who is soliciting which vendors, merchants, or service providers. You don't want to annoy the very people who are donating items by having multiple people approach them after they have already made a donation.

When soliciting, it is important to talk to the owner or manager and get a firm commitment in writing. Have a very basic agreement that can be signed by someone in a responsible position in the store or business. Also find out how and when you can pick up the item or display the service that will be provided. Sometimes a restaurant will give you a menu or a service provider will have you display his or her card and a brochure.

The items don't have to be expensive. One popular trick of the auction trade is to put smaller items together into a theme package. For example, a "Night on the Town" package might combine dinner at a fine restaurant, theater tickets, and even free baby-sitting. Food baskets and even handmade items or baskets of goodies put together by children can also be very popular and fun prizes.

And, finally, don't forget to give credit to all of the people who donated goods and services at the auction as each winner is announced and thank the donors at the end of the evening.

Sales

A simple and effective means of raising money has always been to sell items. From candles to grand pianos, the variety of items sold for fundraising purposes is quite vast. The Internet now serves as a valuable resource when looking to purchase bulk quantities of candy, candles, key chains, T-shirts, or any of a thousand items for fundraising purposes. In fact, many one-stop-shop fundraising Web sites (see Appendix A) serve as portals to numerous vendors and merchants.

ALERT!

Before ordering from an online vendor, try to find out which vendors other nonprofits have used. Call and get shipping terms, timetable, and return policy, and ask questions before ordering from an online vendor.

While door-to-door sales are a thing of the past for most of us in today's environment, children and adults have found that networking through friends, neighbors, and relatives is an effective manner of selling goods. Wrapping paper and magazines have become favorites with schools and youth groups. Since over 2.2 million people buy magazine subscriptions annually, it is a safe bet that your group can sell a few subscriptions.

Before you start out, do some canvassing to see what similar fundraising drives are taking place in your community. The third magazine drive of the season is likely to be a bust in a small town. Be prepared to counter other sales trends. For example, if every school in town is selling magazines, then be the first in the neighborhood to sell items like light bulbs or toilet paper (everyone needs them, right?).

The keys to successful selling for a fundraiser are:

- Selling an item that provides you with a high enough markup to reach your goal
- Having a realistic sales campaign in a realistic time frame
- Making sure the buyer knows which group, school, or organization you represent (have literature and a badge or some type of identification)
- Being convincing, but not pushy, salespeople
- Being able to describe the value of your product to the consumer
- Keeping accurate records of sales and making sure buyers receive their goods in a timely manner

A sales drive can be effective for a wide range of fundraising groups. The choice of item and means of selling will depend on your target audience. Research the buying habits of your potential target audience.

Carnivals

Another popular fundraising activity is an age-old favorite, the carnival. YMCAs, youth groups, schools, church groups, charities, and associations have all run successful carnivals. A carnival takes meticulous planning and preparation since it is a one-time event with numerous details involved.

QUESTION?

Where does the initial funding (or "seed" money) come from to start off an event like a carnival or fair?
To run a carnival, a group or organization will need to either dip into its treasury or seek sponsorship to cover the costs of the activities or the whole event. Vendors or sponsors can set up their own booths or rides. Activities can also be donated by membership or from existing resources. Be creative and resourceful.

Scheduling a carnival requires looking closely at other activities and holidays on the calendar to make sure there is no overlap and that you will be able to draw a crowd. It requires that you have a secure location that is accessible and has parking available. Games and activities will need to be carefully planned so that they are safe for children as well as adults and are run in a fair manner. Prizes must be fairly distributed. Rides need to be carefully inspected to make sure they are safe. Police and fire department officials need to know what is taking place and will generally provide support, providing, of course, that you have any necessary permits or licenses to run a carnival. Look into local licensing and permit requirements well in advance.

Games and activities like ring toss, bean bag races, baseball pitching, shooting baskets, rope climbing, bowling, face painting, dance contests, and numerous others can be initiated with little expense and without bringing in major carnival rental equipment. The use of professional carnival activities should be decided well in advance in conjunction with your budget and funding needs.

Carnivals require a significant amount of preparation because there are many tasks involved, including finding the site, promotion, setup, selling tickets, manning activities, and cleanup. Plan a carnival well in advance and always have a rain date.

A-Thons

Bike-a-thons, walk-a-thons, bowl-a-thons, dance-a-thons, and similar events are very popular with charitable organizations looking to raise money. For example, the annual Walk for the Cure is a walk-a-thon designed to raise money for cancer research.

The need to determine where this activity can take place is paramount in planning such a fundraising activity. You will need to secure, often with local police and authorities, a safe route for bicycles or walkers to follow. Promotion, prizes (hopefully sponsored), and security and safety measures need to be addressed well in advance.

You also need to print pledge sheets and give participants a reasonable amount of time to get pledges from friends, neighbors, and relatives. Such activities can be excellent fundraisers because they have low initial costs. However, they require a lot of planning, promotion, and manpower.

Remember that the stars of your event are the walkers, dancers, bikers, bowlers, or those doing whatever activity you've come up with. Therefore, it is important that the needs of all participants are met. Water, towels, rest areas, and even medical attention should be available, and encouragement and support should be provided.

These types of events (a-thons) don't end when the event is over. One of the biggest aspects (and occasionally headaches) of the event is collecting the money from pledges. Most people will be forthright and prompt about paying what they pledged. However, there's always one person who takes forever to send you the money. Be persistent and try to collect all pledged money. Ⓔ

Chapter 3

Getting Started

Just because you came up with the brilliant fundraising idea doesn't necessarily put you in charge, or does it? Every fundraising project needs a leader to take charge. The leadership role will require a significant time commitment, and the leader will need the support of the members of the organization to get things moving.

Selecting or Electing a Leader

It is often assumed that, to be a good leader, one must possess the ability to tell other people what they need to do. In stark contrast, however, the mark of a good leader is learning and listening. To lead effectively does not mean guiding a group of "followers," but, rather, taking in data from various sources and utilizing it effectively to persuade others to work for a reason. After all, unless you are leading a military command post, people can simply quit . . . especially volunteers. A good leader knows how to effectively communicate what it is that he or she hopes to accomplish.

Once you have sold your membership on the idea of raising the funds, an effective leader makes the people he or she is leading feel good about themselves and enjoy the work they are doing. The success or failure of a fundraising project can be largely based on the enthusiasm of the workers involved, because they are at the heart of the project.

People Skills

Perhaps the most significant set of skills you will need as a leader are people skills. After all, you can be an expert at setting the budget, following your calendar, and lining up the resources necessary to pull off your fundraiser. However, if no one follows your lead, you are not a leader.

Whether dealing with volunteers or donors, you will need to be encouraging and show a degree of patience and flexibility, even more so than in the office or at your workplace where levels of seniority and internal politics may dictate how things are addressed. You will also have to be accessible so that you can address concerns, answer questions, and solve conflicts that may arise. To do this effectively, it helps to have all of your homework done in advance. Know as much as possible about the cause, your fundraising goal, and how to produce and promote your choice of fundraising activity. Have all of the FAQs (frequently asked questions) answered ahead of time—in your mind or on paper.

Important people skills include:

* Listening when others talk
* Doing your research so you're well versed on your fundraising cause

- Clearly delegating work to others
- Giving people latitude to utilize their skills (Don't micromanage.)
- Seeking out the opinions of others
- Monitoring people's work closely, but from afar (Again, don't micromanage.)
- Keeping others apprised of the progress of the fundraiser
- Remaining calm under pressure and getting along with various personalities
- Knowing when you need to ask for help (Don't try to do everything.)
- Providing encouragement and showing appreciation

People skills are always a work in progress, since you never know who you are going to meet and what they will be like. Whether you are working within an established nonprofit organization or you are orchestrating a grassroots fundraiser for a school or library, you will meet many different personality types, and your people skills will be tested time and time again.

Other Important Skills

While the bylaws of your nonprofit organization may indicate the manner in which leaders are officially selected, the most important attributes for heading a fundraising project are people skills. But whoever assumes the role of leader should possess various other skills, including:

- Organizational skills, such as planning and tracking tasks and activities
- Communication skills, both verbal and written
- The ability to persuade and motivate
- Flexibility in the event that you need to shift gears at any point during your efforts or try new ideas
- Decision-making skills, including listening to various points of view before making a decision
- Listening to the needs of others and to any suggestions or opinions they may have that benefit the project

Not unlike the old circus act where the clown tried to keep all the plates spinning at once, high atop several poles, as the leader you will be asked to handle a wide range of responsibilities even on what may initially seem like the simplest of fundraising efforts.

Even if there is no required time frame for your fundraising effort, you should impose one. By setting a time frame, you establish parameters and inspire people to work harder. An open-ended fundraising campaign can drag on, and the people involved may lose their motivation. Deadlines, even soft ones, spur action.

Depending on the size of your organization and the number of people involved in the fundraiser, you will either be a "hands-on" leader or an overseeing supervisor. As a hands-on leader, you will be doing plenty of in-the-trenches work such as putting up tents, driving the van, or manning the loudspeaker at the carnival. As an overseeing supervisor, you will be in the position of having committee chairpersons heading the various committees established to do the necessary work. Your job, then, is to see that each committee is somehow getting the task accomplished within the constraints of your budget and time frame.

Who Is on Board?

Following your heartfelt pitch to raise money for the Children's Hospital of Miami, you received applause from the members of your nonprofit organization. You then gathered to discuss a fundraising drive that could be launched within the next several weeks. The enthusiasm generated a flurry of excellent ideas and ultimately you agreed on running a community golf tournament, since the activity of choice among many of your neighbors is golf.

However, within the next few weeks following this outpouring of support for your fundraiser, the number of volunteers began to diminish. Who was really on board? Who was ready to pitch in and get involved in handling the workload that comes with staging this successful fundraiser?

Gathering human resources is only part of your equation. Actually seeing the results of their efforts is another. At some point, the old saying "put up or shut up" comes clearly into focus as you question the dedication of those people whom you initially thought would be involved.

Emphasize to volunteers that giving whatever time possible to help the fundraising effort is very much appreciated. Find tasks to meet specific time parameters of your members. Not everyone has to put in the same amount of effort as everyone else. Every little bit helps.

Concepts such as fun, togetherness, teamwork, team spirit, and "a good cause" need to be emphasized to rally your troops. Incentives can be used to lure volunteers, but these can open up a can of worms unless the parameters are very clearly predetermined. You need to spell out what is needed to receive such an incentive. The incentive should help convince someone to work a little harder but should not be so big that it overshadows the real reasons for getting involved. Remember that the best incentive for volunteering to be part of a fundraiser should be the special feeling of satisfaction one gets from doing such a job. However, prizes and verbal or written recognition are right up there on the list.

FACT

Studies show that participation in a fundraising project drops by nearly 50 percent in the first two to three weeks. Most often, people realize that they cannot devote the time and effort necessary. In other cases, individuals lose their initial enthusiasm for the cause.

Initially, you may have a lot of volunteers willing to help out. However, in time, you will have to acknowledge that not everyone who is initially on board will end up there. Such is the nature of many fundraising projects. Unless you are hiring a paid fundraiser, it is very hard to ensure that anyone will stick it out. Therefore, it is in your best interest to evaluate the skills, characteristics, and level of commitment of everyone who has pledged their time, and get your list of tasks together quickly. In fact, you should already have a list of what needs to be done from your time spent researching the fundraising possibilities. Asking people to take on specific tasks in accordance with their interests and skills is a far more effective means of getting the help you need than posting a general call for help.

Evaluating Your Personnel

So, who can do what? That may be your first thought as you look out at an enthusiastic crowd of potential volunteers. Nonprofit organizations often have members with skills in various areas that can help the success of your efforts. If you tap into what people enjoy doing, have experience doing, and have an affinity toward, you can get a feel for who will be best at taking on a given task.

While you may want to utilize an accountant to help with your books and people in other professions to employ their business skills, you should also consider people's hobbies and interests. Someone who crunches numbers all day may have no desire to look at numbers on the weekend or in the evening. He or she, however, may be a marvelous auctioneer, having run auctions for a civic group or in college. Remember, one of the reasons people work hard in nonprofits and for community and charitable fundraisers is because it allows them to use their other (non–nine-to-five) skills. Tap those interests and skills and you'll find great enthusiasm!

Newer and Older Members

Include newer members of your organization and have them work alongside long-time members and even board members. Working together allows the senior members to help train the newcomers.

It is also very important to let new members of your organization run with the ball on occasion. While they may fumble, they may also score a touchdown with a new idea. This applies even in situations where you are not working with an established nonprofit: The parent who has been involved with the school for the past five years—through the bake sale, magazine drive, and nine other fundraisers—needs to let the parent of the new kid in school also take initiative and get involved. This way, as children grow up and graduate, parents of the next generation of students can carry forth the PTO.

Tackling Tasks

Defining and assigning tasks is an important step in any fundraising activity. Each task should be written down and delegated to someone who feels comfortable handling that responsibility. This can be tricky because individuals may not have a realistic view of their own strengths and weaknesses. Personalities and character traits come into play, yet as a leader, you walk the fine line of not hurting anyone's feelings while finding the right person for the job.

Define tasks very early in the process and assign them quickly. The longer you wait to explain what people need to do, the greater the opportunity for volunteers to lose interest and slip through the cracks. Also, this way you can gather alternative volunteers in case someone changes his or her mind about being involved.

For example, if the individual in charge of finding and securing the golf course for the tournament is known to be a procrastinator, then everyone else's tasks may be on hold until he or she completes the job. A good leader will assess, in advance, who might be skilled at doing a particular task and how the person goes about getting things done. In addition, you need to establish an open line of communication. Even if someone is doing a marvelous job, if no one else knows what he or she is doing, others may duplicate those efforts. Communication is key.

Unity and Teamwork

When rallying the troops, you want to capture the initial enthusiasm and direct it into an activity before it fades. As the project takes shape, you will want to harness new ideas to maintain the enthusiasm and keep the tasks fresh for the people who are putting the fundraiser together. You can build on the unity the group feels by having tasks that overlap at various points. This will often be the case in your fundraiser whether you make a concerted effort or not. By overlapping tasks, one group or committee will need to communicate with another to complete its work. Often, the programming and planning committees need to coordinate with the site committee to complete their tasks. All of them will also need to be in constant touch with the promotion and advertising committee.

By limiting stand-alone tasks, you not only increase the unity within the group, but you also make people responsible to each other. This will often encourage someone to get the job done, if only not to let someone else down. Of course, this can be a double-edged sword. If one person, such as the procrastinator mentioned above, has a task that affects the work of other individuals or committees and doesn't do the job, then a domino effect can occur. One task does not get accomplished, and it causes others to topple along the way. However, if you are monitoring the work as it progresses, this can be avoided.

Selling is everything! If you say, "I think Michael would do a marvelous job at finding the site for us," you have a better chance of getting Michael to take the job of site coordinator than if you say, "I guess that leaves site coordination to Michael" or "Mike, you're stuck with finding the site."

As the leader, you'll need to keep tabs on the work as it progresses. For this reason, it is also advisable (if possible) to have a committee rather than one person handling key tasks. Therefore, if there is one weak link, the chain will not collapse, and the work will still get done.

Unity is also the result of frequent meetings and even social gatherings to discuss the progress of the fundraiser and enjoy working together. Show your appreciation as often as possible for the work the volunteers are doing.

Who's on *the* Board?

Board members of a nonprofit organization are usually senior members who have been involved with the organization for some time or high-profile individuals in business or corporate America who have contacts in various industries. All board members should have a strong grasp of the overall goals and mission of the organization and be dedicated to meeting those goals.

The board also provides guidance and oversees the financial well-being and fiscal responsibilities of the organization. Also, the board should help provide access to resources for the nonprofit organization to meet their intended mission.

Whether you are talking about the board of a national fundraising organization such as the United Way or the five people who make up the board of a small nonprofit group with annual revenues of $25,000, you should expect the board to contribute to your fundraising efforts. By giving their own money, they are setting an example and sending a message that they are committed to the fundraising drive or event.

Boards should be at the forefront of the organization, even if they maintain a low public image. Board members should:

- Help identify and contact contributors
- Help in the promotion of the fundraising campaign and the work of the organization
- Provide specific resources for fundraising campaigns or events
- Offer knowledge and guidance based on their background in the organization or in the "for profit" business community

Multimillion-dollar fundraising organizations may have board members who are CEOs of major corporations. Their time is limited, but their high-profile positions and access to resources and funding are quite significant to the organization. Small nonprofits rely more heavily on their boards to oversee daily operations and, in some cases, to handle a portion of the fundraising activities.

FACT

Large organizations often use board manuals. A board manual serves as an orientation handbook and details the board structure and operations. It also includes listings of fellow board members and staff and provides general information about the organization.

The First Meetings

So, now that you have a team together to kick off the fundraising drive, you need to decide how it will work. Whether you are about to launch a direct mail campaign, a beauty pageant, or a car wash, you will need to hold fundraising meetings. Even in this day of e-mail, three-way calling, and conference calls, nothing beats the face-to-face, in-person meeting.

ALERT!

Do not hesitate. Once your committee, group, or posse is formed, get together within two weeks! Don't give volunteers a chance to lose interest.

The key is to keep people coming back to subsequent meetings, maintaining the level of interest and enthusiasm for the fundraising goal. You want to make sure that people feel comfortable at meetings. If people feel good and are in a comfortable setting, they will be more likely to participate in the discussion.

Meeting Preparation

Prepare and distribute an agenda for each meeting that includes a clear purpose for the meeting beyond the obvious "to discuss the fundraising efforts." Be as specific as possible!

Prior to your meetings, set some basic rules of procedure to maintain a sense of order and keep things running smoothly. Many nonprofits use Robert's Rules of Order, or a loose variation thereof, to handle meeting protocol. Depending on the size and nature of the group, you will adapt your own version of this antiquated, but still widely accepted, method of governing meetings.

Meeting Tips

Make sure you have allowed sufficient time for everyone to know about the meeting. Send your letters or e-mails a couple of weeks prior to the date. Invite only the people who need to be there—don't bring a dozen extra people together for a meeting that only pertains to the work of five people. Follow up with people who have not responded as the date approaches. Set a start and an end time, and keep track of the time as you go. Do not allow one agenda item to dominate the meeting unless it is considerably more important than all others.

It is important to try to involve everyone present in the discussion. If new members are present, make sure to introduce them or have them introduce themselves. As the meeting progresses and more people participate, try to keep the discussion from going off on tangents, and limit unnecessary side chatter.

Have someone record minutes at your meetings. Key decisions and a clear list of who is responsible for which task should be on paper . . . or computer disk.

And, finally, have refreshments! However, try not to let refreshments get in the way. Position them away from the main meeting area or set a specific time for a refreshment break.

Even an informal group should run the first meetings with some sense of structure and a touch of formality. It sets a tone that will be helpful later once everyone has become more comfortable with one another. What frequently happens is that, once the members of a group get to know each other, more socializing or nonproductive discussion will dominate the meeting and little will get accomplished. If you start off with some formality, then there is a separation of "meeting" and "socializing" because a structure has been set.

Running a successful fundraising meeting also means keeping one eye on the goal at hand and the other on the clock. Remember, if people leave a meeting feeling that they got something out of it besides cake and coffee, they will come back for the next fundraising meeting . . . which should be planned before you adjourn the present one. If people leave shaking their heads because the meeting ran until midnight, they won't be back.

To keep the meetings interesting and the members coming back, you may try varying your meeting place. Sometimes, small nonprofits and other groups engaged in fundraising efforts will meet in people's houses. This alone can draw people who are curious about seeing each other's homes. If your nonprofit or school board has a standard meeting place, you might try a variation by having a lunch or dinner meeting. A new twist on an old theme may keep people coming back.

It is important to schedule both a start and an end time for the meeting. This way, you let everyone know that the meeting is carefully planned around the agenda and that you are cognizant of people's need to end at a reasonable time. Two or two and a half hours is a good length for a meeting.

Goals of the Meeting

Your first fundraising meetings should set the plan in motion. If you are seeking donations for an auction and no one has gotten any donations by the third meeting, then either the approach is wrong, the cause is not being clearly identified, or your members are going after the wrong donors. Likewise, if you are embarking on a phone or direct mail campaign, you can get early feedback from those doing the calling or receiving the return mail. Early in the planning process, meetings can provide a chance to evaluate and remedy unproductive situations before they continue.

When planning a fundraising event, the early meetings give you an opportunity to establish a timeline to work toward the specific fundraising dinner, auction, or bike-a-thon. Again, you will be able to evaluate your progress from meeting to meeting and see how you can get back on schedule if you have fallen behind.

And finally, schedule enough meetings to maintain enthusiasm and keep everything running on time. However, do not hold meetings for the sake of meetings. Many groups meet again and again without rhyme or reason out of force of habit. This is not productive.

Motivation

Start motivating by establishing a level of communication and trust between members. People are motivated if they feel that the cause is important and that others whom they care about are relying on their efforts. Enhance your abilities to motivate by first introducing the project team to one another and letting everyone know who is on board. Next, make sure that everyone understands the goals and objectives of the project and that each person is clear about the tasks that need to be done and how they are integral to the overall fundraising objective.

You'd be surprised how setting the wheels in motion properly from the very beginning will help you motivate people at a later date.

Numerous books are written on motivational techniques. Some emphasize rah-rah team spirit and others have more detailed theoretical insights into what motivates an individual. While such books may come in handy over the long haul, the simple approach is to look at who is working on your fundraiser and what it is that piques their interest and enthusiasm. Children may be motivated by an incentive or prize at the end of the road—so might many adults. However, adults may also be reaping cognitive benefits such as advancing their education or learning new skills.

The Truth about Motivation

Motivation is usually not rah-rah speeches from a podium, but pats on the back, thank-yous, certificates, and, most importantly, a step back to look at the core situation—why are you all gathered here to raise funds in the first place?

If you can research and find results in the field in which you are doing work, such as a decrease in student dropout rates, then you may hit the motivational nail on the head. A PTO president cut an article out of a newspaper and put it in her drawer for just such an occasion when there was a need to motivate. Then, midway into the current fundraising drive for textbooks, when morale was declining, she stood up at a PTO fundraising meeting, pulled out the article, and read that last year's reading scores in the district were up by nearly a full grade level from the previous year. "This," she exclaimed, "is largely due to the new textbooks received by the students at the beginning of the previous school year. It is a result of *your* efforts." Applause followed, and then she reminded everyone that they could do the same thing again this year with money for new math textbooks. From there, they established a slogan of "one grade higher" and used it as a motivational reminder of the article and the meeting.

FACT

Professional motivators have been proven primarily successful in nonprofit situations only if they are active in the cause that the group is working toward. For that reason, a nonprofessional speaker who has a good story to tell involving the cause at hand will usually be far more effective than a professional "motivator."

Motivating from Year to Year

If you've had a relatively successful fundraiser in the past, you can motivate both your membership and outside attendees to come back next year by building on your theme. For example, if one year you hold a dinner with entertainment, the next year you might add in an auction as well. Then toss in a raffle the following year and add a dance contest. Once you have an audience that enjoyed a fundraiser one year, you can motivate them to return the next by building on, or "leveraging," your fundraising event.

If you can become known as the organization that holds the best annual golf tournament or become famous for an offbeat fundraiser, you can distinguish yourself in a hurry. Think outside the box and come up with twists on tried-and-true events.

If a fundraiser was only marginally successful, welcome members to build a "think tank" and find new ways to build on a theme. People love being asked for input and to have a say in the building process of any project or fundraiser. Taking something and making it better is the perfect way to pull people together. Building on a theme is an effective way to motivate people to step up for an annual activity.

Motivating is part of being the leader, and the best way to motivate others is to stay motivated yourself. Keep one eye firmly on the project goals and the other on everyone involved.

Fundraising Consultants

Consultants have become a fixture in our modern world. They are prominent in many fields. Do you need to hire one for your fundraising efforts? Perhaps. The size and scope of the nonprofit organization is one determining factor. Another factor is the success or failure of recent fundraising efforts. And, finally, there is the magnitude of what you are trying to accomplish in conjunction with the resources and manpower you have.

If you want to take on a fundraising activity much larger (or much different) than any other you've done before, some professional advice might be very welcome. (And it might help you avoid disaster.) In some cases, an organization is pressed for time because they have ongoing work to do in conjunction with the fundraising activities. This might also be reason to meet with a fundraising consultant.

FACT

The percentage of nonprofits utilizing the services of paid professionals has grown steadily over the past two years, largely due to the increased competition among fundraising groups of all types. There are numerous consulting services available, most of which are highly reputable and successful. Nonetheless, get references before hiring a consultant.

Some fundraisers will ask for a percentage of the profits. This request on top of a flat salary should not be granted. However, if it's a choice between a set rate or paying a small sum plus a percentage of your profits, then you join an ongoing and sometimes heated debate as to what to do. There are staunch opponents of the idea of paying a fundraising consultant based on the success of the event. There are others, however, who feel such a percentage-induced arrangement motivates the consultant to work harder.

Do keep in mind that the people contributing to a fundraiser are contributing to a cause or goal that is posted. As soon as money goes for something else, whether it is to pay a consultant or to cover some internal cost of the nonprofit group, you may find the donors very unhappy. After all, they pledged $50 to help abused children, not to see the money go to a highly paid consultant.

Of course, the other side of the argument is that paying on commission is fair. That way, you spend more money only if the results of the consultant's preliminary work bring in benefits. This is a choice you will have to make if you decide to hire a professional consultant.

ALERT!

Find out if a consultant has worked with your type of organization in the past and with your type of fundraiser. Some consultants deal with government grants, while some deal with day-to-day operations and others deal with special event planning. Make sure to get the right consultant on board.

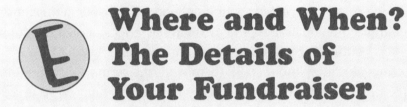

Chapter 4

Where and When? The Details of Your Fundraiser

You know why you are raising the money. Now you need to establish the details of your fundraising event, activity, or drive in conjunction with your planning committee and your board. This chapter looks at what you need to do to fill in some of the key aspects of your project, including locating a site and selecting the date or dates on which to run your fundraising event or campaign.

Location Selection

The choice of location for your fundraiser obviously depends on the activity, but it also depends on your resources and its accessibility so your members and the others can attend.

Whether your planning committee is choosing a park for your two-mile race or a restaurant for your luncheon, all considerations must be made to accommodate the projected turnout. Special consideration may be afforded to major contributors who must attend. List all factors prior to selecting a location and discuss them with one or more board members to see that you have addressed all key concerns. Then, do some research to make sure no other similar event is taking place the same day.

ALERT!

Double-check on the availability of the location as the day approaches. Confirm that the site is reserved for your group—a mistake (on your end or theirs) can be costly if it means you don't have a site the day you need it!

Some fundraisers have seen low turnouts due to closed roads, detours, or heavy traffic. While these factors cannot always be avoided, they are also worth exploring. Find out as much as you can ahead of time. The more difficulties you can avoid, the better off you will be. Remain on top of the situation by being proactive.

Donated Space

One of the biggest expenses of your fundraiser may be in renting a hall, restaurant, or other location. If a member can donate a location or you can use a facility that is owned or leased to the organization, you can cut down on expenses dramatically. Therefore, the more networking your planning committee and board members do to secure a free location, the more easily you will be on track to meeting your financial fundraising goal.

You can also try to negotiate a deal with a site. For example, you may get the room free, or for a minimal cost, for your fundraising luncheon at a local restaurant in exchange for mentioning their name in all of your advertising literature and promotion.

Location Hunting

Go in groups. A simple rule of thumb says that you will never remember all the questions to ask when scouting a site for your fundraiser. Even if you are in your son's school and deciding whether you should use the gymnasium or the auditorium, have another set of eyes and ears to take in the surroundings. You'd be surprised at what another person might point out that you may have missed.

To find the best site for your fundraiser, consider first the potential size of expected turnout. You will then need to compare rental rates— and remember to always inquire about what is included in the rates and what restrictions they may have. For example, can alcohol be served? Can you bring in a DJ or a band? Must you use the catering facility of the hotel or can you bring in an outside caterer? If you find a location that suits your needs, confirm available dates and find out how far ahead you need to book. You should also check out the parking situation and make sure there will be enough parking.

A site coordinator is someone who works for your organization, acting as a liaison between the owner or manager of the site and the organization. From determining when the loading dock will be open for you to unload equipment to finding out who will handle the lighting for your children's talent show, you need to know how the site is run and who can help you handle any problems that may arise. He or she will have a vision for how you can make a location work best for your needs. Choose your site coordinator wisely. Look for someone who has planned activities or events, or perhaps someone who is a designer.

The more familiar the location is to your members and prospective attendees, the better chance of a successful turnout. A fundraiser for the library held in the library courtyard, or a school fundraiser held in the school gymnasium, can help set the tone of the fundraiser.

Many owners or managers of sites are willing to give discounts or special deals to nonprofit organizations or grassroots groups. The more in step with your cause the owner or manager is, the more likely you'll have a low-rate or even donated facility.

The "Right" Date

Selecting a date for your fundraising event or a week for a fundraising drive can be a frustrating task. You'll need to factor in numerous variables, including holidays and the availability of key players in the organization. In addition, you will need to consider the time in which you will draw the most attendees or attract the most donors.

The peak times of year for fundraisers are typically in the spring and prior to the end-of-year holiday season. The spring affords you good weather and lets you get your activity or activities in before the end of the school year and the start of vacation travel. The holiday season is a time of giving and also ends the tax year for individuals looking for an extra tax write-off. People may be more receptive on the phone or by mail as the holidays approach. On the other hand, it is also the time in which thousands of other fundraising campaigns are in effect, so there is more competition.

Start by choosing dates that allow your group or organization enough time for proper planning. A common mistake is to schedule an activity without allowing time for adequate planning and preparation. The bigger the undertaking, the more time you are likely to need.

Obviously, you will want good weather when planning a carnival or golf tournament. However, you may also need to consider factors like hay fever and allergy season. Of course, if the premier golf course in the area can give you a specific date free of charge, you may abandon many of your other considerations—but not all. Don't take a date if it really won't serve your purpose. After all, you can play on any golf course in the Northeast in December, but you probably wouldn't want to. Not that being unique doesn't sometimes work . . . one school held a very successful beach party in January. Of course, they imported sand and held it in the gymnasium.

Organizing and Record Keeping

There are popular software programs used by nonprofits to track fundraising. You can, however, use any organizational software or simply keep records in a notebook or ledger. There are two primary areas that you will want to keep track of. First, make sure you have accurate information on everyone involved in working on the fundraising campaign. You need to have an idea of what everyone is doing and have accurate contact information readily available.

The other key records to be kept are those of sponsors and donors. You want to know who donated money, how much they donated, and when. You then want to be able to send thank-you letters and follow up with these donors in the future. Make sure you have adequate contact information. You need to build your valuable database of people and businesses you can tap into in the future. If you can set up your records so that they can be accessed from a number of different fields, you will be able to look up donors by location, past donations, and other characteristics.

FACT

More than 100,000 new fundraising groups emerged in the United States between 1996 and 1999, and this trend has not slowed in recent years. There is a lot of competition out there for donations!

By keeping accurate records of all procedures and money transactions, you can also update your sponsors and donors on the success of the program. Major sponsors should receive updates on how much money is coming in and what the money is being used for. This keeps them in the loop and serves as good PR for your organization.

Setting up a Schedule

No matter what you call it—schedule, timetable, plan, or program—a successful fundraising activity or event needs to follow some type of defined schedule. The larger the program or event you are planning, the more complex your plan will need to be.

Not unlike managing any other type of project, you will need to list various tasks and, based on the completion date of your fundraising efforts, include a timetable that indicates deadlines for completing tasks. Schedules need to be comprehensive yet not so complicated that other people cannot follow the plan of action. There should also be room for adjustments to be made.

Mapping a Timeline

If you are planning a fundraising drive for next March and you are currently in October, you should map out what needs to be done over the next six months and how long it should take to complete the various tasks. You may plan by working backward from your completion date in accordance with how many weeks it will take to complete each task.

Don't forget to consider the timing of publicity for your event. You will need to time the release of publicity to appear several weeks, or even months, in advance of your fundraiser. Include deadlines in your schedule for getting the word out about your event.

Schedule the most important tasks early on. For example, you would want to find a location before deciding on a local caterer or determining how many tables and chairs to order.

The dates that appear on your timetable, also known as baseline dates, are the initial dates for starting and finishing a task. You will use these dates along with your ongoing schedule to compare when tasks are expected to be completed with where they currently stand. Your timeline should be tied in to your budget (more on budgeting in Chapter 6). You will need to watch the budget in conjunction with the timetable to see how much you are laying out in advance and how much you are spending as you progress through your plan. It's very important to remember that, if you are spending $2,000 a month from a $10,000 planning budget, you will run out of money in five months. If the big push for your event is scheduled to begin in six months, you will be out of funds already.

Keep in mind that just because a job can be done in six or seven hours doesn't mean it will be completed in one day. Elapsed time is how much real time is needed to complete an activity. Someone working on a specific task may need twenty hours to complete the job. However, since he or she will not put in twenty straight hours, you will need to determine how much time he or she can put in on a daily or weekly basis before determining when that job should be completed. For example, a commitment of five hours per week will mean the job will be completed in the twenty-hour total but over the course of four weeks.

Printers' Schedules

Printing is a very time-sensitive aspect of your fundraising project. You will need to know well in advance when the printer you choose to work with needs final copy for advertising and promotional materials as well as day-of programs and organizational literature. Background materials on your nonprofit may already be available, but this may be the ideal time to update such material and run more copies.

FACT

One of the biggest errors made during the planning phase of a fundraiser is not allowing enough time for printing and for mailing services such as collating, labeling, and sorting. All of these need to be done when your printed material is completed. The additional cost for a "rush job" by the printer and the mailing house can eat into your profits. Plan accordingly.

Time-sensitive printing matters need to be addressed early on. Rush jobs will cost you additional money. If you can attract and interest a printer in your cause, perhaps you will save significant money. Including a timetable for printing in your schedule is important in the early part of your fundraising project.

Tracking Your Progress

You need a way to follow the progress of your fundraising project. Therefore, you want to have each task clearly displayed on a schedule or matrix. You should be able to see multiple tasks and their relationship to one another. You also want to be able to see who is responsible for handling each task. All of this should be part of the software program you are using or in the notebook in which you are writing your schedule of activities.

You can track progress on a monthly, biweekly, weekly, or daily basis, depending on the nature of the project and the number of tasks and people involved. Frequently, a fundraising project is tracked less often in the beginning and almost daily as the time frame winds down to the end of the project. Milestones should be marked off as they are reached.

QUESTION?

What is a milestone?
A milestone is a key task in the project that gets completed in the process of planning your fundraising project. For example, the completion of selling all available advertising space in your journal could be considered a milestone. There will be several milestones along the way as you forge ahead to complete the job of putting together your fundraiser.

Don't assume you know how long a task will take. Talk to whoever is going to do the work to find out how long it will take them to complete it. If the time frame sounds unreasonable, research how long it takes someone else to do the same task. For example, if a printer says he can have the job in five weeks but you want it in three weeks, comparison shop with other printers and see what they can offer you. If two other places can have the job done faster at a similar rate, then you should go with one of them. Getting a consensus is a good way to determine how long it should take to complete a job and at what cost.

Schedules can be hard to follow, especially with an organization largely comprised of volunteers and a need for board approval on key decisions. Therefore, you should leave some slack in your schedule so that tasks have a little extra time to be completed beyond the "on paper" completion date.

Contingency Plans

Always have backup plans. One of the most important reasons for keeping track of the ongoing progress of your fundraising campaign is to be prepared in the event you need to switch gears. For smaller projects, where you do not stand to lose money, you may just shrug your shoulders if all goes wrong and say, "We tried . . . we'll try again next time." However, if your organization has invested time and money and put its reputation behind a fundraising campaign or event, then it is important to have some last-minute tricks up your sleeve.

There will certainly be unforeseen developments along the way that will surprise you, but there are ways to reduce the probability of problems that might occur. Look at risk factors surrounding your fundraiser that could directly or indirectly impact your goal. Are the highways leading to the golf course closed for repaving? Are there new zoning laws or ordinances that may affect your plans? Is there a FOR SALE sign on the catering hall you just booked for your fundraiser? Did the wrapping paper company just declare bankruptcy while holding your 2,000-item order? You cannot anticipate all possible scenarios, but if you have backup plans, you can reassure donors that they will receive goods and services or, in the worst-case scenario, have their money returned. It always helps to remind people, when calamity strikes, that after all, their donations are for a good cause.

A contingency plan may be as simple as securing a rain date for a golf tournament or calling Federal Express to overnight an important item to the auction that is late in arriving at the site.

FACT

You may want to take out insurance to compensate your organization in case your event has to be cancelled because of bad weather or other unforeseeable circumstances. While this can be costly, it can ultimately prove valuable.

The bottom line is to think about what your organization will do to shift gears and take a new approach if all is not going as planned. It is also important to have someone in charge of determining when to make such a change in plans so that you can start the process of notifying everyone involved.

Inviting Special Guests

Okay, so you have the place, the date, your timeline, and a contingency plan in case anything goes wrong. Now, what can you do to put this fundraiser over the top? How about a special guest? Let's assume that Julia Roberts or the governor of your state is busy. How about a local celebrity? Chances are that between your board and your members, someone has access to a well-known personality. In some instances, a personality can detract from the matter at hand, but in most cases, he or she will help attract a crowd and generate support for your fundraiser.

To find a "celebrity" of any stature who will be effective, you should first look for someone who believes in your cause. Then find someone who will be in town or accessible when you are having your fundraiser. You might also seek out someone who fits the theme of your event. For example, a professional or former professional golfer to launch your tournament or present the prizes to the winners.

Dealing with Celebrities

If you have a celebrity of any magnitude, be it a local hero or a national sports star, coming to your fundraiser, you should carefully plan exactly what he or she is expected to do (and not to do). Chances are, his or her time is limited, so if there are photos to be taken, an award to be presented, or any such activity, make sure you can schedule it to take place when he or she shows up. Celebrities are prone to the same scheduling snafus the rest of us are, and may be late or even have to change plans at the last minute and cancel their appearance altogether. Double-check that he or she is coming, and do not center your event around his or her appearance unless he or she is already a major player for your cause.

ALERT!

Don't hand a celebrity or a politician a microphone and ask him or her if he or she wants to talk. There are many stories of celebrities and politicians going way off on tangents or monopolizing the time with their own agendas. If your celebrity guest is willing to speak, politely let him or her know you'd be thrilled to have him or her talk for a few minutes about your cause.

It is often to your advantage to invite a local media personality or celebrity who is more in touch with the community and the people than is a "big name celebrity," who may only disappoint when he or she arrives late, has little to say, and can stay for only five minutes.

Use Your Auction

A nice way to work a popular figure into your fundraiser is through an auction. The daughter of a chef in one of New York City's finest restaurants was a student at a local grade school. Dad offered to cook a dinner for eighteen people as an auction prize. Another school had the brother of a professional basketball player in attendance. Big brother agreed to come by and, as a prize, give a twenty-minute basketball clinic to five lucky kids. These are major ways to boost an auction, while letting a personality do what he or she does best.

If someone has a contact who may not be a household name but who is a star in a field of interest, that contact's services can be utilized in your auction. Golf lessons from a pro or a makeup demonstration by a top Hollywood makeup artist are ways to increase the bidding. Determine who your membership can reach.

If you get a talent to donate his or her time to perform at your fundraiser, you should then make a concerted effort to see that everything is taken care of, from sound checks to refreshments to transportation. Anyone who is going out of his or her way for you deserves to be treated well.

Media Representatives

Part of your publicity campaign, discussed in detail in Chapter 10, will include inviting the media to your fundraising activities in an effort to gain some valuable press. While this is wonderful in theory, it can present problems. The media is usually kind to nonprofits, but not always. If members of the media are in attendance, you will need to have someone to guide them around and answer their questions properly. There are plenty of cases of reporters putting a negative spin on their stories or simply getting facts and figures wrong.

Should the media be there to interview people running your fundraiser, try to point them in the right direction. You will want the most knowledgeable, well-spoken representatives of your organization speaking to the press.

Staging Repeat Performances

"We did it that way last year." That statement can be construed as either positive or negative, depending on how well the fundraiser went the previous year. A successful fundraising effort certainly bears repeating. However, how much you should repeat becomes a question that is often debated by fundraising committees and boards. The tendency to fall back on tried-and-true plans can sometimes diminish the opportunity for forward thinking and new ideas. On the other hand, repeating a fundraiser, sometimes with only a few changes, may bring in even more money than it did the year before.

If you repeat a fundraiser, plans, organizational materials, and contact numbers for sponsors, special guests, vendors, and donors should all be easily available in your database. And people who handled specific tasks last year will have a jumping-off point from which they can hit the ground running this year.

But there are also compelling reasons to change direction this time around. New members might have new ideas, additional resources, and contacts to more significant donors. And times change. What was "in" last year may be "out" this year. In addition, you may not have access to the same resources, site, and number of volunteers or the same budget to work with.

FACT

More than 75 percent of nonprofit groups stage the same fund-raising activities on an annual or even ongoing basis. Even fund-raisers that did not raise the money anticipated are repeated more than 60 percent of the time in an effort to build on an idea or theme.

Ultimately, the best answer is often a variation on a theme. A successful golf tournament one year might be a tournament with a dinner the next and a tournament with special prizes for side activities (like sinking the longest putt) the following year. Building on a theme or changing certain key elements that could be improved on is often the manner in which fundraisers are brought back annually.

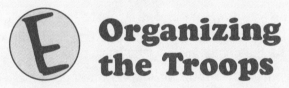

Chapter 5

Organizing the Troops

Now you've got a goal to work toward and a group of people who are excited about helping reach it. How do you utilize your human resources in the best manner to achieve your fundraising goal? You will need to set up guidelines for volunteers or staff members, form committees, divide up responsibilities, and shift the workforce from one task to another whenever it is deemed necessary.

Setting Guidelines

You should set up procedures to follow for fundraising activities. Even if you are not part of a larger, umbrella group, you will need to draw up guidelines prior to setting up your fundraising campaign, activities, or events. The level of formality of such guidelines, and the protocol you will follow, will depend on the size and structure of the organization and the fundraising activities you have in mind. Obviously, five kids running a lemonade stand to raise money for new basketball uniforms will require far less structure than will 2,000 students on a college campus orchestrating a twenty-mile bike-a-thon for several hundred riders.

Be Succinct and Clear

Guidelines should define how the fundraising plan is to be carried out in succinct and clear language. All primary activities should be included, such as promotion, programming, administrative duties, and so on. The responsibilities of the individuals or committee should be outlined, with details included to avoid confusion. While you don't want to pigeonhole people, you do want to provide them with a basic job description to turn to as a guide when doing tasks.

More significantly than how each task will be done, the guidelines should set the tone for how transactions and interactions with other people, including donors, should be conducted. They are a matter of shaping the overall parameters of the fundraiser. For example, areas that need to be addressed might include:

- How to explain information about your goal to a prospective donor
- How specific concerns or complaints are addressed
- What the procedure for moving to a contingency plan is and who makes such a decision
- What to do if someone is injured or takes sick during your fundraising activities
- Who is in charge of ordering from vendors and what procedures should be followed
- What does and does not need to be presented to the board for approval

- If there is no board, who makes the decision on each aspect of the project
- Who can call a meeting, and what the procedure is (and how many people are required) to take a vote

Documentation

Having written guidelines from the beginning can come in handy if anyone questions how you are handling certain procedures or if you are accused of being unfair to a certain volunteer or group of volunteers. It assures that everyone knows what the rules are and how things are being handled.

Having general procedures and guidelines written down can also serve as a guide to future fundraising efforts. Such guidelines will help significantly next year when you start planning your fundraising efforts.

It's to your advantage to have a separate set of guidelines for specific fundraising activities that differs from your organizational code of conduct or bylaws. While you might not have separate guidelines for selling candy versus selling wrapping paper, the bottom line is, your do's and don'ts when making sales calls should be outlined on a separate page and e-mailed or handed to everyone involved in the fundraising project.

Finding Volunteers

Whether you are the executive director, receiving a paycheck, or a volunteer yourself, you will likely be working with a variety of volunteers as you plan a fundraising event at any level.

Recruiting People

Nonprofit organizations often find that volunteerism goes in cycles. Many organizations report that for several years they will have plenty of volunteers, and at other times they will be busily recruiting. The nature of the organization (and why it was formed), the economic climate of the times, the needs of the community, and various other factors may determine how rich your group is with volunteers at any given time.

Most volunteers will come through your membership and through word of mouth. Often, people who are attending meetings but are not yet volunteering need only to be asked if they can help out running events or activities in a small (get your feet wet) manner. When a school runs a fundraiser, word spreads and often announcements in the school papers or on posters will let others know about the upcoming event. This will serve to attract attendees and will also attract people interested in getting involved in making the fundraiser a success. The ongoing fundraising campaigns of major nonprofit groups such as the Salvation Army encourage donations and also attract additional volunteers.

High schools and colleges are often a marvelous place to find additional volunteers. Students are often looking for community service credits, or they may simply be interested in your cause but not sure how to start helping. Make it easy for them!

Keeping People

Volunteers will get involved because they:

- Are passionate about the cause
- Want to give something of themselves
- Want to hone or use skills they may not get to use often
- Are looking for experience to add to their resume
- Want to do something worthwhile for other people
- Are looking to meet people and socialize while doing something constructive

These are among the key reasons why volunteers will come on board. They will likely be turned off and back away if they are feeling that their reason for coming on board is not being met or if they feel that they are engaged in an unpleasant or stressful situation. Unlike a job, where people will endure a lot because they cannot afford to walk away, it is easy to walk away from an unpleasant volunteer experience.

With this in mind, you need to accentuate the positives and ever so gently find ways to correct, or get around, the negatives. Starting new volunteers off with specific, but not crucial, tasks can indoctrinate them into working on the project without throwing them to the lions. For example, you don't want to have a brand-new volunteer out looking to talk with potentially major donors unless he or she is the main contact point for those donors. You will more likely ask new volunteers to help with promotional materials or join the committee in charge of gathering resources or even refreshments. The new volunteer will probably feel much more comfortable starting off in this manner than suddenly being responsible for a major chunk of the contributions necessary for a successful fundraiser.

FACT

It is estimated that more than 60 percent of the population of the United States engaged in some type of volunteer work in the past year. Growing concerns for family, children, and the environment have spearheaded the burgeoning trend in volunteering.

Training Tips

If volunteers are ready to work, you will need to make sure that they are versed in what it is that needs to be done. Not unlike a paying position, job descriptions should be prepared, and volunteers should be trained in how they can best complete tasks. Keep it simple so you don't intimidate new volunteers. Remember also that you will find some people will excel and go beyond the call of their "duties."

It is also important to try to assess the skill level and ability of your volunteers in advance so as not to insult anyone or appear condescending. Find out what they have experience in and, more importantly, what they enjoy doing.

For more specific or specialized tasks, such as maintaining the budget or handling the accounting procedures, be selective from the start and find someone with both the necessary experience and the ongoing dedication to the organization or the cause. Switching treasurers midway through a fundraising effort is not easy and lends itself to errors in accounting.

If you are working with a nonprofit organization, board members should be encouraged to help find someone with an accounting background. If you are running a school fundraiser, you need to network through teachers and school administrators to see if they have someone in mind. Volunteers with experience in a particular area may need training in some aspects of your organization and its goals, but don't try to dictate the job to that person. Rely on his or her expertise in the area—that's why you're bringing him or her onboard.

Present the big picture. Don't just train volunteers to do a specific task. Get them acquainted with the overall work being done by your organization or group so that they have a better understanding of the goals of the group and feel a part of the overall group or organization.

Creating Schedules

It helps if volunteers know when they will be needed. It helps even more if you know when they will be needed. Therefore, a volunteer schedule needs to be set up and carefully maintained. Volunteer schedules often require great flexibility for many reasons:

- Volunteers often need to change their schedule around at any time.
- You may need to change the schedule based on the completion or lack of completion of other tasks.
- External factors ranging from the weather to political snafus are a reality.
- You may have over- or underestimated your need for volunteers.

Schedules should be thought of as works in progress. Start by estimating how long it will take to complete a task, but realize that things may happen more quickly—or more slowly—than you expected. You can reassess your time frame and adjust it to be more realistic once the activity is under way. Always estimate on the long end.

Schedules should be flexible not only in terms of the amount of time needed to complete tasks, but also in regard to the amount of time any one volunteer can put into the effort. Someone may be available for three hours one week, four the next, and seven the week after that. It is an inexact science, so try to have your bases covered with the phone numbers of a few extra volunteers on hand at any given moment, or have a volunteer coordinator handling the responsibility of finding backups or fill-ins for specific tasks.

QUESTION?

Can you fire a volunteer?

In a manner of speaking, yes. While a volunteer is not receiving a salary, you can ask a volunteer to please step down, but only with just cause. If someone is simply not doing a task very well, you should make every effort to help him or her do a better job, or perhaps move him or her to another task. However, if someone is doing something unethical or illegal, you may need to "fire" that individual. Have positive proof of what he or she has done before speaking to him or her; otherwise, you could be sued. Having job descriptions and expected conduct written down in advance can be a big help in these situations.

Working by Committee

A committee is a group of people officially delegated to perform a function such as investigating, considering, reporting, planning, or acting on a matter.

Whatever the makeup of the group or organization running the fundraiser, committees will break down the responsibilities so that they can be handled by smaller, manageable groups. Even if each committee is composed of only two or three people, it lets everyone involved know who is focusing on, and responsible for, each particular aspect of the overall fundraising project. Committees, or even individuals handling tasks alone, will be expected to report their progress at meetings.

Fundraising committees often include:

- A planning committee handling the major details
- A site committee, in charge of finding and securing the location and making sure all of the details are worked out
- An administration, finance, or budget committee, which is in charge of monetary matters
- A security committee in charge of safety (usually for a larger-scale fundraiser such as a carnival or conference)
- A programming committee, in charge of developing the program of activities and speakers
- A sponsorship committee, in charge of making a list of potential key sponsors and reaching out to those sponsors
- A publicity committee, in charge of spreading the word about the event or fundraising campaign with a promotional and advertising campaign

Most often, it is the job of all committee members to seek out donors. However, there may likely be a specific committee finding and talking to major donors.

The need for all of these committees depends on the size and structure of the group running the fundraiser. Very often, even in large membership organizations, there will be only a few people handling these important tasks. In smaller organizations, there may be a fair amount of overlap. One person may be sitting on several committees or a committee may be doing several functions.

Committee Relationships

Usually a committee is formed among people with similar skills who want to do a specific job. For example, someone in the printing business and a couple of people who have a PR background might all join the publicity committee. It is important to establish a general mode of operations for each committee at the onset. Someone will chair the efforts and each person will have specific tasks.

If you are heading the fundraiser, you will need to get reports from committees on a regular basis so that you can look at the overall schedule or timeline and see if the work is getting done in a timely and cost-efficient manner. If a committee is languishing, it may need help. You can offer to work with it, add an additional committee member if possible, or simply make suggestions. While you don't want to overstep your bounds or insult anyone, you might be able to politely find a way of helping the committee stay on track. You may also be asked to play peacemaker among committee members.

Committee Reports

Committee reports can be as elaborate or as simple as you want them to be. The intent of a report is to update all key individuals involved in the fundraiser or in the organization with the latest accomplishments of the committee and where the work stands in relation to the schedule and budget.

A committee report should restate the goal of the committee and provide an update on the tasks involved toward reaching that goal. Include necessary expenditures and the need for additional resources if necessary. Also include expectations such as when tasks will be completed and what else the committee plans to do.

Showing Appreciation to Volunteers

The hard work and time commitment given by volunteers should always be acknowledged. Don't let the volunteers who are working hard for your cause feel that their efforts are going unnoticed. There are several ways to let them know that you appreciate their efforts and to say thank you for a job well done.

If your nonprofit organization has a newsletter, you might mention the individuals who helped, or if you have numerous volunteers, you can at least thank the committees. If this was a grassroots fundraising effort for your school, temple, church, or community center, you might send out thank-you cards.

FACT

Large nonprofit organizations often have annual dinners or banquets where volunteers can be acknowledged from the podium and asked to stand. In some cases, plaques or pins are handed out in recognition of a job well done. This type of dinner can also serve as a successful fundraiser if the honorees invite guests who pay to attend.

A simple and frequent show of appreciation following a school or similar community-based fundraiser is to take everyone out for coffee and dessert. It's a small dip into the profits to pick up the tab for a mini-party to make sure everyone feels good about the job he or she has done. Such a gesture goes far when lining up the volunteers next year.

No matter how you do it, it's important that volunteers know that their work is appreciated. Saying thank you is part of the pay rate for volunteers, and it is an important part of the job.

Hiring Professionals

The rule of thumb throughout the fundraising community is that, if you can get the job done through volunteer means, you should do so. If, however, you are pressed for time or cannot find someone to adequately handle a specific (and necessary) task, you can then hire someone, requesting some consideration because you are a nonprofit group or simply a group of people staging a fundraiser.

ALERT!

You should not work out a deal offering to pay someone contingent on the success of the event or fundraising campaign. Professionals are doing a job for you—they should be paid for the service you hired them for, regardless of factors out of their control (such as a low attendance rate).

Most often, a professional, who could range from a clown to entertain children to a lawyer to handle a major lawsuit, will be paid through your organization's treasury, regardless of the success of the fundraiser.

If you find professionals who are interested in your cause or mission, it is more likely that they will be more accommodating with their fees.

The bottom line is, you need to be able to justify paying someone for services. Can this person bring you closer to your goal? Do the policies, bylaws, guidelines, and, most importantly, the members of the organization support the hiring of a professional? Whatever your answer, and your final decision, use it to set an ongoing precedent for the future. ⓔ

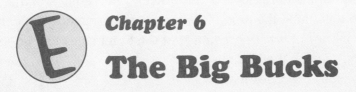

Chapter 6

The Big Bucks

Fundraising is all about, of course, money! How will you convince people to open up their checkbooks or get out their wallets? This chapter looks at how to actually make money and secure donations for your cause. But you will have to spend some money before you can start making any.

Assessing Your Costs

In the ideal fundraising scenario, there would be no costs—everything you need would be donated or sponsored. While this can occur in some cases (usually smaller activities or events), it is likely that you will need to spend money to make money. Whether that means buying refreshments, hiring a professional auctioneer, or catering a dinner, you will need to determine the amount of money your organization can put up as seed money or what percentage of the ticket sales can go to planning and running the fundraiser.

Some of your expenses may include:

- Site rental, including not only the facility, but maintenance and security personnel as well
- Food and refreshments, including servers and bartenders
- Promotion and advertising, which may include printing, mailing, and possibly Web site costs
- Travel and lodging for special guests from out of town
- Equipment such as microphones, speakers, and A/V equipment
- Special personnel such as a square dance caller, an auctioneer, a golf instructor, or a belly dancer
- Items to be sold (Don't forget shipping costs.)
- Telephone bills, including internal calls between committees as well as calls to prospective donors
- Miscellaneous items, from paper clips to raffle prizes

A good goal to start with is to try to get at least one of the major expenditures, which is usually either the site, the food, or the equipment, donated by someone involved with your organization or through a connection to a board member. If you need to pay for every major item, you are often setting yourself back financially before you even get started.

These are just some of the things that will cost you money and mean less profit. The more you can get donated or sponsored (paid for by someone else), the better your profit margin will be.

The trick is to make sure you have budgeted enough for each item that isn't being donated. Also allow for the likelihood of surprise expenses, which will inevitably occur.

Budgeting Expenses

You need to know how much money you are starting with and how much you will need to turn a profit. You'll need to list both the money you'll spend and the money you'll make.

Depending on the activity or event, you will have a variety of ways in which you can raise funds, which include:

- Selling tickets or admission individually or to groups
- Selling refreshments
- Holding a raffle or offering a door prize
- Selling ads in the program or journal that accompanies your event
- Teaming up with a known goods or service provider or vendor to get a piece of its sales

Often you will find ways to utilize several of these means and others to generate additional income for your fundraising activity. For example, a golf tournament can generate money from greens fees (or admission) and/or selling refreshments, raffle tickets, and advertisements in the program. A pre-event dinner can also add revenue. In addition, people can buy items at the pro-shop, with a percentage going to your cause.

Look for as many money-making ideas as possible. However, make sure you are providing value and not just hitting people up for more and more donations. People will buy more and give more if they are feeling that they are receiving quality goods and services.

FACT

It is common for 50 percent of your income from a fundraiser to cover your expenses. More significantly, look for your fundraising budget to be only about 20 to 30 percent of your organization's overall budget.

Typically, a nonprofit organization may spend anywhere from 10 to 40 percent of its budget on fundraising activities, so keep that in focus and don't spend the entire year's fundraising budget on one activity. Also, make sure to stay within the boundaries of any start-up or "seed" money you receive and not spend the potential profits before you see them. Yes, you *may* make $50,000, but if your budget is only $10,000, don't spend $30,000 and hope to make up the difference with profits.

If funding is coming in prior to your actual event from advance ticket sales to your banquet or talent show, you can increase your expenses as needed, but do not build a budget on speculation. Also, remember not to build up your budget based on pledges for participants who will be engaging in an activity. While most people mean well, someone will inevitably forget to look at his or her checkbook, and pledge $10 a mile for your forty-mile bike-a-thon, with only $300 in his or her checking account.

The Ever-Changing Budget

You may be a little more liberal in spending anticipated income if you have staged a similar fundraiser in the past and made a substantial profit. However, you don't know for a fact that the night of this year's auction won't be the night of a major rainstorm that keeps everyone at home.

It's important to keep in mind that your budget will change as you plan and conduct your fundraiser. There will be unexpected costs that you will need to factor into your plans. Conversely, you will add or alter your budget as you incorporate new ways in which you could make money. In addition, you may scrap plans that don't look cost-efficient or are taking you beyond your budget. Flexibility is very important as you work with a budget.

Sponsorship

One of the best ways of getting the money to cover your initial expenses is getting significant portions of your upcoming fundraiser sponsored. If you're having a golf tournament, for example, you can have a different company sponsor each hole. You can then put their names on the scorecard and have signs at each tee area. You can also have sponsors for the lunch you provide or for a demonstration given by the course pro. Everything can be sponsored at your events; you just need to let people know that you are looking for sponsorship.

In addition to helping you end up with a profit, sponsorship from a major corporation bodes well when seeking such sponsorship from other companies or grants from foundations. When a major company sponsors your activities, it lends credibility, so aim high when seeking sponsors.

ALERT!

Most sponsorship is provided in exchange for signage or some sort of mention of the company, which is usually mutually agreeable. However, if a sponsor begins asking for any type of control over your plans, you may have to say no thank you. Remember, your organization needs to maintain control.

Finding Sources of Funding

The key to your success will be finding fundraising sources and tapping them for donations. This is, after all, what your fundraising efforts are all about. Whether your fundraising goal is $5,000 or $5,000,000, you will need to develop a list of prospects. The word "prospects" is often used in the fundraising world to describe potential contributors. Your list of potential prospects may include individuals, businesses, civic organizations, government agencies, foundations, and trade associations. For every prospect you will need to compile information for your database.

Choosing Prospects

How do you develop a list of prospects? Your first list of prospects will be the people who you already know are committed to your cause, your board of directors if you have one, committee members, and all of your current contributors. One way to quickly develop a prospect list is to have people you already know, specifically your board, fundraising committee, or others working on a grassroots fundraiser, write down the names of three to five people they know. These people can be from all areas of their life: family; business or work; civic, religious, or recreational activities; neighborhood, and so on.

Build your list and expand from a narrow list of people to a wider, broader cross section. You might segment your list as follows:

- People involved in the group or organization, such as board members, general members, and everyone working for your fundraiser.
- Contacts, including families, friends, neighbors, work associates, and others.
- People who benefit from, or have an inherent interest in, the work of your group. For example, someone who has a hearing-impaired child will be more likely to give to an organization raising money to help the hearing impaired. Theatergoers will more likely support a theater group.
- Community supporters, including business owners and political figures. While some people may not be as knowledgeable about your cause, they may understand the value of giving as part of a larger community effort.
- The community at large. This can range from your school district to your city, depending on your budget, resources, time frame, and volunteer base. Reach out as far as you can without jeopardizing your possible profits.
- Previous donors. Never forget your database. Go back to anyone who has given before, thank them, and ask them if they will donate again.

The reality is that anyone can end up on your list and in your database. It is in your best interest, however, to start close to home and branch out.

Keep in mind that some volunteers will give time instead of money, which they might not be able to part with at the present time. Don't alienate hard workers by making them feel guilty if they don't hand over a check.

Know Your Prospective Donors

It is also to your advantage to note the characteristics of your prospective donors. Area of residence, occupation, marital status, and other considerations will help you narrow down a target audience. If, for example, you are raising money for a new playground, parents of young children are more likely to see the need than the young singles crowd. Therefore, you will advertise and put more effort toward promoting your fundraiser in neighborhoods where there are families. There are issues that are nearer and dearer to the hearts of women, seniors, singles, and people of various minorities and ethnicities. Baby boomers may be more concerned about ecology issues, whereas working women may respond more quickly to women's rights issues, and minorities may respond more favorably to raising money for civil rights causes. Know how to tap into the community that will be most interested in your message.

Individual Contributors

While corporate contributions of five- or even six-figure checks are the fantasy of every small nonprofit group, the reality is that the vast majority (90 percent) of the billion-plus dollars raised each year from fundraising campaigns will come from individual contributions. Receiving gifts of varying sizes from individuals and maintaining relationships with those individuals form the foundation of successful fundraising. One of your goals, besides raising money, should be building a base of donors for future fundraising efforts. An auction that drew 125 people and generated a modest $4,000 may not at first seem worth all the hard work that went into the planning and staging. However, you now have 125 names to send thank-you notes to and solicit for your next fundraising venture. If you see to it that they have a good time, they will be the first people to attend next year, and you can throw in entertainment to make their evening even better and draw an additional 125 people!

Fundraising efforts generally grow over time. Whether you are working for a nonprofit group or pulling together community fundraising drives when there is a need, you will be able to build on your initial efforts through your database. The person who attended your June event should receive a direct mail letter in November letting him or her know about your upcoming March fundraising drive. The small activities that raise funds for a school when your child enters kindergarten may have grown into big fundraisers by the time he or she is in sixth grade. Keep the ball rolling by maintaining contact with individual contributors, no matter how small their donations may be. Never say, "He or she gave only [x amount]." Each little x contribution adds up.

Have your successes on record. It is important to record the positive aspects of your fundraiser—this gives you a chance to show the donors how their contributions benefited your cause. That will be a major selling point when you solicit people next year.

Foundations

You may turn to a foundation for a portion of your funding. A foundation can be either public, receiving support from a wide range of members, or private, deriving money from an individual, a family, or a company. Foundations are usually nonprofit and are set up to provide money to worthwhile causes and activities, including educational, scientific, and charitable needs. To retain nonprofit status, they usually must donate a specific portion of their money each year.

FACT

Statistics indicate that, most often, foundations provide funding for special projects that help a specific cause. They generally do not fund the ongoing operating expenses of a nonprofit organization. To find foundations, you will need to do research. The Foundation Center, at *www.fdncenter.org*, is a marvelous place to start.

Seeking a grant from a foundation will require not only research on your part, but a well-honed grant proposal in accordance with the guidelines of the foundation. While grants can be a major step for a small nonprofit, keep in mind that there is great competition for grants, and that they are designed to provide a portion, not the majority of, your fundraising needs. Chapters 17 and 18 have more information on grants.

Corporations

Corporate donations can add significantly to your profits. Such donations are usually the result of a connection between one of your board members and a corporate executive. Today more than ever, corporations are responsible to shareholders to report where their money is going. Therefore, before a corporate check will be written to your nonprofit, it is likely that the corporate donors will want to know specifically:

- The goals of the organization and/or specific fundraiser
- The background of the organization or individuals looking for funding
- Exactly how the money is going to be used
- What contingency plans are in place if the fundraising plans are not proceeding on schedule
- How realistic your fundraising plans are and what your budget looks like
- How the efforts of the fundraiser will be monitored and evaluated
- How the company can be showcased in a positive manner

While a wealthy individual may choose to give money and remain anonymous, a corporation will want its name attached. The public relations aspect of funding a good cause is a plus for the company and its concern is, in part, focused on its public image. In fact, as mentioned in the last chapter, companies often sponsor events such as golf tournaments or bike-a-thons that can help them feature their products or their name in conjunction with your cause and/or organization.

One of the biggest problems you'll face in trying to get donations or sponsorship from a corporation is finding the right person to talk to. Often, you'll make a marvelous appeal to an executive who has no real decision-making power. He or she will then need to take it through channels to a series of other executives who will then have to convene with more executives who will forward it to yet more executives and so on. By the time your appeal for funding reaches the source, the cause may be miscommunicated, as in the old game "Telephone" (*"It wasn't to help save Crystal Gayle, it was to help save a whale!"*).

Other Major Donors

Most of the major donations come from wealthy individuals with a passion for your cause. They must be approached carefully and should be courted in person. Naturally, the definition of *major donor* may change from one place to another. For example, a $5,000 donation from a Wall Street executive in response to a direct mail campaign might be a modest donation for an organization that frequently receives six-figure contributions from multimillionaires.

However, if you are thinking of tapping a major donor in a small suburban town for $5,000, when most of the other donations are $50 to $100, then you will treat this donor in a very different manner. It is usually accepted that larger donations for most nonprofit groups are those of $500 or more.

Do some research to learn a little something about potential major donors before you approach them. This will maximize your chances of receiving a sizable donation. When courting such donors, make sure you are armed with backup literature and materials that support your cause and describe your organization. To impress a major donor, you should have information readily available highlighting your mission statement, board of directors, and fundraising team.

Following up leads is important. Sometimes, through researching names and their backgrounds, you will find a connection that results in a contribution. Play detective and look for commonalities between the potential donor and yourself, your organization, or perhaps a board member.

Tapping Your Sources

Yes, "tapping your sources" is just another way of saying "asking for money." Let's face it, in some manner, you will need to ask for money, whether it is asking people to buy something, take part in an activity, or simply donate.

While much of this book focuses on planning your special fundraising events or activities, there are other means of raising funds, most of which are standard practice for nonprofit organizations. Established and even newer nonprofits use three methods regularly: direct mail, telephone soliciting, and Internet contributions.

Direct Mail

Okay, so direct mail brings to mind the junk that fills your mailbox every day. The reality is, however, that it works. If it didn't, you wouldn't be getting that pile of junk mail every day. While most of it may be tossed, an occasional item may catch someone's attention for a number of reasons. The reality is, people do respond to a small percentage of the so-called junk mail, and that percentage makes direct mail worthwhile economically for most nonprofits.

While only a small percentage will respond, perhaps 2 or 3 percent, direct mailing works because you are dealing in volume. The more you send, the more 2 or 3 percent amounts to in profits. In addition, you are spreading the word about your organization and your cause to a mass audience.

FACT

One of the biggest factors in the success or failure of a direct mail campaign is the quality of what is being sent out. Look to professionals who have written direct mail pieces for some guidance. Your message should be clear, concise, and attention-grabbing so it stands out from other mailings.

If your direct mailing is in conjunction with an upcoming event, make sure that it is sent out with a sufficient amount of advance notice.

Include all pertinent information (time, place, admission, etc.). And last, but certainly not least, is the need for a dependable mailing house that can get your mail out quickly and professionally. There's more on direct mail in Chapter 7.

Telephone Soliciting

Telemarketing, as you are probably well aware, is very popular these days, but it has drawbacks. It can potentially alienate prospective donors. So why do people still consider telephone solicitation? It can work if done effectively and to the right people. This is where knowing your target audience helps big time. Volunteers from a school, calling families at 4:30 in the afternoon to ask specifically for Jimmy's mom or dad, and then apologizing for interrupting his or her day, is a better start then making a random call at dinnertime and launching into a sales pitch. Your telemarketing method should be centered on research, personal attention, and honesty.

ALERT!

There are guidelines established by the Federal Communications Commission (FCC) regarding the time periods in which you can call and what constitutes harassment or inappropriate conduct in such solicitations. Get a copy of the FCC regulations and any local laws governing phone solicitation.

The telephone has become less personal over the past decade because of the widespread, unauthorized use of mailing lists. People no longer answer the phone expecting to hear a friendly and familiar voice. Instead, they answer with a "who is this?" attitude, ready for another solicitor. Many people even screen their calls to avoid the intrusive callers.

The bottom line is, telephone solicitation can work only if it goes against what has become the norm—impersonal, scripted (even automated) cold calling. You need to be personal; call people who are involved in your cause and talk to them like real people. Chapter 7 covers soliciting by phone in more detail.

Web Sites

The Web is the way of the new century. It is a source of getting information, buying goods, and even donating money. Because of the anonymity and the ongoing concern regarding Web security, it will be a long time before Web donations rival other means of giving. However, many nonprofits are generating money through their Web sites. Obviously, the bigger the organization, the more confidence people will have in the security provided by the site, just as with e-commerce and online shopping, where established retailers generally do much more business than unknown Web entities.

On your site, make it obvious where the donations can be made and make the contribution process very easy. In fact, it should be possible to contribute from every page on your site.

FACT

While the Web becomes increasingly popular among nonprofits, the old door-to-door solicitation approach has diminished greatly. It has gone from one of the leading methods of raising funds to last on most listings. Safety issues, along with the time factor involved, plus the Internet, have all but eliminated this once viable means of solicitation.

Web fundraising is growing as online security measures grow. However, it remains a smaller source from which you will raise funds. It is, however, a place in which people will learn about your organization and, in many cases, be motivated to send a donation via snail mail. Fundraising over the Web is covered in more detail in Chapter 7.

Giving Something Back

For a $50 donation you get a T-shirt; for a $100 donation, you'll receive an umbrella; and for $200, you'll get a tote bag. This is typical of the fundraising efforts of PBS and other similar organizations whereby you donate money and get something for your efforts.

Giving people an additional incentive can spur on contributions. Having a sponsor who can provide you with T-shirts or some other giveaway item makes this added incentive idea work. It also raises public awareness regarding your organization or cause by the visibility of bumper stickers, T-shirts, caps, mugs, or tote bags featuring the name of your organization. One fundraising group gave a jacket to everyone who put in three hours of volunteer time at its annual conference. This created a professional, united look among the volunteer staff and served to promote the organization.

One of the simplest things to do is simply give recognition. It doesn't cost much, if anything, and it makes people feel good when they are acknowledged for their generosity, say, by being mentioned in the monthly or quarterly newsletter.

Chapter 7

Honing Your Skills for Effective Fundraising

Let's face it, many people have a hard time asking friends, neighbors, and particularly strangers for money. But if you don't ask, you won't receive. This chapter will help you hone your asking skills, be it verbally or in writing, covering ways in which you can put your best foot forward. All it takes is effort, a passion for your cause, and respect for potential contributors.

Fancy Phone Techniques

Telephone solicitation is both a successful and a highly annoying method of raising funds. Most telephone solicitation is done poorly, and the organizations paying telemarketers often receive a low rate of return for the time and cost invested. In some instances such campaigns reflect poorly on the image of the organization.

The question is, how do you do it right? Most people do not want to talk with telemarketers, so you immediately have one strike against you.

Some tricks to doing telephone solicitation successfully include:

- Use a targeted list generated in-house.
- Read names carefully. People are more likely to contribute if you don't butcher their names.
- Use your telephone call as an approach to be followed up with a mailing, because people will usually want to see something in writing.
- Work from a flexible script, one that explains the need for funding but also allows you the leeway to converse on the subject intelligently and answer questions.
- Be well versed in your subject and organization's history. (This is where paid telemarketers often stumble.)
- Listen. Too often solicitors are so eagerly trying to sell that they do not hear what the other person is saying.
- Determine suitable calling times, which exclude dinner hours and weekends. And don't call people repeatedly.
- If people are not interested (or rude even), just shrug it off and move on to the next call.
- Seek a common denominator. What brings them and yourself (and your cause) together?
- Ask for a specific contribution and then have a backup amount or two ready.
- Be polite and courteous.

It's hard for most people to muster up the enthusiasm to do random calling, even for a good cause. It is, therefore, in your best interest to hone a list of good prospects and maintain a database of people who have given in previous years or have sounded enthusiastic about your cause. You can gather names at events, seminars, conferences, or even in schools and universities where the issues you are working for are being discussed or taught. One nonprofit group gathered names for its environmental cause on a college campus, outside of the classrooms where environmental studies courses were taught. They asked if the students minded being called or e-mailed. This way, they were able to get a feel for who wanted to be contacted.

Don't Call Us

There is a rapidly growing national "do not call" movement in the United States. The movement seeks to create a legally-enforced list of people who cannot be called by paid telemarketers. The FCC is supporting such lists, which, if passed into law, could prohibit paid telemarketers from calling as many as 40 million people.

Charitable organizations doing in-house calls are exempt from the proposed list and out of the FCC's jurisdiction on this issue. But because commercial telemarketing firms that solicit contributions for a charity would have to abide by it, all calling would have to be done by volunteers or personnel within the organization. There may also be local restrictions or laws that prohibit you from calling certain areas or individuals. Be aware of any such restrictions.

Handling a Telephone Campaign

Have your volunteers take on a portion of the list and schedule them for reasonable amounts of time. There is a high burnout factor in phone solicitation. Tell your phone-calling volunteers to take their time, learn the basic script, and speak clearly and in a friendly manner. Anyone doing phone solicitation should take frequent breaks, as it can become very tedious.

Remind volunteers not to get frustrated if they do not generate many pledges. Letting people know about your organization and your cause is a start. Perhaps the next time the person hears about the work of the organization, he or she will have enough knowledge and will want to contribute. By calling, you are planting seeds.

When callers do get pledges or requests for written materials, they should take down the name and address of the person and double-check all of the information before hanging up. Remember to thank them for donating.

Make it easy on your potential contributors. If you send follow-up materials in the mail to someone to collect pledges, include a return envelope and a thank-you note.

Direct Mail Campaigns

Direct mail fundraising activities are conducted by nearly every nonprofit organization and political campaign where there is a diversified need for financial support. Such programs have been proven to be effective.

Along with soliciting donations, direct mail is an effective way to introduce a large number of people to your organization and, in the process, potentially gain their financial support at a later date. Direct mail includes both capturing new contributors and increasing your organization's base of ongoing contributors. This method enables a small group or large organization to quickly and simultaneously ask hundreds or even thousands of people for a contribution. A typical direct mail response is 2 percent of the total number of pieces sent. Three percent is considered a good response, and upward of 5 percent is terrific. Therefore, if you mail out 1,000 pieces and get donations from 50 of them, you are doing great.

Drawbacks

A major drawback of direct mail is that it is easy for people to discard. People have less trouble tossing a letter than saying no to a friend who is personally asking for a donation. There is no guarantee that the recipient will even open the envelope, let alone read the letter and take action by writing a check. Furthermore, you may know your good buddy is in a position to make a substantial contribution if you ask him to. However, when responding to a general direct mail letter, he or she may make only a nominal contribution. Therefore, personal contact is still more successful when dealing with people you know well.

Another drawback of direct mail is the competition. Even in this age of high-tech communications, people are getting a wealth of direct mail, and yours is likely one of many they receive.

Plan of Action

A plan of action is required for a successful direct mail initiative. That good response of 3 percent will be achieved when a series of issues, including the following, is researched and addressed:

- Who is to receive the mailing
- How often you will send letters
- The contents of the mailing
- A plan for testing your solicitation materials
- A P.O. box or address where people can reply and someone in your organization can pick up the mail regularly

Too often, people mistakenly think that once the pieces are in the mail, the job is finished. However, it has only just begun. With any luck you will begin getting a response within a few days of your mailing, and you will need to be prepared for such a response—which hopefully will be a good one.

FACT

Community organizations seeking to reach every household or business in a specific zip code can inexpensively purchase a list of addresses—just search on the Web to find companies that sell mailing lists. You can find lists that indicate simply "occupant" (instead of someone's name) as the recipient. These lists are typically purchased for one-time use only.

If you are a grassroots organization and are clear who your compatriots and supporters are, then you are in a position to create a mailing list in-house. The obvious advantage, along with the ability to personalize your mailing (and, if the resources are available, you can personalize specific letters), is that you and your organization already have an existing relationship with the people you are asking for a contribution.

The contents of a typical direct mail solicitation include a letter, sometimes a brochure, and always a reply card and reply envelope.

Typically, the letter will be one page or two sides of one sheet of paper if a brochure is included. When there is no brochure, you may elect to write a longer letter—up to four sides. More on this can be found below, in the "Fundraising Letters" section.

Bulk Mail: Pros and Cons

Another key element of direct mail is using bulk mail. For a one-time fee of $125, a nonprofit organization can apply for a bulk mail permit. There is a minimum of 200 pieces required for a bulk mailing. One benefit of bulk mailing is financial, since first class mail is more costly. Another benefit is the indicia, a code that is on your nonprofit bulk mail number that is also on your carrier envelopes and can save your volunteers the time of licking stamps.

The major drawback is that bulk mail can be *very* slow. Depending on the size of the town or city you are mailing from, as well as the time of year and the number of states and zip codes your mailing is going out to, it might be two to four weeks before all of your fundraising letters are received. Therefore, you must consider your time frame carefully and allow for those extra weeks until the bulk mail is delivered. Plan direct mailings with enough time to prepare your own mailing list carefully; write effective copy; and have your letter, brochure, or other mailing materials edited and proofread. Also allow enough time for the printer to do the job and for you to proofread the materials before sending. Finally, take time to select a good mailing house. Ask for references and find out if the mailing house is reliable and gets the mail out in a timely manner.

If your entire mailing is to be received within one zip code, and you can deliver your letters to the post office that serves that zip code, you may do better than a mailing house would. Experience shows that bulk mailings sent from suburban or small town post offices to a single zip code might be delivered the next day if not within the week.

FACT

One community organization in Pennsylvania led a successful direct mail campaign—increasing their membership by nearly 20 percent while they promoted their cause (trying to keep a particular development out of their neighborhood). They started with a list of 2,000 names, but sent their first mailing to only about 300 households. When they received a positive (2 percent) response to that letter, they fine-tuned it a little and then sent it to the rest of the list. They ultimately had a 5 percent response rate.

Fundraising Letters

The key to an effective fundraising letter is to get your point across in a manner that is clear, concise, and heartfelt. The letter that catches the attention of a potential donor is one that provides facts as well as a personalized appeal. You do not want to beg, nor do you want to confuse people with details of a problem that they do not understand. The letter should feature a compelling statement about your activity or organization that will cause people to take the time to send you a contribution. You also want people to know how their contribution will help you reach your goals.

To be effective, you will want to make it as easy as possible for people to donate money. Be sure to include clear instructions. Finally, people should know what they get for their contribution and if the organization has 501(c)(3) tax-exempt status, so that they can claim a deduction on their personal income taxes.

Determining the demographics for your mailing is very helpful. Writing to a business community will be very different from writing to students in a college town. Phrase the letter or postcard so that you get your point across clearly and in a manner that is appropriate for your readers. In some instances, you may have a different letter for each of a few specific target groups.

You will also need to consider who would be best suited in your organization to write such a letter or letters. Seek out someone with writing experience. Also, look at mailings from other organizations—don't throw out those that appear in your mailbox—and use those as inspiration for wording to use, or for wording to avoid.

Test Marketing

How will you know if your letter is compelling? Testing out your mailing is important. If you anticipate a mailing to 5,000 households, test your letter by sending it to the first 500 names in the database. If your response rate is 2 percent or less, you might consider rewriting the letter and mailing it to another 500 households. If your response is good (say 4 percent), then you will send it through your mailing house to the other 4,500 households.

Use test mailings to determine the strength of your letter. You might even send out two different letters to 250 households each.

ALERT!

If you send two versions of a letter, be sure to keep track of which letter went to which households. This may be as simple as sending "Version 1" to the first 250 names and "Version 2" to the second 250 names. But write it down clearly so you'll know later which version got the better response rate.

Building Your Web Presence

The Internet is a way of generating income for your nonprofit as well as promoting yourself to the world and spreading your message. To build an effective Web site, you need professional help, which may or may not come from within your organization. This day and age, it's hard to find a group of twenty people without there being at least one person who is a computer professional or at least savvy in creating a Web site.

Many of the universal Web standards and usual concerns apply to your organization's site. Your site needs to be appealing to the eye, informative, enlightening, and easy to navigate.

A good Web site has quality content on readable, concise Web pages that allow people to learn about your causes and concerns, read your mission statement, get background information on your organization and board members, and be able to donate money in a safe and easy manner. "Safe" means providing online protection so that people know that their personal information is protected, and "easy" means simple to navigate. People should be able to donate with a few clicks of the mouse—and then receive a thank you (which is very important).

You also need to have a good Web developer to help you create your site, and a server through which to post it. Many services provide both development and access to a server. Otherwise, if you have someone in your organization who develops sites or you have access to Web site developing software, you will need to find a site hosting service to get your site onto the Web. Keep in mind that the bigger the site, the more it will cost.

Whether you build your own Web site from software or have a professional Web site designer come in and do the job, you need to carefully navigate and read through the site to make sure it works. Don't be afraid to alter the site or even tear it down and start it again from scratch. Many computer programs make it easy to make all the changes you will need. WYSIWYG (What You See Is What You Get) programs are fairly easy to learn—these have the benefit of showing you while you're working how the page will look on the Internet.

ALERT!

If you are going to include links to other sites, make sure the links work and that they are in line with your organization. Links may lead to "surprising" places that you do not want to be associated with. Check out all links before allowing them on your site.

Those with a better understanding of the computer may want to learn some basic HTML to better fine-tune your Web pages. When shopping for Web site–building software, know your needs ahead of time and look for a program that meets those needs—don't get carried away buying a program with numerous new features that will not really meet your specific needs.

Also, do not let your Web site get stale. Make sure it is updated often, or people will not return. And take it easy on the graphics. Too many graphics can bog down the site and cause it to load very slowly.

The Internet still trails other methods in generating donations for nonprofits. It is therefore important that you do not bank on your Web site as your primary means of fundraising. Let your Web site be just one of several means of fundraising, but a major means of providing information.

E-Mail

You can use e-mail effectively to communicate with members of your organization and to better establish your relationships with donors. Sending information about what you are working on, updates and reminders of your upcoming fundraising events, and thank-yous for contributions or volunteer work are all great uses of e-mail.

Keep in mind that people do not read e-mails that go on endlessly, so think "brevity." Also, don't send random e-mailings, as people delete unwanted e-mails and this does not ingratiate you to these individuals. Make sure that the recipient consents to your having his or her e-mail address, and don't just add to your e-mail list from other sources.

You should also:

- Maintain an updated e-mail list and add or delete new or old members. Always delete someone who has asked to unsubscribe.
- Respond to e-mails within one or two days of receiving them.
- Avoid jumping at the chance to ask people for money—build a relationship. It costs nothing but a few minutes to send an e-mail, receive an inquiry, and send a response. Build a relationship first, and then ask for a contribution.
- Avoid sending attachments. Computer viruses have made many people leery of opening e-mail attachments.

Public Speaking

It's the banquet you've worked on for months, everything is in place, and everyone is in his or her seat. You've already helped raise money for the organization, and now it's your turn to get up there and say something . . . oh no, you're drawing a total blank.

Public speaking is not easy for most people. Making a speech about your organization or a cause that is near and dear to you is certainly no exception. Whether you are asking people to make a contribution or thanking everyone for the fine job they've done at putting the activity together, you need to be prepared.

Some people work from a written script, whereas others are comfortable with a rough outline. You can also use index cards if necessary, but always spend some time honing your materials in advance. Remember not to hide behind a written script.

Other pointers for keeping your audience interested in your speech include:

- Build a little story to pique interest.
- Emphasize key points.
- Make them laugh.
- Give them something to think about.
- Speak long enough to get your point across but not long enough to have them looking at their watches.
- Remember to pause to let them digest information.
- Vary your tone as you talk—be aware of NOT being monotone.
- Don't fidget with your hands or shuffle your feet.
- Make eye contact with the group as a whole.
- Talk to all the people, not just one corner of the room.

Don't hit people over the head, asking them for money in your speech. There's a fine line between requesting and badgering. A heartfelt and personal request, perhaps using a true story as an example of the need for funding, can often be your best tool.

Annual Campaigns

The keys to a successful annual fundraising campaign are consistency and your database. While people may not be awaiting your call or letter, they may know that you will be contacting them around the same time each year. The Muscular Dystrophy Telethon, Girl Scout cookies, Salvation Army Sidewalk Santas, numerous local walk-a-thons and bike-a-thons, and many mail campaigns take place at the same time each year and in the same (or a similar) manner—and people have come to expect them.

While you may alter your methods, it is important to keep the basics similar from year to year so that people recognize the envelope or pencil in the date of the fundraising dinner on their calendars. Naturally, if your fundraiser was not successful last year or you've found a major way to improve on your results, you'll want to enact that method. Do so without changing everything at once. People like a sense of familiarity. Leave some key elements, such as logo, location, type of event, and time of year the same.

Your database should tell you who donated last year, how to contact them, and how much they gave. This is very important for next year. Keep good records of donors and update such data as it changes, including new street addresses, phone numbers, and e-mail addresses.

Annual fundraising drives can be a staple for your organization and, if done correctly, will grow over time. They are a feature of more than 70 percent of nonprofit groups.

Annual fundraising campaigns:

- Provide ongoing donor support
- Provide a basic blueprint of the fundraiser
- Establish your organization as having an ongoing presence
- Are anticipated by donors who may already be ready to give
- Are easier to run because there are blueprints from previous years

People look forward to annual events or activities, and your volunteers will know when it's time to gear up for putting in more time and energy.

ALERT!

Make changes to your database from information provided by the donor, not off of other lists or information provided by third parties. Make sure your data is updated and accurate by verifying it directly with the donor.

A Public Relations Primer

Effective public relations efforts take some careful planning. The goals are to present your organization in the best light, keep the media informed about your ongoing activities, and dispel any negative press or misconceptions about the work that you do.

To build your PR campaign, you need to consider how you can best present your organization and your mission. You'll need to carefully determine which stories are worthy of media attention. Be realistic. Don't make up a story or try to interest the external world in internal affairs that don't belong outside of your own newsletter.

The best place to start is with stories that illustrate your involvement with the community and those that highlight activities related to your cause. What role have your efforts played in making a change? What is forthcoming that can draw attention to your organization? Press releases should talk about your latest news and key activities. Perhaps the CEO of a major company has just joined your board of directors, or maybe your organization received an award for its environmental efforts. Use this information as a launching point to tell people about what the new CEO will do for the organization or what you did to help the community that won you this award. Perhaps some big-name celebrity has agreed to appear at your upcoming carnival or maybe your fundraising idea was so unique and innovative that it was covered by the local news. Whatever you can turn into a press release can benefit your organization.

Here are a few tips to follow when you write a press release:

- Use a short, attention-grabbing headline, but one that is not misleading.
- Include the who, what, where, when, and why of your story.
- Make sure your facts and figures are accurate—double-check.
- Try to keep the release to one page; two, tops.
- Include a general or "boilerplate" paragraph about your organization.
- Make sure to include contact numbers for more information.
- Keep quotes short and to the point.

Media List

Names, mailing addresses, e-mail addresses, and phone numbers of key contacts for newspapers, television and radio stations, wire services, and Web sites should all be included on your media list. The list will grow over time, and you'll need to update it often since editors and producers change jobs often.

Put your media list together so that you can access contacts by type of media, region, or subject. This way, you can look for all local radio stations, all media outlets pertaining to education, or all local newspapers in your county or city.

To build a media list, you need to do research, which includes using the Web, visiting the library, and digging for sources. Reference guides such as *Publishers Weekly* or *Broadcasting Yearbook,* among others, can help you put together your list. Also use simple methods such as scouting the local magazine racks, checking your local TV and radio guides, and searching the Web under your topic of interest.

Working with the Media

Press releases are one way to get the attention of the media. You can also invite the media to attend events that you are holding or parties that promote your organization's cause. You might also pitch stories about your upcoming activities to reporters and freelance journalists.

If you are just establishing yourself with the media, start with simple, concise information and build from there. Editors and producers have little time to read extensive details, so they won't get to page 2 of a release from a group they've never heard of unless the story is extremely compelling. Since you probably don't have a blockbuster story off the bat, you can simply get them acquainted with who you are and what it is that you do.

Once you have reached the media, follow up and follow up again. The news media are busy, so you must—politely—stay on top of them if you want to get coverage.

Also, you should look for people in the media who have supported your cause before. For example, if a newscaster has been very active in raising money for diabetes, that's the newscaster to contact and personally invite to your fundraising event to raise money for diabetes research.

Before an event, prepare a press kit. This should include some background information about your group or organization (compiled into a document called a backgrounder) plus recent press releases, brochures, or newsletters you have pertaining to the event. You should include all recent stories that have been written about your organization and have appeared in the press.

FACT

The media are more receptive to upcoming news than past news. In their efforts to stay current and on top of forthcoming trends and information, the media tend to accept more stories written in a current or future tense.

You can also write and record public service announcements (PSAs) to distribute to radio stations. Unless they are for a specific event, try to make them as timeless as possible so they can run indefinitely. Either way, keep them simple, to the point, and about fifteen or thirty seconds long. If you do not have the facilities to record a quality PSA, then get a short script in the hands of an announcer. Some stations are okay with using presubmitted PSAs, whereas others want to have their announcers record them. Talk to the stations in your area.

Damage Control

It's not that often in the world of nonprofits or for a local fundraiser, but there are some occasions when you might find yourself receiving negative press. This is when you have to exercise what is called damage control. For example, if someone says your recent fundraising activity was a bust because it did not raise much money, you can point out that while it did not raise the funds you had hoped for, you are pleased with the turnout and are encouraged that the event helped present your organization and raise the level of awareness about what you are working toward. You can add that you are looking forward to building off of this start next year, and you anticipate much greater success. It is important to address the problems or accusations and explain what the situation really was. Try to put a positive spin on such activities, and always point out the highlights of your activity, event, organization, school, or group. Ⓔ

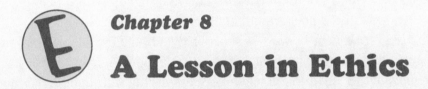

Chapter 8

A Lesson in Ethics

Because fundraising depends on the support and generosity of the public, it is vital that those involved in such activities perform their tasks with integrity and gain the respect of the donors. In the world of fundraising, ethics encompasses a very broad spectrum of how you conduct business, not financially, but regarding morality and fairness.

Establishing a Code of Conduct

A code of conduct is roughly a manual to guide the actions and activities of the members of the organization in their ongoing activities, including fundraising. It is a code that does not need to be elaborate, but should clearly explain the fine line between activities that are acceptable for a nonprofit organization and those that are not.

A code of conduct should outline the manner in which the fundraisers will act in various situations. It should cover monetary and accounting practices as well as practical concerns regarding how to best represent the organization when communicating with donors. Furthermore, a code of conduct will identify who is responsible for overseeing specific problems and activities.

Money Matters

One primary concern of most organizations is the handling of money. In nonprofits, other than salaried employees or administrative costs, money that is raised from donors is not to be used for individuals to profit or for nonorganizational activities such as backing a political candidate (unless you are a political fundraising organization).

There should be no finder's fee, which means no payments or special consideration made to an officer, director, trustee, employee, or advisor of a not-for-profit organization as compensation for successfully soliciting a donor. This is not to say that you cannot reward the top salesperson in a fundraising campaign. Incentives for selling anything from Girl Scout cookies to the winning ticket in a raffle for a luxury car will encourage sales. (In fact, one charity actually matches the winner of a luxury car, giving the seller of the winning ticket the same luxury car as the person holding the winning raffle ticket.)

On the contrary—awards and incentives are a great idea. Such incentives must be spelled out in detail in advance and open to all those participants in the fundraising program. They should also be made known to potential donors.

Another major concern of donors and organizations that should be addressed in a code of ethics is the use of funds by board members, to ensure that funds are not used inappropriately, in areas unrelated to the mission of the organization. It becomes harder to raise money for a foundation if the foundation cannot show that it made sound use of the money that has been raised. Often, a well-intentioned group or organization loses sight of the overall goal in an attempt to compete with other fundraising groups or organizations. And while there is a need to be competitive for donor dollars, it cannot be at the cost of the integrity and responsibilities on which the organization was founded.

It is important that an organization be able to justify all expenses. If, for example, you are throwing a kickoff party to start your fundraising campaign, let it be clear that the money is being used to launch the fundraiser, not for excessive entertainment or valet parking.

Taking Risks

There is a fine line between misuse of funds and taking a calculated risk. One volunteer group voted (after much debate) to fund a film that was being made on a topic near and dear to the members of the organization. While the cause was right, the group had not funded a film before, and this was new territory for it. Nonetheless, the intentions were considered in line with the goals of the group, and the risk was taken that perhaps the young filmmaker could help spread the word about the work of the group.

Risks should:

- Be in line with the organization's goals
- Not result in funds going to a person or company for reasons other than those of the company's missions or goals
- Be calculated and decided on by the board or a vote of members and not be a unilateral decision

The fewer people who know about something, the more likely it can be open to scrutiny by others. Therefore, communication and consent by several members or the board of directors is important for the proper conduct of most organizations—at any level. This ranges from three children selling cookies deciding together who will hold the money, to a multimillion-dollar nonprofit earmarking funds for the building of a new hospital in an underdeveloped nation.

If many people know what is going on, there is less room for misuse of funds, whether intentional or accidental.

Taking Gifts

Not unlike taking funds for personal use, accepting personal gifts should be a no-no. Put a policy in place that prohibits the acceptance of personal gifts or the use of resources that are intended for the organization. This can be hard to monitor, but numerous organizations fall prey to the mishandling of such contributions, so it is worth including in your code of conduct.

In addition, a nonprofit group may be in a situation to receive special discounts, services, and other such perks. Again, these are not for personal use. Volunteers are not "entitled" to a car, computer, or other such organizational resources because of the time they have put into the organization. This includes the $300 someone spent on long-distance personal phone calls made from an organization's headquarters.

ALERT!

Establishing clear policies from the beginning can help avoid temptation later. Be as detailed as possible when setting up guidelines.

Every organization will have situations where people take advantage. They're hard to prevent. One active member of a nonprofit all-volunteer organization was attending a conference in another part of the country and her expenses were to be subsidized by the organization. A month before the conference, her husband suddenly became active and even took on a responsible role at meetings. While some members thought this sudden interest on his part appeared a bit questionable, he was allowed to take on this new job. Within weeks she finagled it so that he, too, was going to the conference on the organization's dollar. After all, he was now an active member, right? Wrong. Two weeks after the free trip, he dropped out of the group as quickly as he had appeared. His free vacation (he attended no workshops or seminars at the conference) was a lesson to the organization. They tightened their policies regarding who could be sent to conferences.

Conflicts of Interest

In one New York–based nonprofit support group, attorneys are permitted to be on the board of governors as legal advisors but not to hold highly visible positions as chapter presidents. In Pennsylvania, a doctor may sit on the board of a medical nonprofit organization, but may not do canvassing for donors. Different organizations view conflicts of interest in their own manner.

The general theme of such a conflict is that an individual's job or title puts him or her in a position to potentially gain at a personal level while working for the organization. The question is, where do you draw the line? Can someone in a profession donate his or her time in a situation in which he or she could stand to gain business, without taking advantage of the situation?

While people do indeed make professional contacts during their work in nonprofits, a clear line needs to be drawn regarding how they deal with their personal business and the nonprofit business. If a potential conflict arises, it is up to the individuals to step forward and present the situation to the board. Usually the member knows if something he or she is doing professionally or personally is potentially a conflict within the group as a whole. Don't let your organization get into a position where any members (or potential donors) may suspect that one of the leaders is doing something for his personal gain rather than for the good of the organization.

Selling Mailing Lists

Mailing lists are very important to the success of a fundraising campaign. Today, mailing lists seem to be traveling from source to source at an alarming rate. No sooner do you sign your name at a supermarket to receive a weekly circular than you find ten other pieces of promotional mail in your mailbox. Online e-mailing has created a situation whereby you sign up for an e-newsletter and suddenly you're the recipient of junk e-mail.

Many organizations have their own membership lists. Members join most organizations and place their names on such a list with the understanding that you are keeping their information private. The more personal the information on the list, the more imperative it is that you safeguard your mailing list. If people lose their trust in your organization, you can lose members, and your prospective pool of donors may shrink. In short, don't sell your mailing list; it's highly unethical and can even jeopardize your organization if it lands in the wrong hands. The FCC and the postal service are cracking down on list-selling activities.

On the other side of the coin is the buying of a mailing list. Some list-selling companies take pride in selling you the proper list in hopes that you will be a steady customer. Others will sell you 20,000 names that are not at all interested in what you have to say. Since mailing list sales are a rather new business, there is still a learning curve that favors the sellers because many organizations have never purchased such a list before. Therefore, it is buyer beware. When buying a mailing list, it is usually for limited use, meaning one time and by a certain date.

Check any list you buy against your own list you've generated in-house to make sure there are no duplicates. Sending two copies of your letter to the same household doesn't make a great first impression.

There are a few questions you should ask when buying a mailing list to be sure you're getting the most useful list possible. First, find out how often the list is updated. Consumer lists age at a rate of 2 percent per month. In one year, 25 percent of the list, or more, can be outdated. Next, ask how the list was generated. It's important to learn from where these names are gathered. If this list is the reproduction of old lists that have been sold many times, the people on list may have been inundated with mailings. And, finally, in what ways can this list be categorized?

Many lists can be broken down by various types of information to help you reach your target audience.

When shopping around for a mailing list, it's advantageous to get referrals from others who have used the company to purchase their list(s). Find out what type of response they received and how current the list actually was.

E-Mail Lists

There are plenty of places to purchase e-mail lists. Here, too, you must beware of what you are buying and from whom. It is easy for almost anyone to build up a random mailing list of thousands of people's e-mail addresses who want nothing less than to get your "junk" e-mail. While there are some legitimate online list sellers, you may have better luck creating your own e-mail list.

Gather addresses by asking people who come to your Web site or communicate with you in any manner if they will give you their e-mail address. (It's unethical to take their e-mail address from another source.) Also, have a privacy policy drawn up to guarantee them that their information is safe in your hands and will not be sold or distributed elsewhere. And, finally, give them something for their efforts. This can range from weekly information about your cause to a weekly, biweekly, or monthly newsletter. However, don't bombard them. People do not want to be harassed. Few people give money to an organization that is annoying.

One of the foremost complaints from Internet users is the inability to unsubscribe from a list. Make sure you allow people to unsubscribe easily if they do not want your newsletter or e-mails.

FACT

It is estimated that over 5 trillion e-mails are sent annually. If your mailing is among them, it must be eye-catching, concise, and feature contact information.

The advantage of e-mail marketing is reaching people very quickly all over the world for little money. You can also be quite current because they will get the message that very day. Too many people forget the immediacy of e-mail and send around the same message month after month. If you add in something that is current, it makes people notice that this is a fresh e-mail and wasn't written months ago.

You can also use chat rooms and newsgroups to spread the word about your group or cause, if the group is amenable. But some newsgroups have policies against solicitation, so be sure to read the forum's guidelines before posting. Even if there are no bans against it, you may want to feel out the situation subtly. Don't just jump in with a sales pitch or solicitation or you might alienate everyone in a second. Remember, it's unethical to use information you gather online without the person's consent, such as copying e-mail addresses from a chat room or other list.

Credibility

Obviously your credibility will become zero if you are caught falsifying records to make your organization appear more financially successful than it is. Receiving a grant is at a premium today, and it's tempting to round off income or try to make your organization appear more credible by adding on funding sources that do not really exist. It's a big risk that you should avoid taking.

Besides money issues, your credibility is always in jeopardy if you make claims that you cannot keep. Like any business, a nonprofit must be able to deliver on a promise, just as donors who pledge money are expected to deliver on their promises. If you claim that your organization has helped many children learn to read, be prepared to explain where, when, and through which program. It doesn't have to mean that every child in the funded program will be reading at an appropriate grade level, but don't make that claim unless there are children who could not read before starting the program your organization has funded who can now read at some level.

On a more basic level, if you are selling something for the holiday season, you must deliver it before the holidays. Don't tell someone that by "holiday season" you meant Valentine's Day, when they clearly bought wrapping paper for Christmas.

ALERT!

Do not allow your organization or group name to be used in conjunction with commercial ventures, or vice versa. Nonprofits should take careful steps to remain independent and not be used to solicit for for-profit activities or use for-profit activities to solicit funds. If a nonprofit organization is too closely aligned with a commercial (for profit) company, it can take away the credibility of the organization and jeopardize its nonprofit tax status.

Activities to Avoid

There are a variety of activities that your organization should avoid altogether to maintain integrity. Most are common sense, but it is worth pointing them out here to get them on your radar screen.

"Creative Accounting"

An effective organization will want to avoid what is sometimes called "slippage." Slippage includes creative accounting, misleading results, overstating your case, marketing hype, deceptions to influence others, concealment of bad news, or false credit for others' work. These are all unethical activities that cannot be permitted for a nonprofit to be successful.

Inappropriate Personal Conduct

There are numerous aspects of fundraising where conduct and ethics will come into play, including how members conduct themselves within the organization and while soliciting funds. If someone has his or her own personal agenda, the functions of the group, including meetings, conferences, and fundraising activities, are not the place to carry out such personal aims. One woman, while putting together a fundraiser, also slipped in that she was job hunting, and used the opportunity to meet people as a means of handing out her resume while collecting donations.

Advertising Plugs

Often, guest speakers may be attending your function in part out of kindness and generosity, and in part to sell their latest book or their services. Policies need to be in place to monitor how this is done, if such activities are permitted. Often a group will have someone speak at a conference or seminar knowing that he or she is going to plug their work in some manner. As long as it doesn't take away from the subject at hand, it is permissible. Again, this is a judgment call that your organization will need to make.

Misleading the Public

Fraudulent practices, such as telling donors that there are plans in the works for which funds will be used when there are no actual plans at all, can get your nonprofit listed among the Internet watchdogs that are monitoring fundraising activities. Internet and charitable fraud has increased in recent years and has found a home, buried within the glut of newly emerging nonprofit groups. Places such as the American Institute of Philanthropy at *www.charitywatch.org*, the Better Business Bureau (BBB) at *www.bbb.org*, Charitable Choices at *www.charitychoices. com*, and Philanthropic Research, Inc., at *www.guidestar.org* rate and report on the activities of nonprofit groups.

They offer research tools that allow prospective donors to look up the mission, goals, financial information, and history of nonprofit organizations. While they do not recommend one nonprofit over another, they often provide grades that can influence the public when selecting where to donate its money.

Harassment

High-pressure selling techniques may also cross the line. These include ongoing phone solicitations or e-mails where solicitors won't take no for an answer. Let's face it—if you've called someone three times and they have politely gotten off the phone each time, they are not interested. In simple terms, there is no place for harassment in fundraising.

Donors have a right to choose whether to contribute, based on the honesty and integrity of your organization as presented by each member. Education about your mission and your organization should be readily available and should be used in place of high-pressure selling techniques.

FACT

Web sites with privacy policies are more apt to generate trust among donors. Any Web site that collects information on people, including the Web site for your nonprofit, should post a privacy policy. It should be clear and easy to understand and should explain (concisely) how personal information is collected, used, and stored and whether it will be sold. Include an e-mail contact in case someone wants more information.

Etiquette is also part of successful sales. After all, if you build up a good relationship with a contributor, he or she may come back and contribute again. If you bully someone into giving you money just to get rid of you, you are not showing the organization in a positive light and will not see further contributions from the individual. Your job is part soliciting or selling and part building up relationships and a positive image for the organization and the work you are doing.

Ethical practices and clear policies that demonstrate to members and donors alike the integrity of your organization are crucial to a successful fundraising effort.

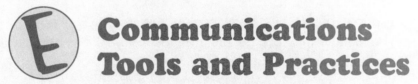

Chapter 9

Communications Tools and Practices

Your system of communications is crucial to your success when planning, plotting, and launching a fundraising event or campaign. This chapter looks at internal communications between members of your group or organization and also takes a more in-depth look at using the Web to spread the word about your fundraiser.

Your Communications Infrastructure

From a handful of phone calls to a massive e-mailing campaign, everyone involved in putting the fundraising activities together needs to be easily reachable. Early in the planning process—possibly as early as the first meeting—you should determine:

- The level of technical knowledge of the group as a whole
- The manner in which people are most likely to be comfortable communicating with one another
- What technology is available within the organization for communications purposes
- The budget (if any) and need for phone systems, cellular phones, or other communication tools to be purchased or rented

Communicating During Planning

Since communication is vital to an effective fundraiser, you will need to ascertain which methods you are comfortable using. You will then need to find a common ground on which to work. For example, if members are computer literate but only at a basic level, then the notion of e-mailing messages should be fine, but utilizing complicated programs or attachments won't work.

Since the vast majority of small to mid-level nonprofits have only a skeletal full-time staff, most people need to be reached at their homes or offices. Mass e-mails are quick and fine for memos, reminders, or even minutes of the last meeting (provided they don't run twenty pages long).

However, more personalized messages or those of a potentially sensitive nature may need to be communicated by phone or at in-person meetings. Many organizations have seen strongly worded e-mails cause friction between members. Often, they were not intended to be taken personally. Remember, e-mail does not catch the nuances that you can convey in a phone call. Therefore, try to minimize e-mail debates on issues concerning the organization (or anything else). Utilize e-mail, but don't overdo it. People will start deleting messages without reading them if you bombard them.

Make sure that once you compile an e-mail list of your member-ship, you keep a safe watch over the list and monitor what is being sent. It is not the place for jokes and other off-topic e-mails.

Put someone in charge of setting up the master list of names and e-mail addresses for the organization. If possible, include a section within the master list to note who does not want to be called after 9 P.M., who does not want to be e-mailed at work unless it's an emergency, and so on. People have their own personal rules and habits concerning how they handle their communications. It is important to respect those wishes.

On-site Communications

At events such as carnivals, conferences, or golf tournaments, cell phones and even rented walkie-talkies may be necessary for on-site communication. Naturally, discretion is needed so you are not ringing someone's cell phone when he or she is teeing off on the course. Individuals manning central locations should be the only ones making contact with one another during your fundraising activity, so as to minimize cross talk.

Since some people frequently check e-mails while others do not, phone calling chains are also still a workable communications system for smaller and grassroots nonprofit groups.

Knowing Who to Contact

Call Sam for information on programming, Fred can handle site-related questions, and Lauren is working with the outside vendors. A phone list or organizer can make life simple. The diversity of tasks and committees makes it important for everyone involved in your fundraising activities to know who is overseeing each aspect of the project and who to turn to for answers.

The smaller the group, the less formal the structuring of such contacts needs to be. A larger group, however, may need to set up a hierarchy of who reports to whom simply to avoid overwhelming any one person with phone calls and e-mails. Determine how many people are working within a committee. If, for example, one committee has forty people, it might be best if one person is not overseeing the entire committee and potentially fielding calls from all of these people. Think about subcommittees and redirecting some of the communications to other people.

Playing devil's advocate early on and anticipating as many potential problems as possible allows you to set up contingency plans and lets volunteers know who to contact or whom they can expect to hear from when there are problems implementing tasks. This will allow you to set up a logical communications system. Some youth groups have local troop leaders who report to regional leaders who report to state leaders, and so on. Most likely, you are not involved in an organization of that size, but a line of communications can help make things easier nonetheless.

Information Storage

Most nonprofit and grassroots fundraising groups have limited resources and have to get the most out of older technology for both communications purposes and data entry and storage. Since your members will likely be at a variety of levels in their computer expertise, you will need to rely on a software system that meets such varying skill levels while also serving your organizational needs. Someone versed in computers may be the person to select and manage your software. However, he or she must keep in mind that buying the latest software with advanced capabilities might not work among people using home PCs that may be two or three years old. Practical considerations and the learning curve of the people involved need to be taken into account before buying state-of-the-art equipment that no one can use.

Networked or Not?

Data storage and retrieval is a vital function of your software. Many small nonprofits have a few key people who handle areas such as membership and contributions. Access to these areas should always be limited to a small number of people, no matter how large your nonprofit grows. You can have separate databases that are maintained individually or a shared database with a system that can be accessed by several people or a network. Ideally, a shared database allows various individuals to make changes so that everyone can see them and others do not have to make the same changes to their individual database. This can save time and allow everyone access to the same updated information. Not having duplicate information means you won't have to wonder which database has the correct phone number for a particular person.

Unfortunately, this does not always work. "The system is down" is one of the most common phrases heard today. Basically, one problem with the software or hardware means that no one has access to the information. Everyone is affected by it. In addition, just as one person can add data that everyone else can read, one person can also make a mistake that everyone else has to deal with. In short, unless everyone involved is computer savvy, shared or joined systems are not recommended for most fundraising groups. If you do use a shared system, you'll need to use password identification. Otherwise, too many people (including unauthorized people) can gain access to your database and use it for personal reasons.

Even if shared or joined software is not necessary for your group at present, it is worthwhile to get a program that offers such features so you have room to grow and change as your organization grows or members become more proficient on the computer.

Determining Your Software Needs

Your database is your lifeline. Since any nonprofit group is dependent on the involvement of various people, you will need to have the storage and retrieval of all key data at your fingertips. Even if you are not using a computer, you need to have information easily accessible on the key people involved in your activities. You will want to store and access information on the following.

- Board members
- General members
- Contributors
- Major donors
- Volunteers
- Vendors
- Organizations similar to yours
- Government or neighborhood leaders
- Media contacts

It is, therefore, imperative that your data storage software be easy to use and have the capacity to bring up information from various data fields. When shopping for such software, you will also need to make sure that the software you choose can work on your computer system and support data from other popular programs such as Microsoft Excel and Lotus. The more people working on the fundraiser, the more likely you will need to input information from a variety of programs.

Buy software that comes with a tutorial or clear instructions on how it is used, plus technical support. Gather opinions on which programs will work best for your needs.

Financial Software

You may be utilizing more than one computer program to handle both data and financial information. While both should be accessible by only a few key individuals, the financial software should be especially limited in usage. Password protection is vital regarding your financial information.

Keep your software needs in mind. Nonprofits may require software for:

- Data entry and storage
- Budgeting, bookkeeping, accounting, and maintaining financial information

- Assembling newsletters and publicity materials
- Project management

The first two are common for organizations of any size; the others will depend on the size and purposes of your organization. Also, always keep in mind the "garbage in, garbage out" mantra, which serves as a reminder that the computer is only as good as the people who input, understand, and know how to utilize the data.

Creating the Database

Information on shopping for fundraising software can be found at NPO-NET (on the Web at ✍ *www.npo.net*), a service of the Information Technology Resource Center, a nonprofit organization based in Chicago that assists other nonprofits in computer and technology data. You might also visit the Computer Use in Social Services Network (an information portal) at ✍ *www.uta.edu/cussn/cussn.html*, the Nonprofit Matrix at ✍ *www.nonprofitmatrix.com*, or Coyote Communications at ✍ *www.coyotecommunications.com*.

When setting up a database, think about how the information will be accessed and used. Always consider the means in which data will need to be retrieved. Think about what information is most beneficial to the needs of *your* group. Review with others and get a consensus of what should be included. Build on the categories as new ideas are suggested and as your organization expands to new areas of interest.

Updating Data

One of the other most significant aspects of software is the ability to update information. You need a system that makes updating information a simple task and allows you to add categories as the information becomes available. Ideally, you want to add new information within a few days of receiving it. For example, if you had a sign-in sheet at your general meeting and five new members listed their names and addresses, you'll want to add the information to your database before the sheet gets lost or misplaced.

Another reason for keeping your tracking and updating procedures simple is that, at some point, the task will be passed on to someone else, who may be less computer proficient than yourself. You don't want to discourage and scare away volunteers by making a job too complicated or intimidating.

Make sure you update your database often, as members will change, new board members will emerge, and committees will be formed and dispersed. All of this needs to be updated monthly or bimonthly. Also, frequently back up all data onto disks or hard copies so that you are not at the mercy of a computer program that could become corrupt.

Updating data information returns us to the topic of communication. A system should be in place to get updated information from members and others in a timely manner. The same holds true for your media lists and lists of local politicians. They need to be routinely checked and updated. Since it's unlikely that the newspaper will contact you when it's been bought out and the *Sun-Times* is now the *Sun-Herald-Legend-Tribune-Times,* it's up to you to keep track of what is going on and touch base every few months with your contacts in the media to make such corrections.

Using a Web Page for Your Fundraiser

Having a Web site gives you the perfect place to communicate information about your upcoming fundraising activities. It's advantageous to set up a separate page linking from your home page that will provide information on fundraising activities.

Provide the details as they fall into place. Put someone in charge of updating material on the Web site frequently. This same person can fill in the data on your newly developed fundraising page. Material sent to this person, however, needs to be carefully checked for accuracy. Establish a process whereby the planning committee communicates via e-mail with whoever is maintaining your database. Get confirmation that the material was received and posted. Double-check it to make sure it has been posted correctly. Many nonprofits are lax in getting timely material onto their Web site because there are too many people involved in the planning and not enough communication with the Webmaster.

ALERT!

Too many data-entry people can spoil the Web site. Limit the number of people who can post on your site. The more you filter the material through one or two central people (unless you are working in a very large nonprofit), the easier it is to have a Web page with a consistent look and accurate information.

Try to make the fundraising activities stand out from other information on your Web site. Without bells and whistles, you can still design the page in a manner that invites the user to check out the information. Graphics, entertaining and informative copy, and all the important details need to be clear. Make it easy for people to sign up in advance or even buy (or reserve) tickets to your event either through the site or by calling a phone number posted on the site.

Even if your organization does not have a Web site, you can develop a Web page for the upcoming event on one of the many free sites offered on the Web. This will let you post information about your fundraiser and provide Web users with an easy place to learn about what you have planned.

Remember, communicating through your Web site is only as effective as the number of hits it receives. And this will happen only with good promotion. See Chapter 10 for more on promotion.

You are better off if you can keep the Web site design and data entry in-house and not rely on outside computer help. Several years ago, people relied heavily on others to handle all of their Web needs. Now, technology has made it much easier to do the vast majority of Web work in-house, including designing graphics and content and responding to inquiries. If you do require outside help, try to minimize your needs by learning as much as you can about how to manage your own Web site. Plenty of easy-to-use software programs are available, and you can find numerous Web sites offering build-your-own Web page capabilities.

The Future of E-Fundraising

Any discussion of fundraising in the new century would not be complete without a look at e-fundraising, where it is, and where it's headed.

E-Fundraising Today

The potential power of the Internet has yet to be properly harvested, but with over 150 million people in the United States alone having Internet access, e-fundraising is worth pondering for anyone trying to reach people and raise funds. A donation of $1 by just ½ percent of this population could bring in some $750,000.

The overhead of e-fundraising is significantly lower than traditional methods such as phone solicitation or direct mail. It costs almost nothing to send mass e-mails, including fundraising appeals, invitations, information on upcoming events, and thank-yous. Your organization can save money on printing, postage, and the services of a mailing house.

The problem with e-fundraising remains skepticism among users. Stories of identities stolen online and fraudulent charities create uneasiness among potential contributors. Nonetheless, once a nonprofit has established its presence and reputation, the Internet can prove less expensive than direct mail campaigns for reaching a mass audience. The site should convince donors that it offers Web security, that no personal information will be shared or sold elsewhere (include a privacy policy), and that donors' money will be used for the reasons for which it was donated.

Often, nonprofits align with well-known sites such as Nonprofitabout.com or other portals to collect money from contributors for several organizations. This allows for the Web portal to handle the promotional aspect of attracting donors while each individual nonprofit builds its own presence. Another growing trend has for-profit businesses providing space for nonprofits or teaming to offer ways in which to donate money to your organization through their Web sites.

ALERT!

State and local governments have regulations and guidelines regarding what is considered charitable solicitation in their jurisdiction. In some cases, it may be necessary to register as a charitable organization in other states before you can solicit funds via the Internet. It is advisable to talk with a lawyer about this issue.

Today, more than 80 percent of qualified nonprofit organizations have some presence on the Internet. The vast number have seen little or no contributions through the Web (some do not yet have a system in place for such donations), but they use their Web site to promote their activities, raise awareness about their mission, and, in some cases, recruit new volunteers. E-fundraising is a drop in the bucket compared with the overall fundraising in recent years since the Web has been popular. Nonetheless, it has proven beneficial when there have been emergency situations such as September 11 or devastating hurricanes or floods. The Internet has provided the immediacy that allows people to donate *now* to help the victims of such disasters as soon as possible.

Pros and Cons of Internet Fundraising

You will find long articles on the subject of e-fundraising, and if you ask the right, or wrong, person (depending on how you look at it), you can get long and detailed answers on why e-fundraising is or is not the wave of the future. For now, it's better to look at a few simple points on both sides of the argument of fundraising over the Internet and what it has to offer.

Advantages of e-fundraising include the following:

- Your organization can reach more people in a shorter time than ever before.
- Costs are relatively low.
- If your e-fundraising capabilities are set up correctly, people can respond immediately to requests for donations.
- Through e-mail you can respond quickly to donors' questions and concerns.

- You can update information on a daily basis and keep people abreast of the latest news and activities taking place in your organization or regarding your topic of interest.

While you certainly *want* to have a Web presence, there are reasons why you should limit your time and efforts toward e-fundraising. The disadvantages are listed here.

- People, in general, are still hesitant about giving money online unless they are confident that you will receive it and that their privacy will be protected.
- There is a tremendous amount of competition on the Internet for donations, and unless you have major marketing dollars, it is unlikely that you will be able to stand out from the crowd.
- Hackers, viruses, and technical problems can wreak havoc with your site and you can lose data, including pledges or donations.
- It takes constant work on your Web page to keep it current.

Many experts predict that online fundraising will increase in the coming years. It is therefore worthwhile to establish some Web presence and have a system in place whereby you can collect donations or at least pledges. In the meantime, if nothing else, promote your site as much as possible so people can read about the work you do and get information about the cause you are supporting.

FACT

More people will find your site when searching the Web if you use the right keywords. Think of a number of such words and phrases that will bring your site up during a search. In addition, get like-minded organizations to trade links with your site.

Requirements for E-Fundraising

To effectively receive contributions online, you will need a service that allows you to process credit cards, a Web page set up to accept credit card information, and a merchant services account with a bank or third-party provider. You should also make sure your Internet Service Provider (ISP) is equipped to help you set up what is essentially a "storefront" for receiving donations. Some ISPs are more familiar with the needs of charities and nonprofit groups, whereas others are more comfortable working only with for-profit businesses dealing in tangible goods, as opposed to online donations. Do some research before selecting an ISP.

FACT

Online contributions have rapidly become an essential component of political fundraising. In the first two months during the 2000 presidential campaign, Bill Bradley's Web site brought in $200,000. John McCain's Web site brought in over $1.4 million in just three days. Online contributions allow campaigns to secure credit card donations twenty-four hours a day at minimal expense. However, as evidenced by these statistics, they don't assure a winning campaign.

Another, more affordable means of using the Web to solicit donations is simply to put up the information as to where people can contribute by mail or pledge by phone. This eliminates having to deal with credit cards or online transactions. And for every person you lose by the added step of having them write a check payable as opposed to clicking online, you gain one person who is more comfortable putting a check in the mail than putting their credit card number online. Certainly, you can offer both options, but this way saves you from having to worry about online business transactions and may also eliminate legal questions regarding donations from other states or even other countries. You might even provide an online form that can be easily printed. Many smaller organizations use the Internet in this manner to request donations and do equally well (or poorly) when it comes to receiving such contributions.

E-fundraising is tricky. Be prepared at your end to handle donations as they come in and thank donors, but don't expect a lot from this means of fundraising quite yet. ⒠

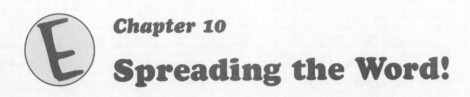

Chapter 10

Spreading the Word!

No matter how long and hard you've worked at planning a carnival, auction, or walk-a-thon, if people don't know when it is going to take place, you won't make money. Advertising and promotion are key elements in making your fundraising efforts successful. This chapter covers ways to get the word out about your event or campaign so you can reach as many people as possible.

Internal Publicity

Internal publicity means spreading the word throughout your organization. In a small group, this can be done via word of mouth, e-mails, and a reminder postcard or letter. Larger organizations, however, should make the most of their newsletter with a story about the upcoming fundraising activities in addition to a well-placed advertisement.

Flyers at meetings and other organizational events can be an inexpensive way to put the information in front of your members. Use your computer to create a flyer that tells people the who, what, when, and where; then make photocopies. Encourage your members to spread the word to friends, neighbors, relatives, and business associates. In a mid- or large-sized organization, you may need to establish an advertising and promotions committee. Each person should work on various methods of promoting your event, being careful not to overlap. You don't want to repeat your efforts and send the same materials to the same source several times.

Get Your Board on Board

Your board of directors should be excited about the event. Provide your board members with the basic information and let them run with it. Along with generating excitement, the job of your board liaison (or fundraising chairperson) is to convince the board that this event is being planned by a well-organized committee and has the potential to be a successful fundraiser for the organization. In the best of circumstances, the board president and the committee chair will have conferred before the presentation at the board meeting about how the individual board members can participate.

Remember, people give to people they know. The board of directors of most smaller 501(c)(3) nonprofits has a hands-on responsibility for fundraising. The bottom line is that successful fundraising events typically have a high level of participation from the board.

There are two ways that board members can participate. The first is to buy tickets, and the second is to help sell tickets. The committee needs to create a mechanism to help board members promote ticket sales.

For example, on big-ticket fundraisers, members of the board are often asked to provide names so that personalized invitations can be sent. Business colleagues, associates, and friends will be more inclined to write a check if they know the board member will also be attending. It makes a big difference if the president of the board will say that he or she is purchasing four tickets, plans on personalizing thirty or forty invitations, and intends to follow up with telephone calls. This type of personal action serves as promotion and sells tickets, lots of them, at all price ranges.

Get Your Staff and Members on Board

Before anyone can help you advertise and promote a fundraising activity, he or she needs to be well versed in the details. Everyone involved in your organization needs to know enough about the fundraiser to speak intelligently and enthusiastically about it and to direct people to the appropriate contact person.

Whatever information you plan to put forth in your upcoming advertising needs to be known by everyone working with the project. Therefore, the planning committee should brief everyone in advance on the details of the forthcoming fundraising campaign or event.

Beyond informing the core group who will be involved in the fundraiser, you will then reach out and invite your membership. Many groups find that mailing invitations is effective. This can range from a formal invitation to a postcard. Quite often a well-designed postcard enables you to reach a large audience at a very reasonable cost, especially if it is sent out as bulk mail. Remember to give yourself enough lead time because bulk mail travels slowly.

Don't tell everyone to spread the word until the word is clearly defined. One of the biggest problems an organization (for profit or nonprofit) can run up against is telling people about an upcoming activity before the plans are confirmed, and then having to backtrack. Set a date for officially releasing the information.

Defining Your Advertising Needs

Advertising and promotion for a neighborhood-based fundraising event such as a school carnival might be as simple as putting up posters and flyers in the display windows of neighborhood stores; on bulletin boards at libraries, community centers, schools, and churches; and even in apartment buildings. Smart organizations will promote the fundraising event not only in their newsletter, but they will also try to get coverage in the newsletters of other neighborhood organizations. Sometimes you can trade postings with other organizations that are also planning upcoming events. The goal is to get your information in front of as many people as possible and as many times as possible.

You must always keep in mind what you will need to do to ensure that your event is financially successful. Selling ads in a program book requires a different type of promotion effort than selling tickets. Furthermore, the advertising needed to sell fifty-dollar tickets for a dinner will differ from that used to sell twelve-dollar tickets for the circus.

Look closely at your target audience and select the most effective advertising and promotional mediums for your particular event. Research which means of advertising will reach your target group. For example, college students are more likely to see an online advertisement or article than an audience of seniors, who might be more easily reached by telephone or personalized letter sent through the mail.

Public Service Announcements

Most often, FCC licensing requires radio and television stations to include some amount of public service programming. As a nonprofit organization, you can run PSAs on radio stations. As mentioned in Chapter 7, PSAs are generally fifteen to thirty seconds in duration, and occasionally sixty seconds. Call the station and ask who handles PSAs and community affairs. Find out what restrictions the station may have and whether it wants PSAs submitted on CD or tape or if it wants the script for its announcers to read.

You may be able to coordinate your publicity efforts with a particular radio or television program. For example, one year, the Philadelphia Old

House Fair (a fundraiser) coincided with a local network's efforts to promote their own home restoration programs. A very short trailer mentioning the Old House Fair appeared after the home restoration shows for a couple of days prior to the fair. The placement was perfect for the audience that the planners of the fair were hoping to reach.

Determine how many people you want to reach. A large county fair may have the capacity for thousands of people to attend throughout the day, in which case the broadcast media can prove very helpful. However, a silent auction in a location that can only hold 200 people does not merit reaching 100,000 people, whom you could not possibly accommodate. Plan your advertising and promotional campaign in accordance with your size and space restrictions as well as your budget limitations.

Going on Air

Almost any city or town has its fair share of talk radio stations. An ideal way to get your message out there without spending money is to try to get someone from your organization, or a spokesperson for your cause, on talk radio. Television is another possibility, but unless you have a speaker who is comfortable in front of the camera, you may do better with radio.

A local celebrity can also be beneficial in promoting your upcoming fundraiser. Contact radio stations in advance, possibly ones that already know you from running your PSAs. Find out which talk shows might work for you. Even music stations are generally required to have some time devoted to community service programming. Unfortunately, this may be at 6 A.M. on Sunday mornings. You'll do better on an all-talk station, where you might fit into one of their daytime programs for a short interview. Most often the program host will ask you in advance what you want to talk about. Prepare questions that you have answers to and that feature highlights of upcoming fundraising activities.

A subtler way of getting your message across is to call in and talk about a topic on a prime time radio call-in show (radio prime time is considered morning or evening drive time when people are heading to and from work) and mention your organization or fundraiser in the course of the conversation.

The Internet and E-Mail

E-mail is a quick and inexpensive way to spread the word to your members. If you have e-mail addresses provided by previous contributors, then they, too, should receive an e-mail. Spam, or the mass distribution of e-mail advertising to an unsuspecting audience, is not permissible—which doesn't stop a lot of people from sending it, but does not put your organization in a positive light. Use controlled e-mail lists of people who you know are willing to hear from you.

If your organization has a Web page, post the information on the Web site. However, you must remember that posting material on a Web site does not help reach people unless the site itself is promoted. You will have to spread the word about the Web site for it to be an effective means of promoting activities and events. Make sure you include your Web site address on all of your literature.

Other ways to utilize the Internet are to send announcements to Web sites that support your mission, post messages on message boards, and mention your fundraiser in appropriate chat rooms.

FACT

The most successful promotion has been recorded by Web sites that drive visitors back to the site. Post stories about your programs or your cause and invite reader feedback. You also might include online polls and surveys. The more interaction, the more likely users will feel a connection to the site. In addition, you can better determine how many people are visiting your Web site and seeing your fundraising promotions.

Online Newsletters

E-newsletters have become an important communications tool between organizations and the public. Numerous for-profit businesses and nonprofits have successful online newsletters. If you decide to publish one, utilize the technology to your advantage. Combine quality content with an easy-to-read layout and use headers and footers to offer subscriptions. Include information about ongoing programs and, best of all, promote what you have coming up. Be careful to have a reasonable balance between content and promotion. People will unsubscribe if you are overselling and underinforming. Also, stay on top of current happenings in your area of concern.

Don't forget to link the newsletter back to your own Web site and always make it possible to contribute with just a couple of clicks.

The best place to get people to sign up for your e-newsletter is from your Web site. The less information you request, the greater the chance that they will sign up. The minimum that you need is the person's e-mail address and name. Beyond that, keep it simple. Long and particularly invasive sign-up forms turn people off, and you will lose them.

You should also include a table of contents at the top of the newsletter so that people can see what is coming up before they scroll down. Use short, catchy headlines and post your fundraiser promotions in strategic, highly visible locations.

The Print Media

Almost every newspaper has some listing of community activities in which you can be included. The print media also includes display and classified ads. Free weekly and monthly newspapers, which typically serve a couple of towns or neighborhoods, are generally filled with advertisements and classifieds. Phone calls to reach the right department should provide you with advertising rates. Display ads will be more expensive and more prominent than classified ads, and you will need to consider your budgetary constraints before spending the money on a larger ad.

Another print media group is newspapers and newsletters that are published by community- and neighborhood-based organizations that extend outside of the immediate membership. One neighborhood organization in Philadelphia has been producing a weekly newspaper for more than forty years. With a membership base of more than 10,000 in a couple of neighborhoods, this newsletter reaches a lot of people within a small geographic area.

When buying ad space, particularly classified ads, remember to be succinct, since classified advertising space is sold by the line or by the word. Advertising rates in local papers and circulars are usually fairly low. As a nonprofit organization you can often get a discount, and if someone on your board has dealt with the publication in the past or knows one of the editors or advertising salespeople, perhaps you can work a favorable deal. Utilize the local papers and look for specialty publications in your field of interest. Give papers thirty to sixty days' advance notice and call to confirm that the ad or listing is running. Make sure to double-check that all spelling and information is accurate. Get a tear sheet from the newspaper once the ad has run to document your advertising expenditures.

Magazine advertising can be more expensive. Look specifically for magazines that cater to your target audience and inquire about classified rates. Again, you should get a discount. You may make a trade-off and let them distribute copies of the magazines at the fundraiser in exchange for a low ad rate. Remember, magazines usually have a three- to six-month lead time.

Articles can provide you with free advertising. Part of the public relations aspect of fundraising is trying to get articles placed in publications (as mentioned in Chapter 7). Look for angles that would make for interesting articles and pitch these ideas to magazine or newspaper editors. Make sure to get the name of the right editor for your type of story.

Signs, Flyers, and Posters

You'd be surprised at how cost-effective simple advertising can be. A simple sign or well-placed poster can be seen by a significant amount of passing traffic and sell tickets. Unless there are specific warnings against posting such signs, you should seek out high-traffic areas where people who might be interested in your organization and your fundraising activities will walk past. For example, a college will post signs for an upcoming fundraiser all over campus and in off-campus establishments that are frequented by students—with the permission of the owner or manager. In addition, you'll see signs and flyers at bus shelters, on lampposts, on supermarket bulletin boards, and on the wooden fences that surround construction sites. Again, don't post if you see a "post no bills" sign.

If people can't catch your headline while walking or riding by, then your ad may not be effective. Keep in mind that white space serves a purpose. Don't overload printed advertisements. Too much copy turns people off, especially in today's sound bite society.

Handouts are also a popular way to spread the word among students or in areas of high foot traffic. Of course, this requires someone to be there to hand out the flyers.

Stickers and other forms of what has become known as guerrilla marketing can also be effective by simply putting the information in front of people. Stenciling information on sidewalks has become a favorite guerrilla method of advertising. Of course, it has also led to legal problems in New York City and other places where it is not allowed. Get an idea of the legal ramifications before you try guerrilla methods.

Posters, signs, and flyers should be easy to read and include all of the key points. Grab the readers' attention as they pass and give them the details in an eye-catching manner.

Promotional Activities

Promotion essentially means spreading the word without buying advertisements. From T-shirt giveaways to launch parties to kick off your ticket sales campaign, there are plenty of ways of promoting your activities that won't cost you as much as advertising.

Promotions That Work

For example, a promotional activity that helped one nonprofit organization increase single ticket sales was for something called the

Lobster Pot, a fundraiser with a thirty-dollar-per-person ticket price. During the entire history of the event, the organization relied solely on its members' selling tickets, and had done well with this method. About 500 tickets were sold each year.

During one summer, there was concern about the ability to continue to reach the goal of 500 tickets, let alone surpass it. The economy was shaky. Because of the way the tickets were sold, not everyone was aware this event was open to the public. And many people thought they were going to have to work harder just to maintain the previous year's sales level.

Promotional activities were introduced for the first time to create awareness of the event before the ticket selling began. The two major promotion activities were press releases and letters of endorsement. Daily, weekly, and monthly local newspapers ran photographs and short stories based on the press releases they received. The letters of endorsement were sent to a couple of hundred businesses in town by one charitable organization that receives financial support from the event sponsor.

The actual ticket selling was done by members of the organization, as had always been done in years past. They made sure to knock on the doors of many of the businesses that had received the letters of endorsement. The result was an all-time record, with ticket sales jumping from 500 to 630!

It never hurts to have a kickoff event to promote your upcoming fundraiser and draw the attention of the media or to create photo opportunities with captions that the print media might want to publish.

In Washington, D.C., embassies have been big players in fundraising events for cultural organizations for many years. On occasion, the wife of the ambassador would host the first planning committee meeting at the embassy, actually in the official residence of the ambassador. Along with being a big energizer for the committee members, on occasion a captioned photograph of the meeting would make it into the social pages, thus promoting the fundraising event by giving it more exposure.

Being Clever

Promotional activities run the spectrum. If, for example, you can procure sponsorship for giveaway items, you can give them away in any number of ways. From a contest at a local high-profile sporting event to handing out freebies in a busy mall, giveaway items and prizes draw attention.

You may be able to tie in your fundraising activity to another local event taking place. For example, one organization that was raffling off a boat arranged with a local boat show to have the drawing at the show.

Tie-ins with sports have proven successful ways in which to promote charities. For example, a promotion might include a donation of $1,000 from a sponsor to a certain charity whenever the home team hits a home run or the high school football team scores a touchdown. These kinds of tie-ins are hard to get at the professional level but are more easily attainable at a local, minor league, college, or high school level.

A well-timed presentation of an award to a local celebrity or community hero is another manner of promoting your organization. Your budget will dictate how much you can spend on promotion. Your creativity can then stretch your promotional budget a long way.

Going to the Extreme

Although you want to stay within the bounds of good taste and safety, you can create new and unconventional means of promoting your organization or upcoming fundraising activities. Unique means of promotion can be traced back many years, if not centuries, and are not confined to nonprofits by any means. For example, back in 1891, Edwin Grozier, in an effort to publicize the Franklin Zoo, located three elephants for sale in Great Britain and announced that any child who wanted to be part owner of an elephant only had to send in one cent. The names of all the children who donated would also be published in the *Boston Post,* of which he was the publisher. Though the paper ultimately paid much of the cost of buying and transporting the elephants to Boston, Grozier received 60,000 contributions, and sold many newspapers to parents eager to see their child's name in print. He hosted a welcome party at Boston's Fenway Park to present the elephants to the zoo, which was attended by many of the 60,000 children and their families.

Over the years, publicity has manifested itself in bizarre ways. Not that you want to try such stunts, but you can get your creative juices flowing by pondering some offbeat methods of promotion.

- In 1909, Maxwell Autos convinced a twenty-two-year-old girl that she could drive cross-country from New York to San Francisco in a Maxwell. She did it in a record fifty-nine days. The stunt hit the newspapers, and Maxwell sales rose dramatically.
- In 1949, the owner of the Physical Culture Hotel promoted his establishment with a parachute jump on his eighty-first birthday, as a means of demonstrating the advantages of physical fitness.
- In 1904, tattoo artist Samuel O'Reilly forever established himself in the publicity-stunt hall of fame when, in an effort to promote his tattoo business, he magnificently tattooed the entire body of a water buffalo.

Think of interesting and original ways to draw attention to your fundraising efforts!

Printing

If you are a small organization or grassroots group, you can use one of the many design and printing software programs such as Printmaster or Printshop to create quality printed materials that attract attention. The key is learning the program thoroughly and having a good layout and some sense of design. Study the spacing, design, and layout of other brochures, flyers, and printed materials to see what stands out.

Whether it's a print advertisement, a brochure, or a Web ad, one of the most common mistakes made is trying to put too much information onto the page. White space can be very valuable and make your ad easier on the eye.

Start with a prototype and show everyone at the committee meeting before mailing out any final products. If you are using a software program, it will be easy to make changes based on the feedback of others.

Hiring an Outside Printer

There are two basic types of printing—photocopy and offset printing. Photocopy uses photocopiers, which can be state-of-the-art machines that create excellent materials in a short time. Offset printing is more costly and slower but can provide higher quality, especially when photographs are involved.

Outside printers can be costly. Make sure you really need what you think you need to reach your sales or revenue goals. Have a reasonable budget for printing and stick to it. Keep in mind, however, that once a printer gets started, more copies can be less expensive. For instance, 100 invitations might be $200, and 250 might be $300. A significant chunk of the cost is the initial layout and setup of the printer's equipment. Once the press is running, the cost to you is primarily paper, so more becomes less per piece.

If you are using an outside printer for journals, programs, or newsletters, make sure to shop around and get several quotes before committing to one. Remember, the least expensive may not always be the best. Don't sacrifice quality for a quick job that may look amateurish. Ask several key questions, such as:

- How long will it take to complete the job?
- Can you see proofs once the job is ready to go to press?
- In what form does the printer want copy delivered? Does it need everything camera-ready?
- Can you see samples of various types of paper?

You will also want to see samples of products similar to those that you are trying to create. Most printing houses will provide you with choices of everything from font to paper quality. Paper stock varies greatly in quality and price. Check out a few before making a decision. The more formal or high-end the event is that you are planning, the more you need to spring for better-quality paper. Try to match the look of the materials—from content to paper quality—to the event you are planning.

Review proofs carefully. Proofs are the "prototype" of the printed work. Although much work is done by computer, there is still a person handling the typesetting process, and errors can always be made. It is essential that you proof the proofs, so to speak!

If you have a program or journal, you might be able to work a deal with the printer, such as offering him a full page at no cost in exchange for a discount on the cost of your printing job. Look to see how you can promote any vendors in a way that might leave them inclined to either give you more for what you are paying or offer you a substantial discount on your bill. Free advertising goes a long way if your product will also reach the printer's target market.

In the end, choose a printer with whom you feel comfortable and confident that you will receive a good, quality product.

Visual Effects

Don't scrimp on the visual image when promoting your event. It is true that a picture is worth a thousand words. In this day and age when people are reading less and flipping channels more, the visual image has a greater impact. You want to make a strong first impression in the mind of your audience. Get a good designer involved, hopefully through contacts within your organization. A good designer will create a visual image that can help sell tickets. Whether your invitation is going out to fifty people or you are printing up 50,000 flyers to promote your fundraising carnival, it is important that your printed product look good.

Working with a Graphic Designer

Before a good graphic designer will go to work, he or she will ask you to provide the text. You will also be asked if your event has a theme. Designers will use this key information as a starting point. The theme lets the designer know how you might address issues such as marketing, advertising, and decorating. They need to know how much space the text will take up on your poster, flyer, postcard, or invitation. A good designer will also tell you if you have too much text or too many design elements in your planned presentation.

Be prepared to advise your designer accordingly if you plan on using the graphic design for everything that you print, which may include post-cards, newspaper advertisements, flyers, posters, napkins, whatever. It is advantageous to create a visual theme that carries all throughout your advertising and marketing.

Assuming that your intended audience will see more than one advertising or promotional piece on the event, well-designed printed materials will help contribute to the branding and the identification of your fundraising event. After a while, people will need only to see the image, design, or logo to think of your organization. It will give a sense of consistency.

Fit the graphics, design, and text to your organization and your fundraising event. If you are planning a trip to the circus for kids, you'll have a far different tone and more colorful design than if you are planning a formal black-tie dinner honoring a longtime board member. Plan the printing design and graphics accordingly.

Photos That Matter

Let's face it—a dozen photos of gray-haired men in business suits accepting awards is boring! Get photos of your group or organization in action, photos of your cause, photos of your neighborhood . . . something that represents your group in an interesting way.

Visually appealing materials are those that say something to your audience or make them stop and think, smile, or react in some manner. The beauty and majesty of a whale is more appealing on a "Save the Whales" flyer than is the face of a committee member who is not known to the vast majority of people who are reading the material.

If you are using photos, get permission from the photographer and let him or her know that you would like to use the photo for a nonprofit mailing. He or she may be inclined to waive a fee for the exposure and for a good cause. If photos are too expensive, you will need to use those in the public domain or those taken in-house by your own members.

Also, be sure to take plenty of photos of fundraising activities—not just people smiling, but people in action as activities are taking place. They look good in the newsletter, on the Web sites, in slide presentations when seeking sponsorship, and in brochures and other printed materials when promoting next year's fundraiser. (E)

Chapter 11

Corporate Fundraising

Corporate America has for many years stepped up to the plate to initiate and promote fundraising drives. Today, cause-related marketing—commercial activity with a conscience—has led to numerous partnerships between major companies and charities. The results have proven good for the corporate bottom line. Studies show that more than 80 percent of consumers when deciding between products of equal price and quality will select the one associated with a worthy cause.

The Role of Corporations in Fundraising

Corporations can play a key role in your ongoing fundraising efforts by sponsoring your events or specific programs. They can also provide grants, which are discussed in more detail in Chapters 17 and 18, or team with your organization to raise money for a good cause through their product marketing.

Yes, corporations are generally looking at the bottom line first—theirs, not yours. After all, they are responsible to stockholders. The incentives for companies to get involved in charity are not completely selfless. Corporate donors are seeking some type of return on their investment.

Donations

Companies, large and small, are not only able to benefit your cause with funding, but they may also offer goods or services. For example, a computer company might donate hardware and software programs to a school computer lab, knowing that, in time, the same students will grow up and buy those same programs to use at home, not to mention computer games. Another example might be BMW, which donated $10 million to Clemson University for a program in automotive engineering. This may be the training ground for future BMW engineers. Meanwhile, it's a major donation to the school and helps it attract students interested in automotive engineering.

FACT

One of the leading reasons for corporate donations is to improve the communities in which they do business. The hope is that, by improving the community in terms of making it cleaner, safer, and better educated, people will not move away. This is good for business.

Giving Back to the Community

While corporations do indulge in philanthropy in part for publicity and business reasons, most are dedicated to giving something significant to the community. The Ronald McDonald House is a marvelous example of the power of a major company to help seriously ill children in great need of love and support. There are many other ways a company such as McDonald's could gain positive publicity, but this is an especially heartfelt example of corporate concern. And, yes, it shows the company in a positive light.

Barnes and Noble provides another example of a company that offers both donations and sponsorship in areas of interest. Their giving policies support organizations that focus on literacy, the arts, or education (K–12).

FACT

Studies have shown that over 80 percent of employees feel a greater sense of pride and dedication to a company that is involved in cause-related marketing or philanthropic endeavors.

Teaming Up

The primary means by which corporations participate in fundraising efforts and activities include:

- Sponsorship of activities or fundraisers
- Forming foundations for the express purpose of philanthropy
- Grant giving
- Staff fundraising and volunteerism
- Partnering with nonprofits
- Corporate donations

If you are seeking any of these means of support from a major corporation, you should consider what, if anything, can be the return on their investment. In your efforts to procure funding, you should offer something in return. You should determine how their participation can show them in a better light or help them in their fiscal goals.

For example, if you are looking for corporate sponsorship for your upcoming charity golf tournament, either through underwriting the event or direct contributions, you should ask yourself or your organization: Will sponsoring this golf tournament help put their name before the public and attract new customers? What can you do to help present the corporation in a positive way?

After all, they are saving you the expense of running such a tournament. Perhaps you could include the company in the tournament name, or feature their products at your pre-event luncheon. There are many ways in which you can team with a company to promote its goods or services while raising money for your fundraising efforts.

It's true that some companies do not make their donations public. They work in subtler ways to do good deeds in their communities. If they are not operating through a foundation, they do not have to make such information public, which makes researching the giving policies of such companies more difficult.

FACT

Companies that do not seek publicity for giving to nonprofits may do so because they do not want to become overwhelmed by requests for funding. They also do not want to set a precedent of being able to give away a certain amount one year, only to be unable to do so the following year because profits are way down.

If a company does not want to receive exposure for its donation(s), then that must be respected, and you do not publicize where the funding came from. It is possible that they are concerned that shareholders will be worried that they are giving too much of their profits away.

Approaching Corporations

You need to put together a strong proposal to approach a corporation for funding. Whether it is a grant (as discussed in Chapter 17), sponsorship, or a donation you are seeking, you need to have your proposal on paper, with plenty of backup materials prepared.

First, it is wise to research carefully to determine which companies might be interested in sponsoring activities such as those that you are planning. See what types of fundraising the company's name has appeared in association with in the past. Determine how sponsoring you would help its image and customer base. Look for a good match.

Who Do You Know?

Let's face it—with the competition among millions of nonprofits to raise money, it is very important to know the right people. The higher the person ranks in the company, the more influence he or she will have regarding spending the company's money on a cause such as yours.

First, take a look at your board of directors and committee members. Who do they work for? Nonprofit organizations may have a number of board members who are professionals in fields such as construction, development, economic consulting, or real estate law. They may work for companies (or even own a business) that are likely candidates to be contributors, newsletter advertisers, or event sponsors. Always remember to provide your board members with the opportunity to get their business more involved with the projects and programs of your organization.

ALERT!

Don't try to slant your mission or misrepresent what you do to fit the parameters of a company's giving policies. You're better off approaching the company honestly. Even if you think it's a long shot, open your dialogue with the company by saying, "I know this isn't the type of cause you usually fund, but . . ." (and be ready with some hard-hitting reasons why they *should* fund you).

The CEO of a major Fortune 500 corporation may sit on the board of several nonprofits, having a very limited role in the activities of each. Unless he or she has a personal interest in a cause, it is unlikely that he or she will have the time to commit to hands-on activities, which is why he or she will seek out a nonprofit that is well run and well established.

If your board does not include corporate executives or you have not yet recruited any, you should talk with board members to determine whether they have any contacts that can be beneficial.

You can create an initial list of companies that may be interested in your cause or build one based on the connections you have from board members and other members of your organization. Again, you should look for the best fits, but remember, "beggars can't be choosers." The reality is that the "who you know" factor is very significant in trying to make headway into the corporate realm.

ALERT!

Don't try to substitute who you know for *what* you know. Just because you know someone in the upper echelon at a major corporation does not mean you do not have to do your homework and learn about the company policies. In fact, you may want to know even more to impress your contact.

Often, it is in your best interest, when dealing with a particularly large company, not to try to reach the CEO (unless you have a direct contact), but to look for influential up-and-coming executives whose decision to sponsor a good cause might help demonstrate to their superiors why they should continue to move up the corporate ladder.

Building Relationships

It may take a year to cultivate a relationship with the right person, but if he or she becomes a major donor, then it is worth it. Five major donors can bring in more money than several successful fundraising events, and at less cost and with fewer hours of volunteering. Of course, courting such high-end donors is difficult and requires face-to-face meetings. You need to build trust by demonstrating that your organization is capable of doing what it sets out to do and by meeting your goals.

Privately held companies are good places for nonprofits to concentrate on. It is easier to reach the CEO and a privately held company will have fewer nonprofits approaching it. A successful individual in a privately owned company may be making $10 million a year and could easily become a major donor for your organization. You need to take the time and establish a relationship with such a company in your community. Time spent establishing and building relationships with top donors is well spent, since their contributions can be significant.

Giving Something Back

Businesses, no matter how large or small, are seeking a return on their investment. For a couple of years, the Preservation Alliance for Greater Philadelphia was the presenter of the Philadelphia Old House Fair. This two-day educational event was aimed at homeowners planning everything from a major restoration to a weekend decorating project. The Old House Fair revenue was from single-ticket sales at $8 each, booths sold for $295, and advertising at a cost range of $75 to $1,000 in the program book. Sponsors of the Old House Fair received a combination of booths, ad space, and complimentary tickets, each of which had a specific dollar value. Sponsors also received additional recognition on promotional materials and giveaways such as press releases, direct mail postcards, shopping bags, program books, and other marketing materials, depending on the level of sponsorship. Each of these items was also assigned a specific dollar value, to help show to the event sponsors that they were receiving a valuable gift that was well worth the financial support they were donating.

The first year that actual sponsorship was sought for the Old House Fair, the prospects were identified from the list of businesses that had been exhibitors and advertisers for several years. The second year, the sponsors included two businesses that were doing business with the alliance. For one of these two sponsors, the size of the event and the amount of exposure the business would receive was instrumental in the dollar level of the sponsorship. The second business, although it was directly involved with historic preservation projects, requested no recognition because it did not work with individual homeowners. Sponsors will differ in their needs, and you should try to accommodate them. The above example also illustrates that you can look for sponsorship from businesses that have supported you in some manner in the past.

Earning Money

No matter how the meeting with a major corporation is set up, through your own efforts or through contacts, you need to learn as much as you can about the products or services they provide. This way, you can present that which you can give back. There are more nonprofit organizations seeking funding than there are major corporations with funds to give. Therefore, you have competition and need to make a strong case for why supporting your efforts is in the best interests of everyone involved in the equation. The more you know about the group you're asking for major donations from, the easier it will be to find ways to show them the benefits they'll gain by supporting your organization.

ALERT!

If you find that your goal is the same as that of many other organizations, align with one of them. Too many nonprofit groups seek the same funding, and there is no need for competition if you are working toward the same overall goal.

Along with giving something in return, you may also consider methods of earning money. The proliferation of nonprofits has created a logjam whereby some groups are not getting donations simply because they are the fifth nonprofit to seek out the same donors for the same cause. Tapping into your membership and determining potential for a type of business within your organization may help your group gain attention and separate itself from the competition. For example, hospitals and other nonprofit organizations often open thrift shops. Try to find a means of earning money that does not have a high cost factor on your end.

Developing Partnerships

Not unlike two for-profit companies developing a strategic alliance, nonprofits and for-profit corporations are working together today in a similar manner. The result has corporations in the new century giving over $10 billion annually to charities.

Corporations provide money through foundations or directly through giving programs, and your goal is to build a relationship that will provide ongoing support. They usually focus on a specific problem or area of concern such as improving elementary education, doing research to fight cystic fibrosis, or spreading the antidrug message to teens.

In many instances, a major corporation will set up a specific program and then work with nonprofit organizations, schools, or charities. For example, the community relations development office of CVS Pharmacy focused its efforts on health and education. It teamed with schools to offer three-year grants and ongoing technical assistance to both elementary and secondary schools. CVS employees donate their time, skills, and services as volunteers to work with schools in the program.

Another example comes from Kraft Foods, which has taken

significant steps to combat the serious problem of domestic violence. They began funding programs that help battered women. In Chicago, Kraft has supported Mujeras Latinas en Accion, a nonprofit program designed to empower Latinas to become role models and resources in their communities. Meanwhile, in Texas, Kraft provided a grant to The Bridge, a program based in Pasadena, Texas, which helps create job readiness so that victims of domestic abuse learn and hone skills that enable them to stay away from violent relationships.

Coca-Cola and the Boys and Girls Clubs also work together, as do many companies and nonprofits. The companies find nonprofits, such as yours, that are working on the issue on which they have decided to take a stand.

Trade and Professional Associations

Consider developing relationships with trade and professional associations. The Old House Fair mentioned earlier developed a partnership with the Philadelphia chapter of the American Institute of Architects (AIA). The alliance provided the AIA with four complimentary booths in a prominent location on the exhibit floor and extensive exposure for the AIA and its members in the program book through listings of participants and stories that addressed how to hire an architect and a description of the training, expertise, and role of an architect.

In turn, the AIA purchased several pages in the program book and provided a great bookstore, an attractive exhibit on recent restoration projects, and dozens of architects providing free design consultations and lectures. The free consultations were promoted extensively and successfully attracted many people to the two-day event.

Trade and professional associations look for publicity and can provide your organization with a rich network of contacts that includes professionals in various businesses.

Employee Donations

Numerous companies have employee contribution programs, many of which are in conjunction with the United Way, which serves as an umbrella group for such donations.

Weekly contributions from employee paychecks provide over $1 billion in charitable donations annually. A number of companies also match the donations made by their employees, or at least a percentage thereof. If your nonprofit stands to receive such donations, you should remind your donors that their contribution might be matched by their employer and be tax deductible, if you have qualified 501(c)(3) nonprofit status.

Sit down with whoever is in charge of such employee giving programs in your company and provide him or her with literature about the nonprofit to which you belong. In some cases, such an employee program may not yet exist, and you may start the ball rolling within your company.

One major financial company has a matching gift program whereby they will direct money from their foundation to meet the donations of their employees. They match donations of $50 or more, up to $2,000 per year, for full-time employees who have been with the company for a specified amount of time. The donation can be made to a single organization or to several organizations as the employee sees fit. The organization must be a 501(c)(3) nonprofit. This is typical of many such programs instituted to promote employee giving and company involvement.

It is also in your best interest to talk with people about the companies they work for. Often, if an employee has worked for a company for several years and is involved with a nonprofit organization, the company may be interested in contributing or sponsoring some activity. Even small businesses may want to begin their involvement with fundraising efforts, and employee interests are a wonderful place to start. It helps boost employee relations and morale when a business shows an interest in the concerns of its employees.

Let your involvement in a nonprofit be known around the office, particularly to whomever is in charge of charitable contributions. They may not be in a position to respond immediately, but should they be looking to donate to or form a partnership with a nonprofit organization at a later date, yours may come to mind more quickly because of the employee connection.

The United Way

The granddaddy of corporate giving programs comes from the United Way. Originally known as the Charitable Organizations Society and founded in Denver in 1887, the United Way now raises over $3 billion annually. As an umbrella group, the United Way pools the contributions of thousands of employees made directly through payroll deductions. The money is then distributed to numerous nonprofit organizations nationwide. Many long-established notable organizations such as the Red Cross receive a portion of their funds through United Way contributions.

FACT

For many years, the United Way was called the Charitable Organizations Society. It eventually became known as the Community Chest, and finally, in 1963, the name was changed to United Way, Inc.

Donating to the United Way can be like investing with a mutual fund, only you are not looking for a monetary return on your investment. Instead of your money going to one nonprofit, it could be going to any of a number of organizations. There are also situations where you can specify to which charities, from the United Way listing, you want your contributions directed. By aligning with numerous organizations and corporations, the United Way has established itself as the premier organization that serves as a liaison between the employees and charities.

Nonprofit groups are eager to get a piece of the billions raised every year and apply to the United Way for such consideration.

It is recommended that you contact your local United Way to learn if it is still accepting applications for 501(c)3 nonprofits as designated recipients and what the application process entails. If your organization is accepted, you can then let your constituents know that you are a participating United Way organization. They can then set up automatic payroll deductions through their employers to make regular contributions to your organization.

Chapter 12

Community Fundraising

Whether it's collecting funds to help refurbish a rundown part of town, build new playgrounds, or clean up the parks, local nonprofit groups spend time and money to maintain their communities. Such community groups and neighborhood associations form and grow based on the common desire to maintain or improve the quality of life in the community. The goals of subsequent fundraising efforts are to meet the pressing needs of everyone from preschoolers to seniors.

Involving the Whole Community

No, not everyone will donate money or volunteer, but if your community-based nonprofit group studies the issues that affect your community and researches the changes that can be made, you can involve much of the community in your efforts and potentially affect everyone with your results.

Start by doing your homework. Research the issues that affect your community and look for the source of each issue. Is there a lack of funding? Has redevelopment changed the face of the neighborhood? Is there a need for more police or a community watch?

FACT

Focus on everyone, not only high-end potentially big money donors. Statistics have shown that 85 percent of all individual donations come from families with incomes of $50,000 or less. Therefore, raising money from the middle and working class should be a significant goal of your fundraising campaign.

Look at the map and determine what makes up the community boundaries. Then explore the makeup of the community. What cultural groups are represented? What are their needs and concerns? What is the overall look and feel of the neighborhood? Are there abandoned buildings and boarded-up stores? Are there areas that need to be revamped or rebuilt? Are there historic buildings that need to be preserved? Are local merchants losing business to a nearby mall in a neighboring community?

Get a feel for what retailers and business owners want and need. You may be able to help them while they, in turn, help you solve community issues and problems.

Establishing a Nucleus

Somewhere between the idea of forming a group to deal with neighborhood concerns and the actual researching of problems and input from the community as a whole, you will need to establish a group within the group. These are the core members who may have been instrumental in the formation of the ideas, or who have the resources and experience to get things done, or both. This core group may be half a dozen people, and they are key to building the organization.

Your Core Group

For the nucleus of the group, you will need to seek out people who are committed to dealing with the cause or problem(s) at hand, able to make a time commitment, good at communicating with others, and open to various opinions. You'll find people for your core group by talking to community leaders, taking part in community activities, and looking in local newspapers for names of people who have impacted the community in other ways.

Once you have established a core group, hold meetings before opening up your doors to the community at large. This way you can get a consensus of opinion on the issues and determine a broad approach to making changes. While you will want input from the community, you will first want the opportunity to build a framework for running the organization effectively. For example, you may want to list some of the practical means of raising funds, such as a community fair or block party, and eliminate less practical ideas. This will give your core group a little time to address concerns such as the need for permits, should the larger group decide a county fair or block party is a good idea. You can divide up responsibilities and determine who will kick off the fundraising campaign, who will be leading the promotional campaign, and so on. You can also set up the agenda for the first public meetings that involve the community as a whole.

Once your core group has been formed and you have begun your community-minded planning, you should determine which community newspaper, local groups, churches and temples, and/or government groups should know about your organization and get some basic materials printed to alert them to your presence and your mission. Then follow up with fundraising information as it develops.

The idea is essentially to get the organization or fundraiser off the ground. By having a mission statement, setting goals, and formulating ideas of what you want to achieve and how you want to achieve it, you establish basic parameters and build a structure from which to operate. Core group members should do research and be knowledgeable about the issues and the community. They should be ready to head up committees, if need be (although your committee chairpersons don't have to be members of this nucleus group). This creates a framework that the larger community-based membership can step into.

Of course, it is important that the core group does not try to dot every *i* and cross every *t* or the general membership will not feel a sense of involvement. People are more likely to join a community organization that is, to some degree, a work in progress and not a finished product. This way, they can have a say in some of the decisions and feel a sense of ownership in the cause or problem being addressed.

In addition, the membership may present very qualified individuals who are not in the core group but could step in and head up committees and handle other important functions. By not having everything completely in place prior to opening up the doors to the community, you leave a little room for such key new members to get involved and, more significantly, present ideas that might work!

The Community Meetings

Once you have established a core group, you can set up a time and place for larger community meetings. You'll need to find a hall or auditorium to accommodate a larger group. You may turn to schools, churches, libraries, or community centers that have facilities available that will not cost you rental money. You should also seek out some donations from your core group for refreshments or promise signage and promotion to a local bakery or coffee shop in exchange for some freebies. Remember, it's always advantageous to spread the word about the new community group to local merchants—some might want to get involved.

Identifying the Issues

While some community organizations are multipurpose and deal with a number of community issues, many are formed around one central issue. For example, there may be a need to address increased drug use by teens, the influx of neighborhood gangs, or the need to preserve historic buildings. Such focused organizations do not need to seek out issues, because they already have one. It is, however, still necessary to research the issue.

Your initial neighborhood concerns may also be the springboard for larger-scale projects over time. Start small, get people on board, and build you group's enthusiasm through small successes. In time, you'll be able to tackle larger community issues.

Gathering a consensus regarding the problems in your community will help you identify the issues of greatest concern. Conduct polls or surveys if necessary.

Making Things Happen

Once you identify the problems, take a realistic look and start seeking constructive, realistic plans. If, for example, you determine that a neighborhood problem is the lack of places for young children to play, then your goal might be to build a small park or a community playground. You'll have to determine where it can be built, how much it would cost, who would build it, and how long it would take.

FACT

Surveys are a terrific way of finding out where your community interests lie. If you can distribute and collect well-placed, easy-to-fill-out surveys asking people what community concerns they would like to see addressed (in conjunction with the type of work your organization does), then you can get a feel for the issues the public will want you to focus on.

Finally, you will need to determine where the funds will come from. If fundraising is your answer, you will then need to construct a plan and, as discussed in Chapter 2, determine what manner (or manners) of fundraising would be beneficial. If, for example, your town is like Armonk, New York, a very small town with a very large IBM facility, you might go to the obvious source for a grant or donation. Know your community and the available donors and resources. In most instances, you will need to look at several key sources, including merchants, residents, and even the local government. Start looking for funding in your own backyard, so to speak.

Of course, fundraising is only part of the job of a community group. Groups can use fundraising activities to reach out and communicate with the neighborhood to make changes. Community groups and neighborhood associations publish neighborhood newsletters, organize events, and implement neighborhood improvement projects.

Working with Your Community Board

A community board is generally made up of volunteers who represent and look out for the best interests of the community at large. Most often the members of such boards represent a cross section of the population found in the community. The board holds meetings to discuss pertinent issues. It follows set rules and procedures but is usually mandated to provide an open forum for the public to participate at meetings, discussions, forums, and/or hearings.

Involving a community board is one step in the process of building awareness of a community issue that needs to be addressed. Do your homework before approaching the community board so that you know exactly how to request its help or support.

Before you can raise money for a community issue, you should try to get the local governing board on your side. Have several members appear when you address the board to present your project or program if you need board approval. Designate one person as the speaker and make sure he or she plans a concise but effective presentation backed up with supporting facts and figures.

If, for example, your group has gathered to discuss the building of a library and you are ready and willing to do fundraising toward that goal, address the need for a library, the location that might be most suitable (and why), and how you plan to go about raising the kind of money necessary to achieve this lofty goal.

ALERT!

Watch for conflicts of interest when dealing with a community board. If you have members who sit on the community board and the board of your organization, they may need to dismiss themselves from taking a vote on such issues. Other people may not sit on both boards but may have ulterior motives, which are sometimes political. Full disclosure is advised in any circumstances that might come back to haunt you later on.

Finding Local Sponsors

One way of benefiting the neighborhood might include cosponsorship of activities with local merchants and institutions. Perhaps the clothing drive will be run from the front lobby of the library or the candy sale will take place in the local mall. Retailers may team with you to provide space and resources while your promotion helps them attract more business. The advertising and promotion done by such local sponsors can also help ensure that you will get a good turnout. You can use these relationships as both a networking opportunity and a way to get in-kind donations.

By getting different sponsors on board, you can help cover the costs of your event. For additional support, contact your local chamber of commerce, block association, or other local merchant groups. If you do one strong pitch to the chamber of commerce, it can then reach out to all of its members, saving you the time and effort of talking to a couple of dozen merchants one by one. Often you'll see a snowball effect whereby once a few local retailers get on board, others will also want to be included, particularly if a major store has agreed to be a sponsor.

There are also situations in which a major store or local business may donate money to, or sponsor the activities of, many local nonprofit organizations. This keeps the business highly visible in the community and is an excellent means of public relations. By spreading the word about your work and letting everyone know that you have plans that are significant within the community, you can become one such organization on their list. For example, one local supermarket in Westchester, New York, donated over $250,000 last year to 290 different local nonprofits!

Selecting the right fundraising activities goes a long way. Often "a-thons" are a great way to draw community interest and utilize local businesses. For example, a bike-a-thon can be sponsored by a local bike shop and draw people to the downtown area on a Sunday, which will be good for store owners. A bowl-a-thon or aerobics-a-thon might include sponsorship from a bowling alley or fitness center.

Local associations are generally a good place to look for funding because they represent a segment of the community. You can also look for foundations that are dedicated to providing funding for community needs and seek a donation or apply for a grant.

Neighborhood banking institutions, including local branches of major-name commercial banks, often pledge to return a portion of their profits to help the communities in which they are located. You might turn to a local branch manager or other bank officer to inquire about funding options. See what type of program they have and ask for an application.

Many major retail and fast-food chains such as The Gap or McDonald's are also places to turn. The manager of a local franchise can often tell you how the corporation handles donations and how to apply for grants. The Foundation Center can help you find local sources as well.

Laws and Ordinances

One of the areas of concern when planning local community-based fundraisers is making sure you know what you can and cannot do. Local laws and ordinances vary tremendously from county to county. Some are not well known but may be enforced.

It is your responsibility to check with the county clerk's office, city hall, or any city permit offices to make sure that you have all necessary licenses or permits. Among the areas that may require permits are:

- The sale of liquor, including wine or beer
- The sale of raffle tickets
- Bingo or other "games of chance"
- The use of rides or amusement park activities
- Soliciting of any kind

Depending on where you are holding your fundraiser, you may need additional permits. Give yourself some time to apply for and receive such permits. There may be a wait of several weeks or, in larger cities, even a few months before you receive the licensing you require. In addition, find out how long the permit is good for and if you need to reapply if you hold a similar fundraiser in six weeks, six months, or a year.

FACT

In some cases, the sale of food and beverages requires a permit from the local board of health, unless you are working with an established food provider (a caterer or restaurant) who already has such a permit. In other situations, you are required to use a specific vendor who is under contract to the facility that you have selected.

Promoting Locally

Local PR is important in promoting a community fundraiser. Good planning can allow you to generate media coverage. For example, one Ohio-based neighborhood economic improvement organization planned ghost and historic walking tours during a new weeklong neighborhood festival. The planning included a nighttime investigation of a municipal building for paranormal activity. The act of requesting permission during a public council meeting to investigate the neighborhood's municipal building for paranormal activity resulted in a local newspaper story. The investigation resulted in two more stories. The result was that people in the town were talking about the ghost tours before the tickets went on sale. The program received considerable coverage before the major promotional push in the press even began.

How far in advance should you promote your event?
Give yourself three to five months to promote your fundraiser. This will allow enough lead time for newspapers and magazines to place ads or write articles. It will also allow you to do pre-event public relations.

Postevent coverage is also important. Reading about the event you attended a few days or even a few weeks ago leaves people feeling good about their participation. They feel that they were a part of something newsworthy and look forward to attending next year. Postevent coverage is also positive acknowledgment for those who sponsored your event.

Another reason why coverage after the event is important is that it goes into the media/sponsor packet for next year's event and can help you when promoting other fundraisers or even soliciting for donations, grants, or sponsorship.

Don't forget to thank media representatives for attending and for writing you up. It's important to maintain an ongoing relationship with the press and not forget about them as soon as the event is over. You will need them again.

Becoming Established in the Community

Sometimes, it's a slow process that helps an organization plant firm roots in a neighborhood. By doing community service and promoting the fact that your organization is working on behalf of the neighborhood, you can establish your presence to a point where people will actually come to you when there is a problem facing the neighborhood.

The upper west side of Manhattan has several community and environmental groups that have worked together successfully in the past to block projects from being built, including a West Side highway, that would create more congestion in an already crowded area. The groups have been so successful that, when the proposal for the 2012 Olympics came up, with the inclusion of a stadium to be built on Manhattan's West Side, many New Yorkers, including some in the media, immediately knew these groups would step up to face the issue. They had established themselves through their previous work and planted seeds so that if they needed to mobilize to raise money, they could do so quickly.

Remember to promote what you have done and keep up your neighborhood profile so that people know you are there when they need to turn to you for help. The Red Cross does this by keeping its name in the public eye, and therefore, when there is a hurricane or another disaster, people immediately know they can turn to the Red Cross for help.

Another example of an organization firmly planting its roots in the community comes from Washington, D.C., where $12 million was raised in several months by Cleveland Park neighbors to purchase a six-acre historic estate named Rosedale, which was in their neighborhood.

According to Andrew Hamilton, president of the community organization Friends of Rosedale, there were several tools available and in place by the time the funds were needed. The neighborhood was already organized and engaged in defining itself. Some people say the organization had unofficially begun in the 1950s when the neighbors had stopped an expressway from coming through their backyards. The community was clear about their shared values, particularly relating to land use, and an opening existed to debate these values. There were several community and government organizations that had worked together successfully in the past to intervene on a number of development issues impacting the neighborhood over the years. The active citizenry of this area of the city had a track record in utilizing existing citywide historic preservation and zoning laws to maintain the quality of life in their neighborhoods.

The most recent effort came about to protect three acres of lawn and gardens on the Rosedale Estate, which includes a 1794 farmhouse listed on the National Register of Historic Places. The lawns, garden, and farmhouse were part of a six-acre tract of land that was on the market.

The Friends of Rosedale and the group of neighbors who worked together acted to defend something the community valued. The Rosedale neighbors operated in a way that built trust as they worked to protect a community asset. They told their neighbors in the community that their objective was to preserve the land as open space for public use, and they were seen as working to benefit the neighborhood. As they went along, everything was explained to the community, in the process creating trust over their objectives.

The successful fundraising effort was the end result of building a base of support, which may have dated back some five decades to the battle they won over the expressway coming through the neighborhood.

An Award-Winning Community Effort

The following article from the *Borough News* magazine (volume 2, issue 6) in Harrisburg, Pennsylvania, was written by journalist Rebecca Sultan. It illustrates a community effort to revitalize a local town center.

The "Townie" awards are presented annually by the Pennsylvania Downtown Center to member communities whose successes, it says, "stand out in the crowd." In the case of Main Street Hatboro's "Townie" award, success began with a crowd.

Created by residents, business owners and civic leaders who recognized that a healthy downtown means a healthy community, Main Street Hatboro launched a series of town meetings to find out how to attract more shoppers—and shops—to a tired-looking downtown, weary from fending off the mega-malls, strip centers and superstores nipping at its heels.

The answer was a vision—a Streetscape—flowers, banners, and new lighting to create a pedestrian-friendly atmosphere. The latter would be the tool to bring a cohesive look to the eclectic mix of buildings in the business district and make after-dark dining and shopping more desirable.

But a vision is costly. Aging highway lights would need to be replaced with pedestrian-oriented streetlights. Another town meeting brought a consensus of opinion: Along with new overhead "cobra" lights, Victorian era streetlights would give just the right look to a downtown proud of its history and tradition. The cost? $800,000—a hefty price tag for any municipality, let alone a tiny borough of 7,200 residents.

Fundraising began and, with the assistance of State Sen. Stewart Greenleaf, $495,000 in state grants was secured. The Borough of Hatboro pledged $100,000, but $200,000 more was needed. So was an investment by residents and businesses. The Greater Hatboro Chamber of Commerce led the way with a $50,000 matching grant, which served as the catalyst to raise funds from the Hatboro Community.

In December 1997, Main Street Hatboro launched "See Your Name On Lights," a program offering streetlight sponsorships for $1,000 each. Plaques affixed to each light pole named its sponsor or sponsors. Individuals or groups could pay $125 to share a pole with others, or pay the total fee for solo billing. Streetlights were dedicated to loved ones, "given" as family gifts, "purchased" by civic and service organizations, and used to memorialize many who, during their lives, contributed significantly to the community. Friends and relatives of a long-time local newspaper columnist, for example, sponsored a light in her memory and specifically requested the pole outside the site of the former newspaper office.

The streetlight project and the "See Your Name On Lights" campaign generated exceptional press coverage and several newspapers published the application for sponsorships at no cost. More than 130 contributions from individuals, local businesses, civic organizations and major corporations—ranging from $10 to $25,000—brought in $158,000. The Chamber's $50,000 "challenge" grant boosted that total to $208,000.

All was well until unanticipated costs relating to submerging cable and telephone lines surfaced. The $800,000 project price tag jumped to $1.2 million. That's when the Hatboro Borough Authority stepped in. Reassured by the support the project had received from Hatboro Borough Council, the Authority—a foundation established with proceeds from the sale of the assets of the Hatboro Water Authority to fund capital improvements throughout the borough—committed more than $530,000 to complete the work.

When the Victorian lights were switched on in October 2000, it wasn't just Downtown Hatboro that basked in the glow. The Streetscape project cast a luster on the entire borough. Main Street Hatboro generated the energy that drove the project, but the premium wattage it produced resulted from a "buy-in" by every segment of the community: residents, business and property owners, civic groups, all levels of government, even a church and school. The project brought focus to downtown revitalization efforts and fostered pride and a spirit of change that continues to invigorate business, community and government leaders. It showed the power a small borough with big vision can have when it taps into its collective talent and pools its resources.

In Hatboro, "Let Your Light Shine" is not just words on a page.

This article was reprinted with kind permission from Borough News.

Chapter 13

Grassroots Fundraising

Maybe you aren't involved in a non-profit group or other organized group, but you have a cause. Small groups of people can effectively raise funds to help their community in many ways. This chapter addresses the specific needs of these groups of real grassroots activists who are not officially listed in the phone book or who have no major Web sites, but are simply people trying to help raise money in their neighborhoods.

Small-Scale Efforts, Big Results

No, you won't be approaching major corporations, writing up bylaws, or making large-scale plans. You have no plans to elect officers, file for 501(c)(3) status, or even establish yourselves as an "ongoing" organization. Yours is simply an effort of five concerned friends to raise money to keep the local boys and girls after-school program afloat for the coming year, or perhaps to help a neighbor rebuild after a fire destroyed his business, or even to provide some holiday cheer to children at the local hospital.

Your goals are simple—get some money together to help someone in need. You do not want to work with complex budgets, just a basic outlay of funds, if necessary. Nonetheless, planning is key to your success.

Brainstorming

This type of grassroots fundraising requires, first and foremost, a meeting of the minds to discuss what you can do as individuals and how you can combine your efforts to maximize results and solve the problem at hand.

Benefits

One way to fully utilize the collective intelligence and experience of everyone involved is to brainstorm ideas. Companies and organizations use this method of generating ideas, so why shouldn't you? You benefit by having input from a variety of sources. The person who called the meeting might be considered "in charge" by default or simple courtesy.

To effectively brainstorm ideas, all who are in attendance will need to understand the basic problem or issues. They also need to remember five things in brainstorming:

1. Everyone's opinions and ideas are equal in value.
2. Ideas, not individuals, are to be discussed or criticized.
3. No one should be "married" to their ideas.
4. It is not a competition to see who provides the best ideas.

5. A simple democratic vote should be available at all times to resolve deadlocks.

While brainstorming works at all levels, it is particularly effective in a small group situation because you can generate a large number of ideas without being overwhelmed. You can then list every idea as it is presented.

Inevitably someone will need to "lead" the meeting in some manner. As noted above, it may simply be the person who asked that everyone get together or who thought of the idea to repair the church roof.

Set some basic parameters that all ideas must meet before brainstorming so that ideas don't run amok. For example, it must be something that we can do as five people or something we can do without laying out more than an agreed-on amount, such as $400 donated by the members involved—or whatever amount you decide on.

Procedures

To begin, you write down all ideas on a master list, making sure everyone has had the opportunity to contribute. Then evaluate the logistics and practicality of the plan (based on manpower needed, cost, time frame, etc.).

Then, eliminate ideas as you go, based on logical reasons. If the group is split on whether an idea should be taken off the board, vote on it. You add positive elements to ideas that stay on the board and eliminate ideas that are considered impractical. You then repeat the cycle as many times as you choose to, until you arrive at your best idea.

Since there is no hierarchy in a newly formed group, there is no political agenda and no one should feel too intimidated to participate. It is a process that allows everyone to feel included, appreciated, and valued.

Brainstorming creates an environment to foster raw ideas and then mold them into profitable outcomes.

Dividing up Responsibilities

Unlike a large organization with committees, a small group will have to throw the various tasks onto the table and see who wants to handle them. Most often, a person will take on the tasks he or she feels most confident performing.

Each person needs to make a personal pledge to do the job, because there is no formal structure, no board members, and no bylaws. In this type of situation, everyone is simply responsible to each other and to the project at hand. Failure to do a task can strain relationships and friendships.

Conversely, if someone does a job as they see fit, it is the responsibility of everyone else to accept that job or politely make suggestions as to how to improve on it. This can be a touchy area. Planning is important, and each person should agree that he or she will not go off and make unilateral decisions.

While many tasks will be divided up, everyone will likely be involved in the overall job of raising funds though selling, performing a service, or simply asking for money. Carefully determine your plan of action and decide where you will each be soliciting funds. If, for example, you are soliciting for contributions, you do not want all five of you contacting the same people. Similarly, if you are selling candy bars, decide who works in which territory, where you will convene, and who will collect the money you have accumulated.

FACT

While you may turn the money over to a qualified 501(c)(3) charity, you cannot advertise that donations are tax deductible because you are not "officially" a nonprofit organization. Nonetheless, you can, and should be ready to, provide individuals with a statement of receipt for their records that you sold them an item or provided a service.

How Much Should You Do?

A critical aspect of your fundraising efforts is knowing how far your efforts should extend. Nonprofit fundraising organizations generally have a system in place for raising money and then for distribution of funds or goods.

Do your responsibilities include raising money to give to the school librarian who will buy the books? Or will you raise the money, buy the books, and then donate them to the library? You need to determine where your efforts begin and end. Does the storeowner have a staff that is more than willing to rebuild the facility, or is the storeowner in need of money and builders? Can your volunteers help?

The responsibility of handling the money raised is also a major one. You do not have a treasurer in place already, so you'll need to appoint someone to be the trusted individual who collects the funds. It is also very important that you have confidence that the money you raise will be spent as intended. You need to ask yourselves a few questions:

- Should we give the money to an established nonprofit organization to handle it (such as the United Way or the Red Cross)?
- Do we have a source (such as the pastor of a church) to give the money directly to?
- Should we utilize the funding ourselves to achieve the goal (build the new roof)?

In answer to the first question, you need to make sure that the nonprofit organization you are giving the money to is on the same page as you and that the money is going to help the cause for which you raised it. If, for example, you raise money for library books in the local grade school, you may feel very comfortable handing the money to the PTO with an explanation of what this money is intended to be used for.

FACT

Following the attacks of September 11, nonorganizational fundraising pulled together millions of dollars thanks to the efforts of schoolchildren nationwide, who took it on themselves to create means of raising money or simply asked for contributions. The money was then sent to several major charities spearheading the fundraising efforts.

In government-run agencies, a bureaucratic process may filter funds to certain groups. To circumvent this, you may be able to buy tangible goods and donate them instead of money (which could end up being spent on something you didn't intend). For example, a local boys and girls club in a small city was affiliated with six other such clubs and run by the city government. The individual club was not allowed to take monetary donations. All money had to be filtered through the main office located downtown. The process was slow and the money was divided up among all of the facilities. It was, however, permissible for the director of an individual club to accept donated items, such as sports equipment or uniforms. Therefore, the local grassroots fundraising group who had raised $600 bought the equipment to donate so they could be sure that their neighborhood group was the beneficiary of their efforts.

In answer to the second question, you need to feel a sense of trust in a person involved in the cause or with the facility that you are helping. Often, it is this person who initially came to you with the problem. It is a judgment call. Will the individual handle the money responsibly and as you believe he or she should?

In the third case, you need to make sure you are achieving the goal in the proper manner. In fact, you may need to hire professionals. For example, if the five of you are not at all skilled in building, you should take the money you raise and hire a builder to repair the store destroyed in the fire rather than try to do it yourself and do a poor job. Of course, you can do this only with the permission of the storeowner. Don't try to surprise people with a huge job they weren't expecting.

Maintaining Focus

Usually a completely grassroots fundraising effort, as defined in this chapter, comes about to serve a local and immediate need. Therefore, the time factor is short and the focus remains fairly consistent. It is, however, up to at least one person in the group to always bring the members back to why they are getting together, particularly if you are meeting several times at private homes and are likely to go off on tangents.

At meetings, you need to allow for socializing, and refreshments of some type are a must. Have each person pitch in or volunteer to bring the refreshments to the next meeting. Set aside an hour and a half to two hours to talk "business," and appoint someone as leader to enforce this rule and keep the discussion on track. This can be a different person for each meeting, if there are several budding leaders in the group, or one person with whom everyone feels comfortable in the leadership position. The leader needs to be very flexible and take the role as more of a "guide" to keeping the project on track. No leader should make unilateral decisions.

FACT

"Hub" events are a great choice for grassroots fundraisers. A "hub" event is a situation where you hold an event and think of several ways of raising money within that event. For example, you hold a picnic and ask all who attend to bring their own food. You provide free drinks and activities. Then, within the picnic, hold an auction, sell desserts, hold a raffle, or play games that bring in funds. Each person then contributes a little here and a little there as he or she goes about enjoying the overall event.

Credibility

Let's face it, anyone can ask you for money, and you have no way of knowing if the person asking represents a legitimate charity or organization. The question of credibility is even more pronounced when you have no specific organization to back you up. For this reason, performing a service, such as walking dogs or washing cars, can help convince others to spend their money on your fundraiser, because it provides the contributor with something for his or her dollar regardless of what you do with the money. The same holds true for selling items at a garage sale or flea market.

Making Connections

Credibility comes from your standing in the neighborhood, community, school, church, or whatever presence you or someone in your grassroots fundraising group has to offer. If no one has made any particular impact on the community, then you might want to seek someone who is trusted and respected by the core group of potential donors whom you hope to attract.

Is there one key element that makes the difference in getting a donor to contribute?
Probably the most significant element is a personal appeal. If you build a relationship and talk to people on a personal level, they are more likely to donate even if the actual cause is something you are more passionate about. This is because they have gained a sense of trust in *you* and believe in *your* dedication to the cause.

For example, three grade-school children trying to raise money for their school to buy new equipment for the gym wrote a letter to a local radio host asking if they could come on his show and talk about their efforts. He was impressed and had them on the program. Besides the free publicity, the kids had an extra boost of credibility because a radio station found their efforts worthy of going on the air. In fact, the radio show host even came down to present the money to the school with the children and talked about it on the air.

Local celebrities, merchants, or political figures can be drawn into what you are working on and are often interested in "helping the little guy" or "the new grassroots group" as the case may be.

Some grassroots groups raise their credibility by their individual associations within the community, which might be with a school, a religious institution, or a business. Even though the fundraising effort is separate from the institution, people may see you in a credible light if you hold a position in a respected place in the community. For example, a teacher may have the goal of raising money to help a family in need. Her credibility as a teacher will prompt more people to give money. Of course, she needs to clear with the school that she can take on this outside mission on her own. As mentioned earlier, whenever there is a possibility of a conflict of interest, or in this case, doing something that may not be allowed by the school or local union, full disclosure is advised.

Be Visual

A picture is indeed worth a thousand words when dealing with a pressing issue that others are not familiar with. Take photos of the church roof that was demolished by the storm and let people see what you are talking about. Since you do not have a long track record and brochures with logos, you may need to use a visual presentation to make your point and emphasize what you are looking to accomplish.

There are plenty of variables that will factor into your success when taking it on yourself to raise funds. The awareness of your issue is obviously a key factor. If the town has been hit hard by storms and tornadoes, and you are raising money to help, people will see your cause all around them. In a case like this, you may not need to "prove" to them that you have a worthy cause.

Your Secret Weapon: The Warm Fuzzies

It doesn't matter how good you are at washing cars or how tasty the pies are that you are selling at a bake sale. The biggest reason people are buying your items or services, or simply donating money, is that "it's for a good cause." Giving to a friend or neighbor is self-satisfying.

Why does someone help you when you're struggling to change a flat tire on the highway or give you booster cables when you're stuck? What makes one child help another off the soccer field when he or she is injured and crying? People, in general, do not sit idly by when others are in need. That's what sparks the plethora of fundraising organizations and volunteer groups around today. Not everyone, however, has the time to commit to attending meetings or following a plan of action. But you'll find that more than 50 percent do some kind of activity to help others, beyond donating money through an employee plan at work or simply writing out a check.

No matter how much calculating and profiling an organization may do to find the ideal donor or how much time a corporation may spend determining how their charitable efforts will best portray them in the market, there is no underestimating the simple power of the warm fuzzies. It is simply giving for no other reason than for the sake of giving.

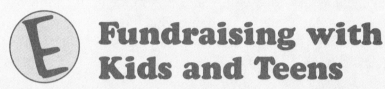

Chapter 14

Fundraising with Kids and Teens

Fundraising and volunteerism are becoming part of the real-world curriculum that is shaping more and more of America's youth. In conjunction with their schools and religious institutions, young children and teens are becoming part of the fundraising community and making an impact. This chapter looks at the role children and families play in fundraising.

Getting Kids Started

While a great many children are introduced to fundraising through candy, wrapping paper, or magazine sales drives in their schools (covered later in this chapter), they can also become indoctrinated into the world of fundraising and volunteering through their parents. Most fundraising projects include tasks that even young children can do, and what better way to share some family time than having fun together working on a project, whether it's sticking labels on envelopes or raking leaves together in a neighborhood cleanup drive.

Teaching the Principles

The basics of why we raise funds and the need to help others can be very easily taught to children. Simple lessons of a character having a problem and then figuring out how to solve it are commonplace in books and easily created for a child. The only other element that needs to be added is that of having to buy something—hence the need for "funds." Henry the Dinosaur lost his blanket and can't afford a new one. Can we help him get a new blanket? "Where can he get one?" you might ask a young child. At some point, a child will usually respond, "at the store" or "at the blanket store." Then you can explain that he needs to pay for it but doesn't have enough money. Since it is hard for a dinosaur to get a job, perhaps we could do something to help him earn the money. The basic point is to nudge children gently and encourage them to help. From analogies and play activities at an early age, schoolchildren, usually as early as the first grade, will move to understanding real needs and real situations where they will want to help other people.

Helping in Times of Tragedy

The terrorist attacks of September 11 made the need to help people very real, and many children were inspired to get involved in helping others. The images on TV were frightening, and the notion of wanting to do something to help was a healthy way of working through the horrors of that time for children as well as adults.

Kids pitched in throughout the nation and raised money and goods for the families of the victims and the rescue crews. In a high school in Winter Park, Florida, students teamed up to give money to local citizens who were affected by the attacks. In Austin, Texas, schoolchildren held various fundraisers and amassed over $70,000. In Newton, Massachusetts, third-grade students held a yard sale and raised $1,000 for the relief effort. The money was also matched by a community bank in the area. In nearby Falmouth, Massachusetts, public school students brought in red, white, and blue yarn and put it in baskets where other students could make the yarn into bracelets and leave a donation for the Red Cross. At a middle school on Long Island, students ran bake sales and tag sales to raise money to donate to local families who had lost loved ones.

Garage sales, toy and clothing drives, bake sales, car washes, school talent shows, breakfasts for the community, and many other creative fundraising ideas were not only suddenly part of the school calendar, but were taking place in community youth groups and other organizations for families and children for many months after the September 11 tragedies.

Teaching Kids the Ropes

No, a youngster won't get the gist of a grant proposal, but he or she will understand the idea that raising money means having a good product or service to entice people into giving a donation.

The idea of working together as a group to come up with and implement a plan for raising funds will be effective if the parents sell it by emphasizing the fun aspect of FUNdraising.

Children can learn teamwork and responsibility by planning and implementing a project in a group setting, and they can have a good time doing so. By showing kids how to divide up tasks and involve everyone in the project, kids learn how a fundraising project operates. Everyone takes part and holds up his or her end of the project.

The actual task of asking for money is hard for many adults and, depending on his or her nature, may be difficult for a child as well. However, kids can make great salespeople. If they are determined to sell a product, they will provide enthusiasm and an honest sales approach. Of course, you will need to remind them that they must be polite, accept no for an answer, and write down orders clearly when they make a sale. Too often, schools put children in the awkward position of selling candy, wrapping paper, or some other item without teaching them the responsibilities that go with the job. Flashing an incentive and telling kids to go out and sell teaches them more about competition and less about the meaning of fundraising and responsibility.

It is advantageous to teach children how to make sales presentations to friends, family, and relatives. From a song to a skit to a pretend commercial to a simple short sales pitch, kids can have fun creating their own means of selling a product. If they're having fun, they should need no greater incentive. It is important to remind children that if they are selling to strangers, they should have an adult present or be on school grounds within the assigned location, such as the gymnasium or wherever the bake sale, book sale, or other such activity is taking place. Sometimes schools will combine the fundraising effort with another school activity, such as selling candy for charity prior to the varsity basketball game or the choir's annual holiday recital.

ALERT!

Make sure you have a plan of action for distribution. Some fundraising programs will send the product directly to the buyer whereas others will send the product to the school. If 500 rolls of wrapping paper are going to show up soon at your school, make sure you have a place to put them and an easy means of distributing them to students.

It can also be very worthwhile, when a PTA or PTO is planning a fundraising activity that will involve the children, to take one afternoon and teach them why they are selling candy and how to keep track of who ordered and how many each person gets.

Among other lessons, fundraising can help children learn the following.

- Decision-making
- Record keeping
- To follow instructions carefully
- Time management

A vast number of schools are adding community service to their curriculum. Fundraising is an aspect of public service and volunteering. There are, however, differences that need to be taught. Community service in the form of helping people in need by reading to the blind or visiting children in a hospital are valuable lessons at any age. Fundraising, however, is stepping away from the actual people in need and approaching others to say, "let's help them" or "let's do something to make a change in the neighborhood." Therefore, both lessons need to be taught: Volunteering to directly help others and raising money to help others through funding.

There are also school-based lessons in subjects such as math that come from fundraising activities. Teachers in many schools incorporate a number of lesson plans into their fundraising. For example, students learn to tally daily and weekly sales totals and multiply the number of items sold by a dollar amount to get a total amount of profit. Students in higher grades can learn what percentages of people are buying items, and they can use the concepts of mean, median, and average in real situations. Weight and other measurement skills can also be learned by real, hands-on examples of selling products.

Kid-Friendly Possibilities

Among the many possibilities for fundraising with kids, in schools or with other organizations, are:

- Auctions—silent, traditional, or Chinese in style, or a combination
- Community service, including car washes, dog walking, and other such activities
- Dances, including raves, disco nights, barn dances, retro nights, etc.
- Fairs, carnivals, bazaars, picnics, or barbecues

- Cookbooks, compiled by students, teachers, and/or people in the community
- Competitions such as hot dog eating, dancing, basketball shooting, etc.
- Student-teacher sporting events or school Olympics
- Exhibitions, including photography, art, crafts, etc.
- Bake sales, book sales, video sales
- Garage sales, flea markets, antiques fairs
- Holiday parties or Easter egg hunts
- Talent shows or karaoke nights

Selecting the activities should be based partly on the suggestions of the kids involved and partly on the practical realities of what the group can realistically do from a financial and resource standpoint. Parents, teachers, school administrators, or group leaders will need to be involved in making sure the plan is realistic and practical.

FACT

Girl Scout cookies have been a successful fundraiser for more than eighty years. All of the revenue earned from cookie sales, after paying the baker, goes directly to the local Girl Scout council, with a portion (roughly 15 percent) going to the individual troop. While the type of cookies, style of the packaging, and methods of tallying up orders have changed over the years, the concept of selling what has become one of the best-known fundraising products remains the same from generation to generation.

The kids should also be involved in selecting the date, location, and other aspects of the overall plan. It should then be up to everyone involved to pitch in and help make it a reality.

Various plans help spice up fundraising. A carnival in the summer and wrapping paper sales in the fall give children two diverse types of fundraisers, one that presents activities and one that focuses on selling, taking and fulfilling orders. It is advantageous to introduce new fund-raising ideas and try to vary the type of activities from season to season.

It is also, however, a successful formula, when working with children, to bring back a perennial favorite. Kids look forward to certain activities and can aim for a higher level of success than the previous year. Girl Scout cookie sales are perhaps the most famous example of a fundraising effort that never dies.

Many schools and youth organizations try to maintain some of the same fundraisers from year to year while introducing something new for specific projects that come up during the year. For example, there may be an annual bake sale every spring to raise money for underprivileged children. However, a sudden one-time need to build a new playground, library, or something else for the school may bring an opportunity to try a new fundraiser that hasn't been done before. Mix up the old and the new.

You may, however, find that using similar fundraising approaches to introduce new projects is helpful from a learning perspective. For example, a first-time-ever holiday ornament drive might use the same tally forms and order-taking system as the annual candy drive.

School Fundraisers

Grade schools, middle schools, and high schools coast to coast have fundraisers that involve their students. The response to 9/11 was initiated by an overwhelming tragedy that affected everyone. In parts of the country, hurricanes, floods, and other natural disasters have brought schoolchildren together in an effort to help their community.

However, schools also have a need to raise money for their own purposes. The PTA or PTO will, therefore, initiate projects that are either parent-run or student-run activities or, as is often the case, a combination of the two.

FACT

The difference between PTA and PTO is national versus local. There is a national PTA, and school organizations that belong to it pay dues to the national organization. A PTO is an independent group formed in a single school or perhaps representing a few schools in a single community. In 1962, there were 12 million people involved in the national PTA; today, there are about half of that total as more schools elect to go it alone.

Schoolchildren today raise over $1.5 billion by selling items to friends, family, and neighbors, which amounts to about $30 per schoolchild. An Internet search under "fundraising" will bring up a vast number of companies ready to meet your fundraising needs, selling you— in bulk—all the goods you could ever need with all sorts of deals whereby you get the bulk of the proceeds! (Be careful, some of these companies are more reliable than others.)

Selecting a Fundraising Company

There are more than 1,500 companies in the United States and Canada selling fundraising items for resale, along with providing order forms and other tools of the trade. Some offer incentive programs, and others provide fundraising advice.

So, how does one select the right fundraising company to work with? First, remember that it is certainly not *necessary* to work with a fundraising company. Instances where a PTA has had homemade goods or organized a flea market utilizing the contributed items of many students (and their families) have also raised lots of money, as have many other innovative plans. Nonetheless, if you choose to rely on a fundraising supplier, you can find tons of them on the Internet or by looking in a business directory at your local library.

FACT

The Association of Fundraising Distributors and Suppliers is an international association with more than 650 member companies that manufacture, supply, and/or distribute products that will be resold by nonprofit organizations. Member companies must conduct business on a professional level and adhere to a code of standards and ethics. Companies can apply for membership once they have done business in the nonprofit sector for at least one year.

References

Whenever committing yourself to an outside vendor or company, you should always get references. You can ask the company for references or first contact other PTOs or nonprofit organizations that have conducted sales fundraising campaigns in your region and ask what companies they've used and been satisfied with. Find out if the company delivered on its promises and met all expectations. Also inquire about the relationship between the people running the fundraiser and the company rep. Was it a good relationship? Did he or she take an interest in the organization's needs? Did the company tailor the program to meet your needs, or was it a boilerplate program? Was the rep available to answer questions or solve problems?

Percentages

Find out how much of a percentage the company takes and how promptly the merchandise was delivered. Inquire about the quality of the merchandise and the condition. Keep in mind that just because one company may give you a greater percentage of the money raised, it does not mean it is the best company with which to work. If the material is not delivered on time or there are complaints about the quality of the product, you could get a worse deal by taking the higher percentage.

When teaming with any fundraising company, the most important information for your purposes is the reliability, financial stability, and reputation of the company.

QUESTION?

How do you know what the products are really like if you've only seen them on the company's Web site?
Ask for a product sample kit, some sample product, or at least a copy of the catalog from which people will be ordering. Don't just take the company's word for it—get more information on each product before you sell it.

Services

You will also want to find out what services are provided. Do they help with tallying or meeting specific orders? Ask how they handle sales-tax laws (since they may be in a different state). Inquire about their return policy and find out how long they've been in business. Also, inquire how the products are shipped. Do they fill each individual order or deliver one huge order of 500 rolls of wrapping paper on your front steps? It makes a big difference. You'll have a lot more work to do if you need to divide up boxes of cookies or rolls of paper.

Look for a company that is easily reachable, preferably by phone as well as e-mail.

If you find a company on the Internet, look for an address and phone number. This allows you to check on the status of the company with the Better Business Bureau (look for any complaints) and provides a means of reaching them other than online. This is becoming a general rule of thumb, as fewer people are doing business with Internet companies that provide no address or phone number for checking their business status.

Licensing

You can, and probably should, check to see that a fundraising company is a licensed business in whatever area they claim to be located. Don't forget that someone with 500 candy bars in his basement can build a nice-looking Web site and try to pawn them off on you even if they are stale. Again, look for an affiliation with the Association of Fund-Raising Distributors and Supplies (AFRDS) and double-check that the company is a member.

A good fundraising distributor/supplier knows that most schools will do annual or semiannual fundraising campaigns and would prefer that you turn to them again and again for your fundraising needs. They will do what they can to win your business and keep you coming back year after year.

FACT

One common complaint about working with fundraising companies or vendors is surprise costs. Inquire about all possible costs when working with a fundraising company. You don't want hidden costs for freight, prizes, tally sheets, or anything else to cut into your profits. Get everything in writing to avoid such surprises.

The Products

Evaluate not only the company, but look over their selection of products carefully and see if they have something that your group is interested in selling. Besides wrapping paper and candy, other popular sales items include candles, cheesecake, scratch cards (where contestants can win a few dollars), and holiday decorations. Magazine subscription drives are also very popular.

Look at the age of the sellers and the target audience and determine what item is best for your group. For example, young children may not understand how scratch cards work and will be more enthusiastic about selling candy, since they can endorse the product with great enthusiasm. Just make sure they don't eat into your profits, literally.

Along with having the right products for your sales force and your neighborhood, you want to get a feel for what other schools are doing in your area. Some neighborhoods are besieged by schools selling magazine subscriptions or wrapping paper, and people can only buy so much. Therefore, sales can suffer as a result of a glut of fundraising campaigns.

It is also important to make sure that order forms and tallying are kid-friendly so that, with a little explaining, the kids can handle their own paperwork. While parents may want to check the math and make sure orders are filled and money is handed in properly, the children should play a significant role in all aspects of the fundraising process.

Rewarding a Job Well Done

Incentives are nice if kept small. However, simple rewards can also make an impact. Announcing the names of all of the helpers on the project and having them come up onstage at an assembly is an easy way of showing gratitude. Getting the school newspaper to write about the volunteers or publishing a small article in the neighborhood paper does wonders for morale and self-satisfaction. The bottom line is that children will feel good about fundraising and embrace the meaning of what it is all about if they feel appreciated.

ALERT!

Be careful with incentives for children. While you want to motivate them to sell, you don't want them to lose the valuable lesson that comes from selling to help raise money for a good cause. Keep incentives small enough so as not to push the competitive edge but interesting enough to encourage kids to sell more. Also, have many prizes and not just one, so that many, or all, of the children feel rewarded.

In addition, you should, if possible, show children the fruits of their efforts. For example, if the funding was used to clean up the neighborhood, take a tour of the neighborhood before and after the project to show the difference. Show photographs of children in a hospital opening the presents donated from the fundraising drive or have a special party in the new library built by funding raised through the PTO. Sometimes this will be simply by showing them a newspaper or magazine article. It creates a more realistic understanding of what fundraising is all about when they can see the results.

The same holds true for the parents and teachers that took part in the hard work. Let them feel appreciated. While the reason for fundraising is to help others, everyone still likes the pat on the back, hearing the words "thank you," and seeing the fruits of his or her labor.

In the end, fundraising with children in school or in other groups, such as Boy Scouts or Girl Scouts, helps create a new generation of future fundraisers who understand the process and purpose of giving to others. Ⓔ

Chapter 15

Political Fundraising

Anyone running for political office knows that it takes a strong campaign to make a successful run for office, and it takes money to campaign. This chapter looks at some of the basic how-to's—from a practical and process-driven approach—of raising money to support a political candidate.

The Campaign Fundraising Plan

Winning candidates at all levels of politics will often need to spend 50 percent of their time fundraising. Since time is crucial in a campaign and rallying support and, ultimately, votes is the objective, a detailed plan for fundraising needs to be put in place prior to the announcement of candidacy for office.

A campaign fundraising plan, not unlike other fundraising plans, should include how much money needs to be raised, the time frame in which the money is needed, and what the funds will be used for. The plan should also include the manner(s) in which the funds will be raised.

One common means of campaign fundraising is a kickoff dinner or party to launch the campaign. This should be prepared prior to the campaign announcement and included in the initial plan of action. It is a way of gathering together initial support for the candidate. All those people who endorsed the candidacy of this individual, along with family, friends, people from the local business community, and local politicians should be included in this launch party, which will raise some initial funding.

Various Approaches

It is nowhere more evident than in political fundraising that there is a need for different types of fundraising activities. A politician is seeking a cross section of voters and will need to reach this diverse audience with a fundraising plan that covers a broad range of interests and reaches supporters at various financial levels.

Big-ticket-only dinner parties at $500 a plate are not likely to attract the nine-to-five working crowd. Therefore, small-ticket fundraisers such as a picnic for $25 per family will bring in another realm of constituents. While the majority of funding may still come from a minority of people, a campaign needs a majority of people to get out and vote in favor of the candidate. Therefore, fundraising and campaigning go hand in hand. Events will bring in money while selling the platform of the politician.

In addition, a politician will need to plan fundraisers that draw a multicultural audience, which creates a wider diversity of supporters and garners votes from various ethnic groups.

ALERT!

Stay in close contact with the media. The media can make or break an election. The public relations team will be in charge of handling inevitable media snafus, but you can utilize positive media stories to your advantage. Play up all such stories and use them to help generate funds.

Political fundraising will include phone solicitation, special events, and direct mailings. However, because the goal is to raise money *and* generate votes, the approach is slightly different. Unlike ongoing nonprofit groups that may be wooing major donors over the course of years or waiting for months for a grant proposal to be accepted, supporters need to be pulled on board in a short time and donations need to come in quickly. Among the many tools commonly used in political fundraising are:

- The fundraising letter
- The house party
- Personal appearances
- Big-name support

You'll read more about these tools later in this chapter.

Establishing a Finance Committee

The fundraising plan for a campaign is usually the work of the campaign manager, the candidate, and the staff they have assembled. A finance committee, however, is generally made up of a group of supporters who work hard to find donors. Each member of the committee is expected to support the candidate with his or her own contribution and then turn to his or her contacts and connections to get other donors. Such committees often include people who are prominent in the community.

This committee helps to build the donor base and works in conjunction with the campaign staffers to build a donor list.

The Donor List

Most fundraising efforts need to utilize a list of potential donors. Political fundraising is no exception. Whether you intend to raise money from events, direct mail, personal solicitation, or a combination of all three, a list of potential givers is always necessary. In all fundraising, you need to have that core group of givers who will be motivated by your message. Your list for upcoming mailings should begin with party supporters. You can, therefore, start out by contacting other politicians in your party and getting hold of their lists of contributors and/or volunteers who worked on their campaigns. You can also get a list of local party delegates and contact them.

Finding a Receptive Audience

In addition, you'll find Democratic and Republican organizations as well as other groups that support your campaign. A third-party or independent candidate may need to rely more heavily on such nonparty lists from likeminded supporters of specific causes. For example, an independent candidate supporting many environmental issues may cull names for his or her mailing list from local environmental groups.

Depending on the size of the town or city, you can use research and demographic data to determine where party pockets are located. Generally, within a city, there are areas that vote for a certain party. Don't make assumptions. Look at previous data and get a feel for which areas are already leaning in your direction.

Working the Donor List

Political campaigns are both ongoing and time sensitive. Therefore, contacting names on the donor list at key times during the campaign is usually part of the plan. While a major donor giving a lump sum of thousands of dollars may be maxed out in terms of how much he or she can give by law, smaller donors can pitch in as the campaign builds. Therefore, a push for funding when the campaign kicks off is only one of the times to tap donors. This is where the initial enthusiasm is high and the initial platform is first revealed. Backers are gung ho and ready to talk about their candidate to whomever will listen. The first wave of funding should ride in from the initial campaign launch party and the first pitch to the donors.

FACT

Knowing where the money is centered in your town or region and understanding the party demographics are keys to making the most of your fundraising efforts. On a national level, for example, New York is the strongest magnet for politicians in search of cash. In Manhattan, the Upper East Side alone has been responsible for contributing more than $10 million to each of the last two presidential campaigns. Know the hotbeds of funding in your area.

Once the early numbers are in and the campaign gains some steam, you may want to tap your donors once more as you reach the midpoint of the campaign. Now you can show that the candidate has gained momentum and generated attention. He or she should, at this point, have answered some tough questions and through publicity established his or her name around the community.

The third and final time to tap into your donors is when the campaign is nearing the homestretch and the candidate is making a serious bid. The pitch now is that with the last-ditch fundraising, he or she can get over the final hurdle and win.

It's also worth mentioning that the candidate, no matter how much he or she dislikes seeking out campaign funding (and many politicians do not like this part of the job), should tap into the major contributors personally. Who qualifies as major contributors will obviously vary from one campaign to another. The candidate should talk directly to the people with the money in his or her region, whether you're talking about millions, thousands, or hundreds of dollars.

Don't Ignore the Smaller Donations

Minor donors can be very valuable to your efforts because they can give money at different times in the campaign. This is important because you will need continuous funding throughout. It takes strong budget-management skills to handle the budget for a political campaign, because the size and scope of the campaign grow as it picks up steam and funding is needed at each turn. The initial 200 people who came to the kickoff party may be 2,000-plus by the time the election approaches. It is an ongoing process.

Keep donors informed. A regular newsletter, e-mail, or a mailing of some type to supporters should keep them informed on how the campaign is going. The more connected donors feel with the process, the more likely they will donate again.

Legal Issues

Campaign funding has become a very hotly debated issue. Therefore, contributions to political campaigns are being closely watched.

The federal government, all states, and even most counties and towns have their own laws regarding campaign financing. These laws detail who can contribute, how much they are allowed to contribute, what the money must be spent on, and how contributions and expenditures need to be reported. It is imperative before starting the campaign that everyone involved in fundraising efforts understand the laws and regulations that will affect the campaign. You can be sure that any missteps will be picked up immediately by your opponents.

If you have someone with a legal background involved as a volunteer or supporter in any manner, this may be the person to ask about following up on such laws. It is important to appoint at least one person to check and make sure that each aspect of fundraising follows the letter of the law.

In 2002, a new set of campaign finance laws was enacted, called the Bipartisan Campaign Reform Act. The bill bans soft money to national political parties. "Soft money" is the term used to describe contributions not regulated by federal election laws. The original exemption was made to encourage "party building" activities, which benefit the political parties in general but not specific candidates. The money was supposed to be used for political activities supporting the platforms of the parties, from bumper stickers to ads trying to encourage more people to vote. The result, however, allowed very wealthy donors (who could otherwise not contribute more than the legal maximum to a single campaign) to contribute heavily to a party, and the money would then filter into high-tech office equipment and other means of helping a specific candidate. It was also used by the party to back a candidate in a key state during the midterm year in the presidential election.

Unlimited contributions to the national political parties will no longer be allowed. In addition, contributions from corporate or union treasuries will once again be outlawed in federal elections. This will have a major effect on the financing of the Democratic and Republican parties.

The contribution limits for individuals giving to federal candidates and political parties were also increased. Individuals can now give $2,000 to a candidate for an election, which is twice the previous limit.

FACT

According to the Campaign Finance Institute, the raise from the $1,000 to $2,000 maximum individual contribution will more likely help the challengers and open seat candidates who, in recent elections, received 22 percent of their donations at the maximum $1,000 level, or 4 percent more than the incumbents received.

The Fundraising Letter

One of the most important tools of your campaign fundraising activities is a good fundraising letter ready to go out to everyone you can think of. The candidate should be ready to reach out to all those whom he or she knows, from friends and neighbors to doctors to owners of stores he or she frequents.

Party politics aside, people are often drawn into supporting someone they actually know in person. The candidate needs to tap into as many people as he or she can, and a letter is a strong way of starting the process.

Your letter should explain why the candidate is running, what he or she hopes to do if elected, how much money is needed for an effective campaign, how the money will be spent, and how soon it is needed. Finally, a specific amount should be requested, or two or three suggested donation amounts should be provided.

It is important to seek money as early as possible. In politics, most vendors will want money up front, including printers and other resources you may need, because of the volatile nature of political campaigns. They can end abruptly, when a candidate drops out or runs out of money. So, if you are planning to do mailings to get the vote, be sure to get the funding in advance of approaching the printer.

The letter should be heartfelt, sincere, and to the point, meaning a couple of pages with short paragraphs that are reader-friendly. A personalized letter will be better received, and it is even recommended to use actual stamps over an ink indicia. However, this is not the place to go into details about political reforms, only to generate interest and give people a broad overview of the campaign.

The letter should be accompanied by a self-addressed stamped envelope. The return address can be that of the candidate, in a small town, or to the person sending out the letters on behalf of the candidate. Keep it personal. Not unlike a wedding invitation, someone should hand address the outside envelopes (unless the candidate is running for office in a major city) and include a reply card to return in the envelope.

The House Party

The banquet dinner is commonly thought of as a way to attract major donors and raise big money for a campaign. However, at a smaller, more easily manageable community level are local house parties. These are simply get-togethers in the home of a supporter to help generate some much-needed cash. After work is often the best time to hold a simple reception, but a weekend gathering may also work (although Fridays are not advised). The determination will be based on the makeup of the guest list and the availability of the candidate, who should certainly be present.

FACT

Signs, stickers, banners, and bumper stickers are all part of the political campaign. Use funds early on to get these basic sources of promotion printed in advance of launching the campaign. Lawn signs are popular and should be present outside of a house party and in supportive neighborhoods. Have plenty of items with the candidate's name on them ready to distribute.

Generally, it is not up to one person alone to pull off such a personal fundraising party, but a committee that helps make the arrangements. Someone needs to first be able to open up his or her home to such an event. It is best if this is someone who is centrally located and has the space to host such a party.

It is important to print and send out professional-looking invitations and include a reply card and the host's return address.

Various levels of support should be requested so you fulfill the objective of such a party, which is raising funds. The candidate should make an appearance and speak to the gathering briefly. He or she should mingle and shake hands with as many guests as possible.

In larger towns or cities, such house parties may become impractical, so receptions move into larger venues. The principal idea is the same, but at a grander scale.

Personal Appearances

Campaigning requires a lot of personal appearances for gathering votes, which gives you extra routes for obtaining funding. Supporters of the candidate should set up a means of donating money to the campaign wherever possible and allowable by law. The trick in these situations is not to detract from the quest for votes. Campaign staffers do not want to draw attention away from the candidate but do need to be taking contributions.

A personal appearance schedule for a candidate can be rigorous, especially in a larger town or a city. He or she needs to be focused on making a positive impression and gathering votes. If nothing else, each visit can help promote an upcoming fundraising event that will be open to the audience in attendance.

Big-Name Support

Perhaps the biggest fundraising tool of all is support by the right people. In politics, having significant party members on your side for campaigning and fundraising is extremely helpful. For this reason, George W. Bush, and before him, Bill Clinton, spent many hours crisscrossing the country (on taxpayers' dollars) to attend fundraisers for party candidates. They are still appearing at such fundraisers, as are politicians on all levels. It lends credibility to the candidate and links him or her with a party member who has garnered the support of the constituents.

Celebrities, whether local or national, are also a big plus at fundraising events for politicians. Politicians or celebrities can make speeches on behalf of the candidate, shake hands, sign autographs, or simply smile and make their presence felt. The bottom line is that they are endorsing the candidate, and you can use this to raise funds.

However, don't let the celebrity or well-known politician take the spotlight away from the candidate. If the candidate is overshadowed, people may give money at that moment because they are caught up in the frenzy of support. However, the donors may be less enthusiastic the next time around when the well-known politician or celebrity is not present. The focus needs to remain on the candidate.

Image Is Everything

In politics, image is almost everything. Yes, it helps to have a good platform, but image is still the key ingredient in a culture that often has little time to fully digest the issues. Image building, ripe with consultants and the right photo ops, requires funding, and this is also part of the fundraising package. The candidate needs to project the right image to ascertain funding and then turn around and use such funding to improve on that image and promote the platform.

Having the camera crew ready for every image-building moment costs money. Fundraising efforts, therefore, need to focus on a cost-effective means of image building in conjunction with the ongoing campaign. In addition, public relations and the flip side of image building, damage control, will need to be part of the fundraising plan. It's more than bumper stickers, lawn signs, and rallies. Fundraising also lends itself to hiring the right political publicists.

Combating the Self-Funded Candidates

The division of wealth in the United States over the past decade has shifted to a situation where nearly 90 percent of the personal wealth in the country is in the hands of just over 10 percent of the people. It has created a scenario whereby the super rich can now pour their own multimillions into running for office. There have always been rich candidates, but today, the high cost of running a campaign is daunting, and because of the vast discrepancies in wealth, a candidate without the personal funds to pour into the campaign is at a major disadvantage.

New York City Mayor Michael Bloomberg is a prime example of someone wealthy enough to finance the bulk of his own campaign. Regardless of whether he is considered a good mayor by the people of the city, the fact is, he had the upper hand by not having to do a great deal of fundraising, and he was able to pour more major amounts of money into the primary source of advertising today, which is television.

As the costs of running a campaign get increasingly higher, the multimillionaire self-funded candidate gains more power. The Ross Perots of the world can do a lot more than the peanut farmers in modern-day politics. Of course, it doesn't mean the richer candidate will automatically win, especially if a campaign is carefully run and the opposing candidate is diligent in his or her fundraising efforts. Combating the multimillionaire candidate is sometimes a matter of pointing out the fact that your candidate is financed by the people. Use the concept of working hard to raise funds as a campaign point.

FACT

One idea advocated by those seeking election-fundraising reforms is to push television stations to provide free time to candidates so they can get their message across without having to buy high-priced airtime, which favors the wealthy candidates.

Trying to push through clean money reforms is the other means by which to offset some of the influence of corporate America and special interest groups. This doesn't slow down the self-made millionaire train, but it does put the campaign financing back in the hands of the voters by reducing campaign spending and encouraging more people to throw their hats into the ring.

Involvement in campaign fundraising is unique among fundraising activities because of the emotional highs and lows that peak at election time. It can be a very rewarding experience, win or lose.

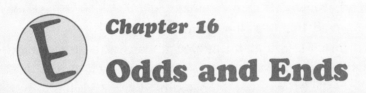

Chapter 16

Odds and Ends

No matter how large or small your fundraising campaign may be, there will be plenty of "little" details associated with the success of the project. Some are tangible, such as ordering nametags, and others are learning experiences, such as honing your skills in asking for and collecting money. This chapter covers all the things you don't want to forget about.

The Art of Collecting Money

Almost anything you read about fundraising emphasizes one key point: You have to ask for money. It is unlikely that donors will simply give unless they have a personal reason and seek you out. Therefore, you need to ask, and asking for money is not easy for most people. In addition, fundraising adds a new wrinkle; you may have to ask for payment of money that has already been pledged.

There is an art to asking for money. It starts with firmly believing in your cause or reason for asking. The words get stuck in your throat if you don't honestly believe that people should give their hard-earned money for your cause. If you are willing to put your own money in, then you will feel it is easier to ask others to do the same.

Practice your approach, and if you're reading from a script for phone solicitation, work on the inflection and the timing and try to sound as confident as possible.

If you are trying to collect money from friends and the situation is awkward, keep the discussion on the organization. While you want them to know you are a member, you can always approach from the organizational point of view, saying, "they are collecting" or "we are collecting" as opposed to "I am collecting." It is true because the organization is doing the fundraiser, and it takes the attention and awkwardness away from you personally asking someone you know for money.

Owed Money

Requesting money and actually collecting it can be two different animals. As noted previously, you may need to contact people who have pledged money and gently remind them that you need to hand in the funds and you haven't yet received their payment. If people continue to owe you money, you can politely become more persistent with reminders. However, you should also realize that they may be unable to pay or may have pledged money that they only *thought* they could afford to pay. In this case you should assume the money is not forthcoming and just let it go.

Collecting money for your fundraiser should be treated as you would treat any business. However, since you cannot hold people responsible for a promise, be reasonable when ascertaining whether a collection seems attainable and when one does not. You don't want to waste time chasing down a fifty-dollar donation when you could just as easily find other contributors.

Auction Prizes

Many people find it hard to ask for auction prizes or sponsorship of activities for their fundraising event. The easy way to get the ball rolling is to start off by sending a letter (this can work for all fundraising activities). This way, the person you are asking has a point of reference, and you don't have to start from the very beginning.

The conversation can be structured around the auction or similar activity as a whole and you can include some of the other prizes you have received or are hoping to get. The more you already have, the easier it may be to get more people on board. After all, no one likes to go first. You might also ask for a donation without specifying a specific item. That allows the individual to think of the price level of what he or she wants to donate and also provides an opportunity for the person to be creative. For example, rather than a gift certificate to a food boutique, the owner might surprise you with a fabulous basket of goodies to auction off.

Ordering from Vendors

Whether it's items to resell or party supplies to make your dinner party a political hit, you need to work professionally with vendors. You should:

- Check to see that a vendor is licensed.
- Get referrals.
- Inquire about additional costs above and beyond the product or item, such as shipping and handling.
- Inquire about a return policy if you need to send something back because it is broken or does not work.
- Find out the method(s) of payment in advance.

- Make sure to let vendors know that you are a nonprofit organization. You won't have to pay sales tax if you are tax exempt and have your 501(c)(3) letter to prove it.

One of the biggest problems organizations run into is the issue of timing. It's not the vendor's fault if he or she clearly explains that it takes two weeks to ship and you have not given yourselves enough time. You're always better having things delivered too early than too late, so shopping around and comparing vendors well in advance is highly advisable.

ALERT!

Make sure to see what you're buying. It's too easy to get inferior-quality products. Get a sample, or at least a good picture with the dimensions of the items clearly listed. This way, you are not in for a surprise when the dresses you ordered for young girls turn out to fit American Girl dolls instead.

Also look for vendor closeouts or discount rates that may be offered seasonally. For example, one school group took advantage of the week-after-Christmas half-price sale on holiday cards and ordered 500 boxes of cards at the discount rate. In fact, when they explained that they were ordering for fundraising purposes, the card manufacturer gave them an additional 20 percent off, making the total a 70 percent discount on cards that normally ran about $10 per box. The group stored the cards in the assistant principal's office closet for about nine months, and then as the following holiday season approached, sold them at close to full price, thus making almost $7 per box of cards or roughly a $3,500 profit for the school. Had they ordered the cards a few months in advance, the cards would have only brought them a $3 per box profit, and they would have made only $1,500.

Utilizing All Available Resources

The premise of the play *Six Degrees of Separation* centered on the idea that everyone is connected to each other in some manner by no more than six links. The same theory holds true for resources. Anything you need to locate can probably be found through six connections or less. The trick is making lists of the people you know who might know people who have what you need.

Generally speaking, people give up too easily. Chains of connection can come up with remarkable results and that is something you need to emphasize to your organization. Auctions have brought in celebrities and raised thousands of dollars for schools because one child's father's boss was good friends with a TV celebrity or the wife of the assistant principal had a brother who went to college with a major sports star.

FACT

When reviewing contacts or researching for major donors in any manner, *Who's Who in America* and the *Standard & Poor Directory* can be valuable resources for finding information on high-profile business donors. You can also utilize software or the library to help locate public records for top executives and CEOs of major corporations.

As for "available resources," there are usually items in the school, church, temple, community center, or homes of your members or volunteers (or their friends or families) that can help make a fundraiser work without having to go out and buy or rent everything. The trick is to make a scavenger-hunt type of plan whereby everyone looks for what is necessary in advance. Too often groups realize they need supplies at the last second and have no choice but to buy them, only because no one took the time to make a detailed list well in advance and start the hunting process. From paper clips to pickup trucks, if you search for most items, you'll find them.

Successful fundraising organizations report that upward of 75 percent of their resources, including manpower, goods and services, venues, and so on, come from sources within the organization. The most common resource needed from the outside is entertainment.

Shipping

Don't overlook the need to establish how everything will come together to make your fundraiser work. If you are ordering items that need to be there by the date of your fundraiser, you'll have to plan well in advance and have a contingency plan ready in case what you ordered does not arrive by a certain date.

Shipping costs can add up. When researching vendors and/or fundraising companies, make sure to inquire about shipping costs and find out at what point they may be lower. Many companies provide free shipping if you order more than x amount of goods. You can also try to negotiate if your need does not meet that magic number.

Printed materials need to be delivered with enough time to then send out invitations or post signage. You need to establish a calendar detailing specifically the date you will receive what you ordered, a follow-up date, and a last "must have" date, after which time you will no longer accept the delivery because you've spent more money to get a rush order from another printer or company.

It is, therefore, very important that you provide explicit shipping details. You need to:

- Have in writing exactly what date the items will ship out
- Have in writing by what date the items will arrive
- Provide a shipping address and backup address if necessary
- Have someone ready to accept the shipping order(s)
- Get explicit details as to whom you can contact if the order is wrong or late

Don't rely on someone's good word when the success of all of your hard work depends on that individual's delivering the products on time and to the right place. Make a detailed plan and have it in writing.

If you are taking orders for wrapping paper or magazine subscriptions, the orders will either be delivered to one location for you to distribute or sent to each person who bought the paper or subscribed to the magazine. In the first scenario, you need to make sure you have a central location in which someone can receive the shipment, organize it, and store it. A volunteer may say it's fine to deliver to his or her house because he or she is at home during the day. However, when 800 rolls of wrapping paper show up, that volunteer might wish he or she had not volunteered to receive the goods. Make sure there is some storage space available.

Baby-Sitting and Child Care

Volunteers need to put in plenty of time making a fundraising project a success. This can include meetings at night and on weekends. In addition, you may get a larger turnout at a dinner or other activity if you can provide some help with child care. If parents bring young children along to meetings or other activities, they need to be responsible for them. Having kids present, you run the risk of an injury or accident, which can result in a lawsuit. Therefore, you should not try to provide a child care facility. The best you can do is to simply make your environment child-friendly.

If you are having an event in the winter, make sure there is an adequate coatroom for your guests. One of the amenities at the 1999 Philadelphia Old House Fair, held in a National Guard armory building, was a coat check service for the 3,000 visitors. Many appreciated the opportunity to take off their bulky winter coats. This was also part of the strategy of extending people's stay at the event.

One organization had extra space at their monthly meetings and invited people to bring their children, who watched videos for the two hours of the meeting. Of course, the adults took turns manning the "video room," and it was understood in advance by the group that the parents were responsible for their children.

When the provision of group baby-sitting is not possible, programs and activities for kids accompanied by their parent(s) is a way of having your event be more family-friendly and attractive to more people. The "Zoo on Wheels" at the Philadelphia Old House Fair was enjoyed by kids and adults alike. While the fair was geared to adults seeking information on old house maintenance and restoration, the purpose of the zoo was to give the parent(s) a break and a place to have their kids entertained. Likewise, a school event filled with children's activities might have something for the adults to do, which might simply be a place set up to have coffee or read. Always consider your primary audience and then consider others who may also be present.

Security Concerns

Far from being a "little" detail, it is something that needs to be carefully considered from several standpoints. First, you need to make sure attendees are safe and that security is on hand in the event of a problem. Second, you need to make sure the funds you have worked so diligently to raise are safe. Unless you are working on a political fundraiser, where security will be more prevalent, try to maintain a low level of security that is discreet, yet present at all times.

ALERT!

Not all of your events and programs will be held at easily identifiable locations. Make sure people know where to park and how to find the entrance to where they are going. Good signage is important if the entrance to your event is not obvious. If parking is an insurmountable problem, a valet service may be a good solution.

Rehearsals or Walk-Throughs

Hold a pre-event "dress rehearsal" or at least a walk-through. Prepare a script or action plan for the event that spells out what is happening when and who is participating. Have a pre-event conference with all the key players and review the action plan. This is an excellent way to confirm who is doing what, identify concerns, and address them in advance. It also lets all volunteers know the lay of the land. People attending your fundraiser will ask all sorts of questions, including very simple ones such as, "Where are the rest rooms?" Your volunteers should be able to provide an answer.

Note fire regulations and other potential crowding situations when doing a walk-through of your site. Make sure there is always a path to fire exits and that there is a smooth traffic flow so that potentially dangerous overcrowding situations do not arise.

There are many details to consider when planning a fundraiser of any size or scale, but you're one step ahead of the game now! Ⓔ

Chapter 17

All about Grants

Remember that grants do not provide the bulk of fundraising money; individual donations still account for nearly 90 percent. But you don't want to overlook grants as a great potential source of getting the funds you need. This chapter gives you an introduction to what you need to know to find and apply for grants.

Finding Grants

A grant is an act of bestowing a subsidy. In the world of fundraising, it is a much-welcomed gift of support usually bestowed by a foundation. The big question is, where does one get such a generous subsidy?

Do Your Research

Procuring a grant will take some research on your part. The rule of thumb is that you narrow down a large list to those that are the best matches and apply to a select number of foundations rather than blitzing every foundation you can come up with. Targeting your list will almost always provide a better response and increase your chances of finding a good match.

There are over 40,000 places from which you might secure a grant. However, only a small percent will even consider your proposal. Why? Foundations have guidelines and criteria. Some may serve only the greater San Francisco area whereas others fund only scientific research projects. Some may insist that your nonprofit have at least a three-year history, and others will fund newly founded nonprofits. Narrowing down your list keeps you from wasting time and money sending grant proposals to foundations that aren't a good match.

Three key things to know about the foundation are: the geographic area(s) in which they bestow grants, the type of grants they give, and the areas of interest of the foundation.

The Internet and the library are two primary sources of information on foundations and grant possibilities. The Foundation Center, now some forty-five years old, has five main libraries and 215 cooperating collections throughout the United States, all of which can help you research foundations. They also have a comprehensive Web site and are the most highly recognized source of foundation information. Other sources for grant research can be found in Appendix A.

What to Look For

First, consider geographic restrictions. Many foundations operate in areas close to home, so you are best off starting with foundations near your home base. Explore the ones in your community first. The Foundation Center and other online grant research Web sites will help you search by geographic region. You should also go to a local library, since many foundations (more than 50 percent) are either not yet on the Web or maintain a low profile. The *Guide to U.S. Foundations* and the *Foundation Directory* are valuable sources for locating foundations.

Next, you need to consider the guidelines of the foundation. What types of projects do they fund? What are their areas of interest? If you read about a foundation that funds science and technology and you are looking for a grant to help maintain a children's day-care program, don't waste your time applying.

You should also take a moment to consider what the grantee looks for in an organization that they may fund. Along with looking at the need for funding, they want to see that your organization is well known in the community and that it addresses an existing need. Sound fiscal management, a strong, involved board, committed volunteers, qualified staff, and a realistic budget are all very important considerations.

There are also public and private foundations. It's worth noting that private foundations may allow you a more personalized approach as they may be less formal than public ones. It may be easier to talk to someone about what is required and there may be less bureaucracy involved. However, an advantage to public foundations is that, because they are public, they will have materials on public record, including other (accepted) grant proposals, that you can look at.

You should research other grant proposals. Grantsmart.org is a Web site that provides an online source for this information. Another way to learn about the recent grants given by a foundation is to call or write to it and request a copy of its annual report.

While some foundations offer support on a general basis by providing operating grants for the day-to-day operations of the nonprofit, many foundations prefer to fund particular projects or activities. This makes it easier for the foundation to monitor the results of its grant and know the money is being used as it had intended.

Policies of Foundations and Grant Providers

The funding goals of many foundations change from year to year. The most current information on the foundation's giving policies may be available through research on the Web, but it might also be best learned from a program officer. Call the program officers at the foundations that you are interested in and ask questions:

- What are your key areas of interest for this year's funding?
- What are your geographic preferences, if any?
- What kinds of restrictions do you have?
- How many grant awards do you plan to make this year?
- What are your application deadlines?
- When will the awards be announced?
- Can you explain the overall evaluation process and criteria?

Ask to receive a copy of the foundation's guidelines, which may also provide answers to many of the questions listed above. Read them several times to understand how the foundation wants the grant application to be submitted.

QUESTION?

Can foundations provide grants to organizations that have not applied for 501(c)(3) nonprofit public charity status with the IRS? Yes, according to federal law, public schools, libraries, other government and nongovernment organizations, as well as individuals, can receive grants providing the foundation follows specific rules detailing their expenditure responsibilities. The foundation will be required to file reports to certify that the funds were spent only for the charitable purposes outlined in the grant.

Renewal Grants

You might also look for foundations that provide renewal grants, which means they will offer the same grant for the same project(s) next year. If you think that you will be running the same project on an ongoing basis, keep this in mind. However, just because a foundation offers ongoing grants doesn't mean that by receiving a grant you automatically qualify for renewal. The renewal is based on the performance of the organization and how the initial grant money has been spent. Also keep in mind that most foundations do not want you to be solely dependent on their grant for funding. They will usually want to see that you are seeking funding from other sources.

The Application Process

To apply for a grant, you need to write out a proposal in accordance with the guidelines of the foundation. The proposal, typically around five pages, will be the cornerstone of your application. The other materials you will need to fill out are primarily for administrative purposes. Remember, follow instructions carefully.

The Data

You will need to do advance preparation for your proposal. This includes gathering your backup support materials and making sure that the data you are about to include is factual and up-to-date. While many people labor over the wording of their grants and may hire professional grant writers, even the most carefully worded professionally written grant proposal will be unsuccessful if the data are incorrect or the claims that are made cannot be substantiated.

Your proposal should make key points in a manner that is clear and compelling. Your objective is not to dazzle them with vocabulary words, nor is it to try to tug at their emotional heartstrings. It is to make sure that whoever makes the funding decision understands the significance of your cause or mission and the need for funding at this juncture. You must also explain how their funding will help in specific and practical terms.

When writing a grant proposal, don't make the common mistake of focusing more heavily on the wording than the credibility of those words. Putting the right substance into a concise and attention-grabbing package is the key.

The Specifics

Include the specifics, first regarding your mission. Then include some facts about your organization, followed by the specifics of your program. How long will this program run? Be realistic in what you feel can be accomplished in a set time frame.

Make sure that you have both backup information and the clearance of whoever needs to approve such activities before you put anything in writing. Don't assume that your organization or school board will go along with whatever you ask for. You should also explain the various tasks that will be carried out in the project and the experience of the people who are slated to handle these tasks.

The Guidelines

While working on the proposal, have the funding requirements and guidelines open at your side, and follow them closely. If the foundation provides research grants, don't try to explain how a building grant will be a research grant because the building may be used for research. Likewise, don't decide that your project is so important that you can take ten pages to explain it when the requirement is five. Remember, if the foundation is going to provide five grants this year and they have 200 proposals sitting in front of them, you can be sure that one manner of narrowing down the huge pile is to eliminate the proposals that do not adhere to the guidelines—without even reading them.

Also keep in mind that the application may call for a copy of the IRS letter regarding your organization's 501(c)(3) tax-exempt status. This is not optional. You must provide a copy.

ALERT!

If your grant proposal is for seed money for the start-up of a project, the foundation will be interested in how the program will be funded in the years after its funding has been spent. Be as detailed as possible. Show them that you've thought it through completely.

Support and Endorsements

You may also seek support for your proposal from outside sources. Individuals in academic, medical, or political positions who believe in your work can help out by adding a letter of support to your proposal package. Endorsement from government or other agencies, organizations, or influential individuals can help promote your cause.

Grant application reviewers will also look for a division of responsibility, should you be collaborating with other organizations. In your grant application process, you will need to present a schedule of meetings for the project and display a clear division of responsibility. Show that the project deliverables (or tasks that make up your fundraising effort) are being produced by more than one entity.

Presentation

While the validity of the mission is the most important part of the equation, presentation is also a factor. Appearance is crucial to success. Your proposal should look good and be user-friendly. Many foundations now request that applicants use a standard format application, which may vary by region. Some foundations participate in regional associations, such as in southeastern Pennsylvania, where the Delaware Valley Grantmakers has developed a standard format that many foundations in the metropolitan Philadelphia area use.

Some pointers:

- Use a popular and easy-to-read font, no smaller than 12-point.
- Use the headings from the grant application.

- Don't crowd your pages or try to cram nine pages of material into five.
- Use words and phrases that say what you mean.
- Use a cover page and keep it simple.
- Include all necessary documents and signatures.
- Include tables, charts, and graphics that are clearly labeled and explained.
- Have all contact information included.
- Don't use clip art, cutesy pictures, or plastic covers.
- Recheck your work several times.
- Use FedEx or UPS, so you can track the proposal and have a guarantee that it has been received before the proposal deadline.

While presentation is not the deciding factor, it will often help keep your proposal in the "to be read" pile. Neatness counts. Edit, spell-check, and proofread.

Timing and Follow-Up

Give yourself sufficient time to research and make an A-list of foundations that you most want to approach. Then, factor in time to write the proposal and run it past board members and other key people in your group or organization. Make sure you are aware of the time frame in which the foundation is looking to read grant proposals. Then prepare to wait.

It can take from several weeks to several months before you receive a response. And don't fret when you get rejection letters. Even the best grant writers in the business receive numerous rejection letters. Like finding a job or selling your novel, it is part of the process. Only in this case, you can get more than one positive response. In fact, the more you receive, the better. Foundations that see you are receiving grants from other foundations may look more closely at your proposal. You've been "accepted," so to speak.

There's nothing wrong with calling a foundation if you are unclear about their guidelines or need to find out information. It helps to be prepared, sound professional, and ask specific questions. It also helps *not* to call often or become a pest. Also, when you call, be prepared to talk in case someone asks you about your organization or project.

ALERT!

If you hire a professional grant writer, make sure he or she is knowledgeable about your organization and your mission. Spend time explaining what your organization's goals are. Too often, professionals come in and use all the buzz words but do not include the right substance because they do not know enough about the organization.

Corporate Grants

Large corporations may have foundations set up to allocate funding through grants to organizations such as yours. This may come from an endowment or through the earnings of the company.

The corporation is very likely providing funding for the sake of good public relations and a positive image within the overall community. Since they need to justify to stockholders why they are giving away money, they may request that they be clearly recognized for their efforts, for example, in an announcement at your event or with their name on your literature.

There needs to be a clear distinction between the for-profit corporation and the nonprofit organization. Does the fact that the corporation's name is associated with your organization change the image or alter the work being done by your organization in any manner? Does it alter the public perception of the organization? For example, if an organization that helps and supports families and children receives a grant from a company that manufactures alcoholic beverages, could that be seen as a conflict or an improper sponsorship?

Consider which companies do and do not serve as a good match for your organization. If the public perception will be more focused on the corporate sponsor than on your cause, or if the company is asking to have a say in how you proceed with your fundraising agenda, then they may not be right for you. Money with strings attached can end up costing you more in the long run. Most companies won't ask to be involved, just apprised of the progress being made in your organization. The public relations goal of the company usually means simply acknowledging it in some manner that puts its name in front of the public but does not interfere with your mission.

Federal Grants

If you are seeking a grant from the federal government, you may look at the *Catalog of Federal Domestic Assistance* in either a library or on the Internet at *www.cfda.gov*. Federal agencies provide various types of grants as well as other types of assistance in the form of loans, insurance, and federal relief in the case of disasters. You can search the Web site for federal assistance by subject.

There are fifteen types of government subsidy assistance, each of which includes a number of programs. Among these are:

- Formula grants, allocated by law for activities of a continuing nature not confined to a specific project
- Project grants, allocated for specific projects including research, training, or planning grants
- Direct payment for specialized use, which means federal assistance is provided directly to individuals, private firms, and other private institutions to encourage or subsidize a particular activity
- Direct payment of unrestricted use, which is federal funding to recipients who qualify without restrictions on how the money is to be spent
- Direct loans, which may or may not require the payment of interest

As is always the situation when dealing with the government, there will be plenty of paperwork in the application process. Request a grant application kit from the agency you are interested in pursuing. You might try to strike up a conversation with support staff on the phone and get to know some of the grantor agency personnel. Sometimes this can be helpful. The more people who can provide suggestions and feedback for your ideas, the better able you will be to structure the grant to the agency.

FACT

Most grant applications are scored using a point system. Ask for a written evaluation so you can learn what you need to improve. Talk with or write to the program officer to learn what was missing if your grant was not accepted.

Once you have made a comprehensive list of foundations and narrowed it down to those that look like the best match, you can begin writing your grant proposals. Tailor them to the individual foundations as opposed to writing a blanket proposal for all foundations. Chapter 18 focuses on the actual writing of the proposals and what you need to include.

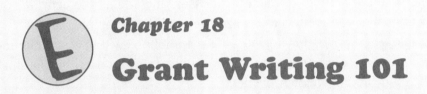

Chapter 18

Grant Writing 101

Like any other type of writing, grant writing takes some practice, so don't be concerned if your first try doesn't sound quite right. Your goal is to create a proposal that will entice grant givers to provide you with funding. In this chapter, we look at the elements that need to be included in your grant proposal. Remember, you can (and should) use other grant proposals as examples.

Overview of a Proposal

When writing your grant proposal, keep in mind your goals and objectives. Your goal is whatever it is you plan to do; for example, increase the number of retail businesses in the Main Street district.

Your objective is how you are going to achieve this. How will you increase the number of retail businesses? Include all the activities or actions that you can do to realize the goal. For example, 20,000 employees working for neighboring corporations within a ten-mile radius will be able to go online and view menus from a dozen restaurants in Jacksonville's downtown district.

Writing a grant proposal is like writing a business plan. You want to outline what it is you are looking to do in a manner that attracts someone to fund your venture. The inclination is to jump right into your need for funding upfront and make an impassioned plea. Don't do this. You need to first state a compelling problem, not unlike a narrative sets up the intriguing story line of a novel. You need to reach a point where the reader will be wondering how this significant dilemma will be resolved. The meat and potatoes of the proposal will then explain how you will set goals to tackle this problem. This section will also detail how your organization is capable of doing the work necessary to complete this mission. Finally, you will detail the manner in which your fundraiser will resolve the issues. This is a very broad overview, but it explains the basics of what a grant proposal should do.

FACT

Grant proposals need to identify expected outcomes. These outcomes are also known as measurable objectives, which need to be clearly defined in your proposal and must be achievable.

The topics covered in your proposal should usually include:

- A project summary
- Information about your organization
- A problem statement
- Your goals, objectives, and desired outcomes

- Your plan of action or methodology
- How you will analyze or evaluate your results
- The budget

Sometimes a wrap-up page or two will follow and, in many instances, you will have additional pages of data, which we'll discuss in the final section of the proposal.

The Project Summary

A project summary should appear at the beginning of your proposal. It should consist of two to five paragraphs outlining the fundraising project in very basic terms. Even though it appears in the beginning, the summary is often written after the rest of the proposal has been prepared. This way, you make sure to include what is actually in the proposal and don't lock yourself into trying to write a proposal to fit the summary.

Make sure the summary is worded carefully and encompasses your key ideas *in brief*. The summary must include the overview of the project, the key issues that will be detailed in the rest of the proposal, and how the funding will impact the community in question.

Keep the interests and ideals of the foundation in mind when writing the summary. Do not include any extraneous information about areas not covered within the proposal in your summary. This is why you should put together your summary last, because you may have made changes to other parts of the proposal that need to be reflected in the summary.

About Your Organization

Whether you are a long-standing nonprofit organization, a fledgling newcomer, or a university or high school, you will need to introduce or present your organization to the foundation. Include a brief organizational history, perhaps short biographies of the board members (or key staffers), and your goals, philosophy, and success stories. In addition, you can mention programs that are currently provided.

Sometimes, biographical and other aspects of this organizational data can be moved to the end of the proposal. The idea here is to present the credibility of the organization. Keep in mind that this should be the condensed, *Reader's Digest* version of how marvelous your organization is and not the full three-act play.

FACT

Grant givers will find merit in the accomplishments of your organization as validated by outside sources and the inclusion of additional materials. If your organization has won awards or citations, or if you've received mention in the press, you should mention such honors. You may attach clippings at the end of the proposal.

The Problem Statement

Also called the needs assessment, this is where you make a well-crafted statement of the problem that needs to be addressed. Explain what the problem is, who is at risk, and how your organization became aware of this need. Mention what is currently being done to address this problem and how addressing this issue in greater depth can rectify the problem.

Be factual in your statements, cite sources wherever possible, and include how the issue is affecting economics, social well-being, the environment, or other key areas. Match the needs and interests of the foundation whenever possible without stretching your own limits.

By the end of this section, you should have drawn the reader into the problem at hand. If you are appealing to a foundation that is interested in your cause (you should know this from your research), then a well-crafted problem statement should have its undivided attention at this point.

Goals and Objectives

This section follows the introduction of the problem. It takes the reader from wondering what will happen and presents possible ways in which to solve the problem stated above.

It is important to note the objectives and the goals you hope to reach. The objectives of the program will include the activities in the proposal. The desired outcome is the culmination you hope to see from all the hard work. This section is not defining your actual plan of action, but presenting a broader view of the program, including measurable results. The foundation or organization funding the program will want to see such measurable results.

This is often the hardest part of the proposal to write, because you do not want to state goals that cannot be reached or objectives that cannot be clearly attained. You need to be careful to maintain a level of objectivity and not let your dreams of overwhelming success get the better of you.

Your Plan of Action

This is where you explain your methodology and show in detail how you will achieve your goal. You should describe the specific tasks that will take place, how they relate to each other, and who will handle the various tasks.

While you may have all the details in place, the trick is to present a sound plan while keeping the reader intrigued. Try to make the section flow smoothly as you take the reader on a tour of your plan. Remember to illustrate the logic and reasoning behind your ideas so it is clear why your plan will allow you to meet your goals. All of the aspects of your program should be highlighted, including how you will promote your activities or event, any technology necessary, and any new personnel that may need to be hired.

ALERT!

If you use supporting data, do not overdo it. Too often, grant writers believe that if they load up the proposal with tons of graphs, charts, bios, and other paperwork, it will help get the grant request accepted. It won't. Include only a few pages of the most significant information.

Use supporting data to substantiate what you are claiming will take place. If you feel that supporting material will interfere with the flow of the narrative, then place such materials at the back of the proposal in an appendix.

You may also differentiate why your program will work as opposed to other programs or methods that have been used to deal with this particular problem in the past. Most issues are not brand-new and, therefore, other attempts have been made to solve the problem. Your proposal should not belittle other efforts but should state how this plan is unique or how it compares to other successful plans that have worked in the past.

Evaluating the Program

This is where you explain how the program will be measured to determine the success or lack thereof. First, you will need to describe how the evaluations will be conducted and who will handle the process. You also need to include the method of measurement. Besides evaluating the results of the project itself, you will want to evaluate the process by which you achieved the results. Did the project follow the plan of action? Explain how you will determine the answer to this question.

Federal agencies and foundations will want to see the type of evaluation that you plan to use and at what junctures during the project you will conduct your evaluations or analysis.

You want to show that you are prepared to determine whether the project served the anticipated number of people. You also need to evaluate whether the fundraising project stayed within the initial budget and how it impacted the community, neighborhood, or other affected group(s).

Your Budget

You are asking for a foundation's money for an investment in your project. The program officer needs to know how the money granted by the foundation will be spent. Along with a strong narrative, you need to include a budget.

A carefully prepared budget should justify all of your expenses and be consistent with the activities listed within the proposal. There should be no surprise items entered on the budget that aren't mentioned in your plan of action. Some common budget areas include rental of building(s), equipment and resources, transportation, publicity, insurance, and food/refreshments. Personnel costs are also included and subtitled.

FACT

Often pro bono and in-kind services will be accepted as a source of a funding match. If your proposal states that you'll match their grant with money or donations from other sources, you may be able to use volunteered services (such as free Web site design services donated by a professional) as part of your "other" donations. If this is the case, the value of volunteered services may need to be substantiated in the proposal using prevailing average wages or agreed on in writing as a condition of the funding of the application.

Remember to include only the costs that relate to this particular program and not ongoing administration costs that are not part of this grant proposal (unless you are applying for a general operating grant). In fact, you might even explain what will become of equipment after the project is over. Will it be donated or put to good use for future projects?

Indicate where the project will take place. Are the project personnel working out of an office? Are they using typical office equipment, such as copiers and telephones? If so, do the budget guidelines of the funder allow for space and usage of equipment to be considered as eligible project costs? Will meeting rooms, auditoriums, and audiovisual equipment need to be rented to complete the tasks of the project? These are legitimate project costs. Include them in your budget.

Make sure that you list the various sources of income, including sponsors, donors, sales, grants, and so on. Foundations will want to know where other funding will come from. The foundation providing the grant, as noted earlier, will usually not be your primary source of funding, but one of several. Many grant applications require that the applicant show matching funds and additional resources.

And in the End

To conclude your proposal, you may include a formal wrap-up, or conclusion, but it is not essential. You may want to simply reiterate some of the key earlier points of your proposal so that the last thing the reader reads is something other than the budget. Whatever you choose to conclude with, keep it brief.

In addition, all accompanying documents will be attached in the appendix at the end of your proposal. This should include the bios of your board of directors, your nonprofit status, and the previous year's financial statements. You might also include press releases of your organization's activities, major grants received in recent years, and letters of support for the project goals.

There are many classes and seminars offered on grant writing. Look for ones in your area. You are usually better off taking a course and improving your own skills than hiring someone who doesn't know about your organization to write a grant. However, if you are more comfortable hiring a professional, make sure he or she is a grant writer and not another type of scribe. Also, look at work he or she has done previously and make sure to provide this person with all the data that he or she will need to capture the essence of your goals and needs. In short, make sure the grant writer is on the same page as your organization.

Sample Grant Application

Here is the written portion of an actual grant application presented by a historical preservation committee in conjunction with the guidelines and questions asked on the application of an urban preservation foundation. Most of the above-mentioned areas were requested and included. You'll note that this particular application lumped goals and results with plan of action in part three. Remember, each grant proposal is slightly different, and you will need to follow the application carefully.

1. Project Summary

The Jefferson County Urban Design and Historical Preservation Committee (JCUD-HPC) seeks funding to create a comprehensive plan that is compatible with the overall fabric of the historic context of the region. This project will help us achieve our goal of economic viability and revitalization of the neighborhood and commercial streets in the Jefferson County Historic District.

The infrastructure, facades and signage, mercantile issues and streetscape, including parks and public art, will be addressed. Current and future zoning issues will be examined with the intent of safeguarding this plan. The results will be described both visually and verbally for use by the community in its negotiations and dealings with the district government including the departments of Public Works, Parks and Recreation.

The procedure for producing this plan will incorporate significant input from area residents and citizen organizations prior to and during a two-day neighborhood design workshop. Pro-bono services of local professionals in the fields of urban design, historic preservation, retail marketing and business development will all be utilized. All relevant technical information including maps, photographs, historic guidelines, zoning and scale drawings will be prepared, updated and analyzed. Two weeks after the neighborhood design workshop the final project report will be presented at a community-wide meeting in Jefferson County.

The JCUD-HPC will implement this project with the assistance of a planning group known as Design Unlimited, an organization sponsored by the state commission on the arts and humanities, funded in part by the National Endowment for the Arts and supported by the American Institute of Architects.

2. Description of the Need for Funding from the Urban Preservation Foundation

Funding is being requested because the neighborhood referred to as the Historic District is in need of revitalization. Business and shop owners have reported a decline in customers of nearly 40 percent over the past five years. Tourist traffic in the area is also down significantly. In addition, several of the buildings have been reported to have minor structural damage as determined by the City Buildings Safety Commission. The loss of revenue for the Jefferson community resulting from the lessened tourist traffic and business conducted in this area is projected at nearly $1 million annually over the next two years.

There is also a cultural and historic obligation to the city to maintain the historic buildings that were the cornerstones of the Jefferson community.

This is the first time the community has sought funding from outside the neighborhood to support a project regarding historic preservation. The Jefferson Architectural Bureau has agreed to pledge $5,000. Additional funding of $5,000 is requested from the Urban Preservation Foundation to be specifically used for this project.

3. About the Organization

The JCUD-HPC was founded in 1967 as a privately endowed, independent institution devoted to collecting, interpreting, and presenting the rich multicultural history of the community and the state to the public through exhibitions, programs, research collections, and publications.

In addition, the committee also works to establish historical status for select buildings in the Jefferson County region and works to maintain and preserve the eighteen structures that are already listed as historical landmarks in the Jefferson Township.

4. Describe your goals and future plans for the project or activity beyond the scope of this grant proposal (i.e. how the consultant's recommendations will be implemented, how educational programs will be institutionalized, etc.).

The goals and subsequent results of this project will be to:

- Encourage compatibility of building rehabilitation and new construction with protection of the historic district.
- Enhance pedestrian activity and tourism in the area.
- Strengthen and identify the character and attractiveness of the area.
- Improve and increase retail business activity.
  The project will include a major overhaul of the sidewalks, curbs,

streets, lighting, landscaping and neighborhood park in the downtown historic district of Jefferson. This work, scheduled to begin during the spring of 2004, will work with the already pledged support of the local municipal organizations and the department of public works.

The work is expected to take five months and will include the entire twelve square block area encompassing the historic district. Work will be completed in three parts to avoid inconvenience to residents and storeowners. See attached work schedule. Our committee also recently negotiated with the Department of Recreation and the Office of Business and Economic Development to take responsibility for special projects to improve the public park in the Jefferson Historic District. This work will begin in the fall of 2004 and include planting, new lighting and safe, new playground equipment.

Further, the proposed urban re-design and historic preservation plan of the Jefferson Historic District will be the foundation for the update of the Jefferson shopping district, scheduled to begin in the fall of 2005. This additional project is expected to take nine months and is not part of this specific project and will be separately funded.

5. Evaluating the Project

The JCUD-HPC is seeking project funding, with the average grant in the range of $1,500 to $2,000. In the evaluation process, the JCUD-HPC will confirm the proposed project, an urban design plan for the neighborhood's commercial district, and show continual building progress on a monthly basis as well as accounting for the project expenses. Committee reports will also be provided monthly from the fundraising, planning and project committees.

The "Urban Design Plan" for the Historic District will be completed with information gathered from a two-day community workshop to be held in May. Approximately 125 residents and planning professionals will be invited to participate in the workshop. A report, with drawings prepared by architects, urban planners, and landscape architects will be distributed in July through a community newspaper. A copy of the report will also be provided to all funders.

A search for funding to implement some of the recommendations has already begun. One local foundation has publicly expressed interest in funding projects in this neighborhood and an introductory meeting has already been scheduled.

6. Budget
Estimated total of this project/activity: $25,000
Amount requested from the (name of grantor): $5,000

Project Activity/Income
Source of Cash (specify)

PSF Grant (request submitted)	$5,000
Urban Preservation Foundation (grant requested)	$5,000
Local Business Contributions	$1,000
Direct Mail solicitation in neighborhood	$1,500
Neighborhood Bazaar and Flea Market	$1,500
Raffle	$1,000
Barbecue Picnic Dinner	$1,500
Total	$16,500

Source of donated services and materials (specify)

Printing and reproduction donated by Fast Press	$300
Food donated by area restaurants and supermarkets	$750
Room for workshop donated by St. Mary's Church	$500
Audiovisual equipment donated by Jefferson Media Corp.	$400
Juan Alvarez Architects donation of drafting services	$570
Donation of services of 6 design professionals (architects, urban planners, and landscape architects) for 2 days @ $500 per day	$6,000
Total	$8,520

CHAPTER 18: GRANT WRITING 101

Cost Category	Description	Cost	Applicant Share	UPF Share
Consultant (cash)	Preparing technical/structural reports	$2,250	$750	$1,500
Salaries/ honoraria (cash)	Facilitator, administration, and staff coordinator	$10,020	$10,020	——
Donated services (in-kind)	Professional Design Team	$6,000	$6,000	——
Printed materials	Technical materials, report, and raffles	$3,000	$300	$2,700
Supplies	Office, drafting, and two fundraising events (bazaar and picnic)	$1,200	$1,200	——
Space/ equipment rentals	Meetings	$900	$900	——
Food and beverages		$700	$700	——
Mailing and postage		$130	$130	——
Other	Preparing technical data	$800	——	$800
Total project expenses		$25,000	$20,000	$5,000

You'll note that in the sample budget, under expenses, it indicates exactly what the applicant (the organization requesting the grant) will pay for and how the funds from the specific grant, in this case from the UPF or Urban Preservation Foundation, will be used.

This grant proposal is a sample of the type of information that may be requested and how it might be presented. Remember, grants alone will not save the day, but they can help you in your quest to complete a successful fundraising project. Ⓔ

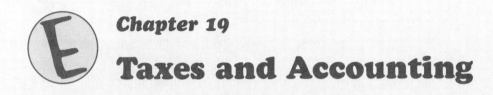

Chapter 19

Taxes and Accounting

Wherever income and funding are involved, there is a need to address the issue of taxes. As a nonprofit organization, you will need to determine your tax status and set up your bookkeeping methods in a manner that will help your organization remain financially accountable. Tax regulations vary from state to state, but this chapter introduces you to the basics.

Your Tax Status

If you are a nonprofit organization, you can apply for federal tax exemption by filing with the IRS. Churches, schools, hospitals, and certain other organizations automatically qualify for nonprofit status because they are considered public charities. They must, however, meet certain criteria. For example, a school has to provide ongoing instruction, have a student population, and have faculty members. A hospital must meet health requirements and have a regular medical staff. You cannot simply call yourself a school or hospital and expect to be recognized as such. For information on which tax-exempt status is right for your organization, you can look at IRS Publication 557, which can be obtained from the IRS or found on its Web site at ✎ *www.irs.ustreas.gov.*

Operating as a nonprofit organization, company, or association, you can obtain tax-exempt status under section 501(c)(3) of the Internal Revenue Code if your purpose is charitable, educational, cultural, or religious. The benefit of having this status is so that contributors can take a tax deduction on their federal income taxes when contributing to your organization.

Applying for Nonprofit Status

To apply for 501(c)(3) status, you will need to file IRS Form 1023 and attach Form 8718 (User Fee for Exempt Organization Determination Letter Request). To make filing easy, you can download Form 1023 from the IRS Web site or call 1-800-Tax-Form and request a copy. You will need to fill out several parts of this form, which asks for administrative information, a description of the activities of your organization, financial statements, and so on.

The nine-page Form 1023 will take a while to complete, so proceed slowly and carefully. Then attach all requested accompanying documents. And remember to attach a check for the fee.

Not all groups need to file Form 1023 to apply. If your organization is part of a larger parent organization that already qualifies for 501(c)(3) status, you do not have to apply. For example, if you are a chapter or branch of a national charity or your PTA belongs to the national PTA, you would not have to file separately. Public charities that have gross receipts that total less than $5,000 a year also need not apply.

The fee for filing Form 1023 depends on your organization's gross receipts. If your income has exceeded $10,000 or you anticipate that it will in the given year, then you will pay $500. If your income has been under $10,000 or you anticipate that it will be, the fee is $150.

If your organization is not a corporation, you will need to submit your constitution, articles of association, or other governing documents besides your bylaws. Whatever you choose to send should include three signatures by officers or leaders of the organization. You also need to send financial data, including an income statement (if you have already had some income) and a two-year projected budget. If you are incorporated, then the articles of incorporation, with the secretary of state's stamp on page 1, need to be submitted.

It is recommended for most independent nonprofits to apply for tax-exempt status because achieving this status is the only way to be assured that the IRS views the corporation as a 501(c)(3) tax-exempt group and, therefore, you can confidently let contributors know that they can take a tax exemption for contributions on their personal income taxes.

If you are a corporation, you will need to have your 1023 application filed and postmarked within fifteen months after the end of the month in which your articles of incorporation were filed. If you file on time, the tax-exemption status is effective retroactively to the date on which your articles were filed.

You will then receive your 501(c)(3) status letter from the IRS determining that you qualify for tax-exempt status. Copies of this letter will come in handy when:

- Sending grant proposals
- Purchasing equipment for the organization
- Dealing with government agencies

- Applying for a bulk mail permit
- Placing classified ads (you can get lower rates)
- Recording public service announcements

Keep copies of the letter handy for such reasons and other situations that may arise.

Incorporating

You may wish to become a nonprofit corporation. To do so, you will first have to incorporate in your state (each state has its own guidelines for incorporating). Depending on state laws, you may need to incorporate in other states where you are doing business.

You will need to follow the guidelines of incorporating, which include establishing bylaws and holding annual meetings of members and directors. Incorporating, however, does not automatically qualify you for tax-exempt status. You will then need to file for your 501(c)(3) as described above.

Despite a lot of additional paperwork, incorporating has some important benefits. As a nonprofit 501(c)(3), your corporation will be exempt from federal corporate income taxes. In addition, you will be able to apply for public and federal grants. Another major advantage of incorporating is that, as a corporation, you get increased protection against liability. This means board members and others involved in the corporation are protected from being held personally responsible should the corporation incur debts or liabilities.

If the corporation has significant assets, it may also be wise to incorporate. Also, should you have income that is unrelated to your charitable cause, and you have to pay tax on it, you will be taxed at the corporate rate.

Donor Contributions

Contributions to nonprofits with 501(c)(3) tax-exempt status are tax deductible. This encourages people to donate money as well as goods and services. The fair market value of the goods or services is also deductible.

If you provide goods or services in exchange for someone's contribution, that person can deduct only the amount of the payment that is more than the value of the goods or services received. If, for example, you sell an item at an auction for $200 that is valued at $50, the buyer can deduct only the $150 difference between the amount they spent (the contribution) and the actual value of the item. If the value of the goods or services is over $75, your nonprofit organization must then be ready to provide a statement to the contributor stating such information.

Should you receive a gift in kind, look for some third party to provide you with an approximate value of the item unless the donor provides you an amount. You need to know the value of the gift for your own income records.

A 501(c)(3) qualified nonprofit organization is not allowed to be involved in politics, so steer clear. Political nonprofit groups operate separately from this classification.

Pledges are a unique type of contribution. In effect, a pledge is a promise (written or verbal) of a contribution to be given in the future. A pledge is usually monetary and may be based on an activity at your fundraising event, such as money pledged for each mile walked by a participant at a walk-a-thon. A pledge can also be a nonmonetary item.

According to the Financial Accounting Standards Board, a pledge needs to be considered legitimate before it is entered into your accounting system. The validity is hard to measure. Did the donor write down the words "promise" or "binding" and sign his or her name? If you feel that you have received what would be considered a legally binding agreement, then it should be recorded. Most pledges are unconditional, but if there is a condition that the organization must meet, then that is part of the binding agreement. Once the condition is met, the pledge becomes binding in the same manner as mentioned above.

It is worth mentioning that pledges can present a misleading picture of your income, much in the way that paper assets fooled a lot of people in the stock market with tech and Internet stocks a few years ago. A total of $30,000 in outstanding pledges needs to be clearly differentiated from

$30,000 in actual income for your organization. An organization that is frequently reporting far more money in pledges than it is seeing in income may look suspicious to the state charity commission.

Deductions

Beyond the obvious deductions that contributors can take for giving money to a qualified 501(c)(3) nonprofit organization (which is up to 50 percent of their annual gross income), there are several variations on the theme and some exceptions. Raffle tickets, for example, are not considered tax deductible. A tax professional can help contributors determine the exceptions to the rule.

If money is given to a government organization, under section 115 of the IRS code, the contribution is deductible, provided, of course, it is used for the public. Public schools fall into this category as long as the money is used for the education of the students (hence, the public).

Your volunteers may also have deductions that they can take in accordance with the work they do. They should keep track of any expenses they incur that are directly related to their work on the fundraiser. Remind volunteers that they can put in for deductions for out-of-pocket expenses. They can also include fourteen cents per mile on travel expenses and include items such as clothing (e.g., a uniform) purchased specifically for the purpose of the fundraising activity. A volunteer cannot deduct his or her time and services.

Filing with the IRS

A nonprofit organization is required to file a Form 990 with the IRS. You must also have copies of the past three 990s that you have filed available for the public to read.

When filing, you will use a fiscal year in the same manner as a for-profit business. You can use either the regular calendar year or a variation. Some organizations may base their fiscal year around the nature of seasonal activities. For example, if you are very busy with fundraising activities from September through March or April, you might have your fiscal year from July 1 through June 30. This way, the preparations and other work that needs to be done before filing your tax return can be done during a "quiet" time for your organization. Whatever your fiscal calendar year, make sure to file by the fifteenth day of the fifth month following the end of the fiscal year, or request an extension in advance of the filing date.

Churches and organizations that receive under $25,000 in gross receipts do not have to file Form 990 by federal law. However, there may be state laws that require you to file. Double-check state filing requirements.

Bookkeeping Practices

When running fundraising activities, you need to keep a careful watch over your books. You want accurate data regarding your income and expenses as they relate to each activity or event you run. This will help you when it's time to file taxes or you need to show financial information to an auditor, government agency, or to foundations when seeking grants.

It is imperative that someone in your organization has basic bookkeeping and financial management skills. If not, you may need to hire someone to handle your accounting. Board members and directors need to keep a watchful eye over this key aspect of an organization. In small groups, one person may find himself wearing many hats, including bookkeeper and accountant, so to speak. Cash management and bookkeeping need to be done carefully and with the utmost integrity.

If you are in a management position for a nonprofit organization or are running a fundraiser, you should have a basic understanding of how to read the financial statements and the organization's books to better comprehend the financial status of the organization. Brush up on basic accounting skills.

Whether you or someone you trust is handling the bookkeeping activities, it is crucial to record all financial transactions in a clear manner. The work needs to be easy to decipher in case there is cause to review your books. Remember, each organization will have its own policies and guidelines for handling financial transactions. Once such a working system has been established, it should be carefully maintained.

It is common for nonprofit organizations to authorize two or three people to sign checks, one being, of course, the treasurer. In some cases, two signatures may be required for every transaction. Some organizations, however, may feel that this is unnecessary because it may be difficult to get the check into the hands of two people for signing purposes when it needs to be mailed out quickly. Whatever system you use, be consistent, and do not give signing privileges to too many people.

ALERT!

Often, because members of the organization do not see each other regularly, checks are presigned to be used when necessary. It is suggested that this practice of presigning checks be avoided. It can lead to serious problems should the checkbook fall into the wrong hands.

Your Accounting System

When handling the accounting for your organization, you can use either a cash-based system or an accrual-based system. The cash-based system is similar to the manner in which you maintain your checkbook, except you'll be using a ledger and posting cash receipts into the cash receipts journal and cash disbursements into the cash disbursements journal. The system, which is more common in smaller to mid-sized organizations, is based on cash transactions.

An accrual basis is one where entries are posted when money is earned and owed. This is usually more common in larger organizations. You will need to utilize this system when filling out financial statements whereby you will list what income is due you and what expenses are owed. Larger organizations, handling more money, can afford to have more money owed, while a small organization will need to have its money readily available at all times.

Depending on the size of your organization or fundraising effort, and the computer comfort level of your treasurer, you can work in anything from a basic ledger to an advanced accounting software program. Many people have used a simple Excel program to create spreadsheets and QuickBooks or Peachtree software to handle the accounting for a small nonprofit group.

Nonprofit organizations need to report account activity for program transactions that relate specifically to services provided. They also need to report supporting transactions, which are more general transactions that are common to all ongoing programs and activities, such as administrative costs.

An audit can provide you with a financial overview. Generally done by an experienced professional, an audit provides an all-inclusive report of the financial procedures and activities of your organization. An audit will provide you with a document detailing the manner in which your organization is handling the finances. Some nonprofits are required to have audits done periodically. Even if you are not required to have an audit completed, it is a good idea to have one done because such a document can help you when seeking grants, sponsorship, and corporate funding. The only drawback is that an audit can be costly. Smaller organizations generally cannot afford to have one done until they have built up significant funding and can justify the need for an audit.

Cash Flow

Often, your cash flow will depend on seasonal activities, including your fundraising campaigns. Membership drives or renewals may provide income at certain times of year, and your special fundraising events will also help you maintain a positive cash flow. In most organizations, income will come in more readily during certain times of year. Otherwise, you will need to plan in advance to have sufficient cash on hand during the rest of the year to cover your operating expenses. This is one situation where pledges do nothing to help your needs.

You will need to plan accordingly when to buy equipment for your office or begin a public relations campaign. However, there will be situations that may arise where you will need to spend some of your funds. Depending on the cause or mission of your organization, you may need to help in the event of an emergency. The definition of emergency differs among organizations. One group dedicated to preserving the ecology of a particular region suddenly found that it needed to help out when an oil spill threatened to destroy one of the region's lakes. A civil rights organization needed to spend emergency funds to send a contingent to Washington, D.C., when a bill threatened to eradicate much of what they had been fighting for. A PTO voted to use some reserve funds to repair the gymnasium after a storm destroyed part of the ceiling.

Many organizations set aside a portion of their funding for such emergency use. The larger the organization, the more that can be put into this special pool of funds. In any case, you need to keep money in reserve and have cash available at all times.

Put procedures in place early on that dictate how and when emergency funds are to be used. This may include a vote of the board or other means of determining that such funds can be used. Make sure the policies are spelled out in advance so you can act quickly when necessary.

Reviewing Your Financial Picture

You need to keep a watchful eye on your financial picture as you proceed through operations and especially through fundraising activities and special events preparation.

Planning Ahead

It is important to examine how much you can dip into your funding and still have enough to continue operations. You always need to plan ahead and cannot "expect" that the next fundraiser will solve your financial woes, even if the last three years have shown the same event to be a major success.

Ultimately, you want to find a balance by which you can maintain enough funding to keep your organization running smoothly to meet your goals and further your mission for years to come. Depending on the needs of the organization, nonprofits report that anywhere from 20 to 50 percent of their money is spent on fundraising.

Organizations do not want to build up excessive amounts of money. If you find that you are operating with significantly more money in reserve than your anticipated needs, you should sit down with your board or key members of your group and decide how to put the money into programs that better serve the community and further your goals as an organization.

FACT

A nonprofit can show money in reserve above and beyond its operating expenses. But this money cannot be used to benefit any individual in the organization or to back a political candidate or a commercial venture. It must be used for the purposes of the designated mission of the organization.

The Numbers

To get a good feeling of where your organization stands financially, you need to review your financial statements. Ask yourself:

- Are you sticking to your budget?
- Are there extra expenses beyond those for which you had planned?
- Are you keeping administrative costs down?
- Are contributions being used for their intended purposes?

These are among the questions you will need to ponder when trying to get an adequate assessment of where you stand financially. If, for example, you find that the percentage of money going toward administration costs is too high, then you will know where to make adjustments that will put more money into the necessary programs and activities of the organization. Naturally, the nature of the organization and the size and scope of the fundraising activities will factor into your analysis.

Also, how new the organization is will be a factor. In the first year, the setup of the office and establishing the presence of the organization will likely require more money than once you are up and running.

It's important to monitor and analyze the finances of any nonprofit organization or grassroots fundraising activity on a frequent basis. Usually an organization with monthly or bimonthly board meetings will require a financial report at each meeting.

Financial Accountability

Besides having your past three Form 990s or 990ez's available to the public, you should also check all state and local government regulations to determine what other documents you are required to have available to the public.

Related Income

You will need to be financially accountable and to show that income is related to the purposes of the organization. If, for example, the IRS determines that income is unrelated to the purpose of your nonprofit organization, then you will have to pay income taxes even if you have "tax-exempt" status. One East Coast charity dedicated to raising money for the treatment of a serious illness also owns a building from which it does its administrative activities. It utilizes only two of the three floors in the building and rents the third floor to another company. This rental income is taxable because it does not relate to the organization's main function. If, however, the floor were rented to a research team that was working on medical issues relating to the same illness, then this could possibly be considered related income.

FACT

To maintain nonprofit status as a public charity, you need to show that one-third of your income comes from the public in the form of either contributions or revenues.

What is and is not considered advertising is also a question that has many answers. If, for example, Bob's Meat Market purchased uniforms for a Little League team, the value of the uniforms would not be considered unrelated income, but an advertising expense. However, if Bob took out an ad in a journal for his meat market, it would depend on the organization and the content of the ad as to whether this was or was not considered advertising and thus unrelated income. Journal ads can be a gray area. Talk with a tax specialist and don't be surprised if he or she needs to look through his or her tax books to give you answers.

Unrelated business income can be tricky, and it is advisable to review with an accountant what falls under that classification and is considered taxable income. When you pay taxes in this situation you will pay under the corporate rate if you incorporated prior to receiving your 501(c)(3) status.

Being financially accountable for a nonprofit organization means maintaining integrity and making sure that all income and expenses are clearly accounted for. It also means upholding the nonprofit status of the organization and being accountable to the IRS in the case of an audit or review of the tax exemption status. You will maintain your nonprofit status, provided your organization:

- Does not engage in for-profit business activities
- Does not have board members or other nonstaff individuals benefiting monetarily from the activities of the organization
- Is not conducting any type of income-generating activity that is not in keeping with the purposes of the organization

With the fast increase in nonprofit groups over the past few years, the government is now watching very closely to make sure such groups follow the IRS guidelines.

Substantiation and Disclosure Requirements

According to the IRS, a donor is responsible for obtaining a written acknowledgment from a charity for any single contribution of $250 or more before the donor can claim a charitable contribution on his or her federal income tax return. This means you are required to provide such written acknowledgment.

You are also required to provide a written disclosure to a donor who receives goods or services in exchange for any single payment of $75 or more. This includes buying tickets to a fundraising dinner or auction. The fair market value of the ticket must be determined and provided to the contributor so that he or she can deduct this amount from the amount spent to purchase the ticket. The remaining total can then be deducted on the individual's income tax return. Keep in mind that just because your organization may have received a discount on the tickets of $25 each, that does not affect the fair market value, which may be $50 each.

ALERT!

While you are required to provide a fair market value on goods or services over $75, you are not required to advise the donor how he or she should deduct this amount from his or her taxes. Do not provide financial advice that can get your organization into trouble.

Sometimes it is difficult to gauge fair market value, but you need to simply come up with a system and a number that you can justify should the IRS ask you to do so. An estimated amount can be printed on the ticket or provided on a separate document, such as in a thank-you letter.

Statement of Acknowledgment

A simple statement of acknowledgement requires only the name of the organization, amount of the contribution, description of a noncash contribution or statement of goods or services provided, and a good faith estimate of the value of such goods or services. Also, make sure the date is included. This can be sent in a letter, computer form printout, or any other clear manner. You should send these acknowledgments out by mid-January of the following year so that people have them for their tax returns (by no later than January 31). Save a copy for your organization's files.

Be diligent about sending out such statements acknowledging donations. While doing their income tax return, people generally look for tax deductions, and if you have 501(c)(3) status, they are anxious to receive a letter from you.

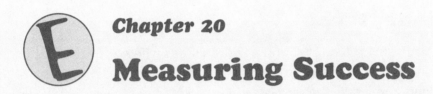

Chapter 20

Measuring Success

After your fundraiser is over, you will sit down with your committee members, volunteers, and board members to evaluate your fundraising campaign. Did you raise as much money as you had originally hoped? Did everything go as planned? Evaluating your results and looking at ways to improve on them next year are important parts of any fundraiser.

Evaluating Your Efforts

The obvious measurement of your success will be whether you raised the funds you originally hoped to raise. This is an easy one to evaluate because it's a finite number. However, there is more to your success or failure than a dollar figure.

Evaluating Funds

First and foremost, you need to assess whether you spent the funds on the fundraiser or on the mission you set out for. A concern of major fundraising organizations is always tracking the money they receive and making sure it goes to the right place.

While organizations try hard to filter their money to the right channels, expenses do add up, and often, unexpected ones tap into the funding that was raised. Many small nonprofits find that the costs of staying afloat eat into their profits on a regular basis.

Postevent evaluations are a valuable planning and learning tool. To maximize the value of the evaluation form, list each of the major components of the event and have two columns. Use one column to indicate "what worked," to reinforce what you want to keep on doing, and the other column to identify "what needs improvement." This format also has the benefit of helping whoever is facilitating the evaluation to keep the participants focused on the goal of improving the event in the following year.

Your evaluation, therefore, has to go hand in hand with the various components mentioned throughout the book. You need to ask:

- Was the original budget a fair assessment of our projected income and ultimately our expenses?
- Did everyone involved in the fundraising campaign act responsibly and is all money raised accounted for?
- Were there surprise expenses? Were they completely unpredictable or did we overlook something in our calculations?

The bottom line is determining whether you raised money and fulfilled the goal of your organization's fundraising plan.

Committees, Board Members, and Volunteers

Along with evaluating your overall fundraising effort, you can look at the various committees and board members involved. You need to assess efforts of each committee and review final reports, which should be submitted in a timely fashion after the fundraising campaign is over.

Make sure all evaluations are done in the same manner and are available for others to read. Fairness and consistency are *very* important when evaluating the work of individuals.

You will also want to review how the board responded to the needs of the fundraising committee and the manner in which it helped raise funds through contacts and resources.

In addition, you should review how the volunteers did in terms of the various tasks. This is the hardest evaluation because volunteering itself is already a positive. It's hard to say that the volunteers should have also done such-and-such. Nonetheless, you can determine which plans of action worked, who really excelled at the task they did, and who should take on a different task next year.

Personal Evaluation

You might also take time to look at the results of your fundraising efforts on a personal level. After all, no one is forcing you into fund-raising. Was the work worthwhile? Do you feel that you accomplished the goals you set out to achieve from an organizational and a personal standpoint? Did you learn anything new? Perhaps you made new friendships or built stronger bonds with people you've known in the organization but never worked with on a project before.

If you were heading the fundraiser, you might want to ask yourself several questions:

- Did I work well with the volunteers?
- How well did I communicate my ideas?

- Did I keep board members and key parties abreast of the progress of the fundraiser?
- Did we stay on schedule?
- Did we reach our goals?
- Was I able to manage conflicts?
- Would I do it again?

Take your time and think it through. Fundraising can be very rewarding, tiring, and enlightening. You can learn about both the process and about yourself.

Evaluation Standards

An evaluation is worthwhile only if you have some set of standards to measure the work against. If, for example, your goal of reaching $50,000 in a school fundraiser was grossly unrealistic, then you are setting an unattainable standard. Conversely, you may set a goal of $5,000 (it's always better from a morale standpoint to keep your goals on the low side) and bring in $12,000. Does this mean that you did very well, or that you set a goal that was too easily attainable?

What Should You Measure?

You need to research what a group your size, working within the same time frame and in similar conditions (from the standpoint of area demographics, geographical location, etc.) should do given the same circumstances. You also need to remember that no plan should seek the absolute highest "perfect" results—you'd just be setting yourself up for disappointment.

Along with setting proper standards comes objectivity, which is often not attainable from those working close to the project.

One of the major problems with any type of evaluation is that it will inevitably become subjective. Someone is doing the evaluating and using an arbitrary system by which to make a judgment. Therefore, factors such as personalities and preconceptions can factor into the equation. If a person thought that he or she should have been doing the job of promotion, then he or she might be more critical of the person who handled promotion for the event.

You may try to compare this fundraiser to one the previous year, but be careful. There are numerous factors, including the overall economy, accessibility of the venue, and even the weather, that will make it hard to do a straight comparison from one year to the next.

Likewise, a school doing a fundraiser for the first time may measure its results against the success of another school in the district. The other school, however, might have more students, a larger PTO membership, or more funding, or might have received $10,000 in donated computer equipment from a parent who just happens to own a computer company. The technology may have made it much easier to run the fundraising campaign.

Look outside of the organization to get a feeling for what people thought about the job that was done. Brief questionnaires as people exit or perhaps in the organization's newsletter or next mailing can provide responses from which you can get a feel for what people thought of your efforts.

Remember, more people will be spurred to respond with negatives than with praise. People who thought everything was terrific often aren't as quick to express themselves as the people with complaints are.

Did You Make the Right Choices?

Okay, so Super Bowl Sunday was not the time to hold the carnival. If the fundraiser fell short, you'll need to review your choice of time, place, activity, promotion, and other variables. Was it the wrong fundraiser for your demographic group? Did you neglect to check on what other schools were doing? Were you the ninth school in the community to sell candy in the last six months? Did you pick a venue that was too small for the party or start too late at night for families to attend? Consider all the possibilities and examine your efforts.

Each fundraising effort by your organization will be a learning and a growing experience. You can have successes even without making money. Nonmonetary positive outcomes may include the following.

- Discovering new talents in membership
- Spreading the word about your group to more people
- Building your presence in the neighborhood or community
- Developing a working system for doing a fundraising project

You should also take some time to consider these outcomes, which may be hard to measure but which are important for the future of the organization.

Common Evaluation Errors

There are several types of errors that are commonly made when evaluating a fundraising project. Some of these are:

1. Evaluating only the final results and not how they were achieved. Numbers don't always tell the whole story.
2. Not getting a broad view. If the fundraiser can affect your whole community, three people's evaluations may not be enough.
3. Not taking good notes. If you don't document the results of your efforts, how can you evaluate them fairly? How can you repeat them next year?
4. Evaluations becoming too complicated. If you've ever been handed a ten-page form to evaluate a twenty-minute lecture, you'll understand the need to keep evaluations within the scope of the project.
5. Looking only at the negative and neglecting to review the positives and leverage those aspects of the event that went well in your future endeavors.
6. Taking too long a break between your fundraiser and your review. People may not remember the details of the bake sale six months later. Hold evaluation meetings shortly after your fundraiser.

While no evaluation is foolproof, try to take some time and step back so you can evaluate the efforts of your organization and the job that was done, using a broad view.

Making Improvements

During your evaluation(s), you will want to review what methods worked and why. You will be able to look at the manner in which tasks were completed and determine if the best methods were used or not. If the process was one that the organization found to be most effective, you will want to carefully review the process so that it can be duplicated in the future. If a task succeeded, but the manner in which it was handled could have been improved on, you will want to list exactly what aspects of this task should be revamped in the future. Determine why this new and improved version would be more effective and what the implications would be if you used it during the next fundraising project.

If you are asking patrons or contributors for their evaluations in written form, make sure your questions are simple and to the point. Ask for direct feedback to specific questions regarding the fundraiser and don't overwhelm them.

Naturally it's important to look at the big picture to determine how close the final results were to those that you had anticipated. Any completed project is rarely identical to the original concept. Trial and feedback throughout, plus testing, tinkering, and numerous obstacles confronted along the way, will change the course and alter the outcome of any project—sometimes for better and sometimes for worse.

The learning process is twofold. Not only will future project teams learn from your detailed accounts, but you will also improve your own skills for future projects.

Judging Weak Points

There are many aspects involved in the success or failure of your fundraising effort. The environment, the scheduling, the budget, the promotion, the products, the services rendered, and even the weather could all be factors. Before you determine what you could do better next time, you'll have to differentiate between those factors that were within your control and those that were not.

If the fundraiser failed because there was a major storm, obviously it was out of your hands. Try to pinpoint each source of success or failure within the project. Ask yourself and everyone involved in the fundraising activities if they can think through the various elements that made up the overall project. Consider the following:

- Was the initial plan too complex?
- Were you missing certain expertise?
- Were there too many or too few people involved?
- Was the communication system effective?
- Was there conflict that went unresolved and slowed down the project?
- Did an outside fundraising company come through or disappoint?
- Were outside "experts" or consultants effective?
- Should key decisions have been made sooner?

These are just some of the many questions you can consider when trying to evaluate how the fundraiser went and what you could do better next year. You want to look for ways to improve on that which did not work for the betterment of the project and ways to capitalize on those aspects that were valuable to the success of the project.

Look at the Positives

Keep in mind that evaluating does not mean looking only at what went wrong. Take ample time to applaud the positive aspects of the job you did staging your fundraising campaign or activity. Look at what worked well so you can find a way to leverage it.

For example, if the raffle was a big hit at the fundraising party, perhaps next year you'll plan to seek out bigger prizes and sell tickets a month in advance instead of only one week. Build on your successes!

You might make one list of all of the positives that you achieved from the fundraising effort and a separate list of new ideas to improve on your work for next time.

FACT

One of the most common postproject determinations made is that there was a need for more test marketing. If, for example, a fundraising letter had been distributed (or test marketed) to 50 people before being mailed out to the entire 15,000 families in the community, the wording or phrasing could have been improved on and the results might have been much better. Now you'll know for next time.

Lasting Effects

There are often times when a fundraising project comes to an end and you cannot determine the overall results of your efforts. If, for example, you raised money to work on beautifying a neighborhood or to help research an illness, the results may not be seen for some time. A year later, you will see if the work did, indeed, help beautify the neighborhood. It may take a long time before researchers make any significant progress in curing a serious illness. However, if you find out that the money helped maintain the research facility over the past year, then you've done a small but meaningful part in helping to seek a cure.

Sometimes progress takes years. Merck Pharmaceuticals donates a medicine called Mectizan to people suffering from river blindness in the most remote parts of Africa. The medication is administered once annually for years. Over the fifteen-plus years of the unique Mectizan donation program, progress has been made as the number of people suffering from this serious, debilitating disease has decreased. However, the program is dedicated to continuing for years, and the results may not fully be seen for another decade. This is also the case when raising money to fight a disease such as HIV. Progress is very slow.

Conversely, a response to a local disaster or a political fundraiser will have more obvious short-term outcomes.

It's worth noting that most fundraising projects that you undertake have a carryover effect. Rarely does a project end with no discernable trace. Even a small-scale school fundraising project that results in a few new textbooks may make the difference between a dozen children making it into college or not years later and finding better jobs.

There are tangible and intangible results that will come from your fundraising project.

QUESTION?

Can you see any benefits from supporting a political candidate if he or she does not win?
Yes. A losing candidate can help rally support for other party candidates by building up his or her profile. He or she can also run in the next election and have a higher profile. Also, a candidate may lose the campaign but win by drawing attention to specific problems or issues.

Wrapping up and Moving On

After a major fundraising drive, most organizations need time to regroup. People often need to step back and detach themselves for a while to catch up with friends and family whom they missed while planning the fundraiser. The larger the project, the more downtime your organization may need. Take time to pat yourselves on the back, whether you raised your projected total or not.

Often a wrap party is a nice way to conclude your busy fundraising effort. You might elect to wait a week or two before such a party to give everyone a chance to recover. The party should be simple and come from the organization's ongoing budget, not from the project.

If you're planning a conference, party, book sale, auction, picnic, or seminar, make sure you include the cleanup process. It's important in any project to plan who will clean up, break down, or disassemble in the end. Put this in your initial plan along with other closing activities such as a final evaluation.

Preparing for the Future

Besides a wrap-up party and evaluating the results of your efforts, you need to make sure everything is in order for the future. For example, do you have a file for each donor complete with contact information and amount contributed? Do you have the names and contact information for each person who volunteered and worked on the project?

Make sure you have all vendor numbers filed, and if you used a fundraising company, you need to have all of the info on hand for future reference.

You also need to make arrangements for items borrowed from friends or neighbors to be returned. Rentals and leased equipment also need to be accounted for.

You should maintain a log or have a computer disk detailing much of what you did at the ready to be used for planning future fundraisers. There's no need to reinvent the wheel every time you do a fundraising activity.

Reporting Results

You also need to post your results in some manner. For example, you might have a story in your monthly or quarterly newsletter about the success of the fundraiser. A press release should detail the highlights, whether it was raising the money you had hoped to or attracting 500 people to the auction. No matter how your fundraiser turned out, you'll want to put a positive spin on the final results.

Board members will want to sit down and listen to a final report including the budgetary details, number of attendees, and so on. Meet with stakeholders, sponsors, and anyone else who was involved in your fundraiser and should be filled in on how it went. After all, if sponsors are pleased with the results, you can call on them in the future.

Paperwork

Finish off all accounting procedures, which will include payment of any outstanding bills and/or fulfilling any contractual obligations. Make sure all bookkeeping is up-to-date and all information is accessible for the board members or whoever else is supposed to review the figures.

You will also need to have 1099 forms ready if you hired someone to work on the project. In addition, you may be responsible to local government offices to file reports, and you will have to follow up on any grant you received by detailing where the grant money went.

In short, there are a lot of odds and ends that need to be tied up when your fundraiser is completed. Plan for these activities ahead of time. Generally, this occupies the time and efforts of only a few key people, particularly whoever was handling the books, budget, and accounting procedures.

ALERT!

When your fundraiser is completed, don't leave a lot of materials behind. While cleaning up, you can determine what may be used for ongoing operations or future fundraising projects. Also, be sure to get necessary information from volunteers, such as the password they were using on the computer or where certain files can be found.

Thank-Yous

We've mentioned it several times throughout the book, but it is worth repeating. Thank all of those who made your party, carnival, walk-a-thon, golf tournament, auction, karaoke night, or other fundraising drive actually happen. Whether you raised the money you hoped to raise or not, people's efforts need to be appreciated.

Nearly all nonprofit groups agree that cards, notes, or even just saying thank you are the number one means of bringing back volunteers for your next fundraiser. Appreciation goes a long way.

From a simple thank-you note to a token gift to acknowledgment in front of a group of peers, a thank-you means a lot. You should make sure everyone involved feels appreciated when your fundraiser is completed and that any thank-you notes that need to be sent to donors or vendors are sent out promptly. Ⓔ

Appendix A

Fundraising Resources

Organizations and Associations

The Aspen Institute: Nonprofit Sector Research Fund

One Dupont Circle NW, Suite 700

Washington, DC 20036-1133

(202) 736-5800

✐ *www.nonprofitresearch.org*

The fund seeks to enhance both the quantity and quality of nonprofit research. Since its founding in 1991, the Aspen Institute has awarded over $9 million to support over 350 research projects.

Association for Research on Nonprofit Organizations and Voluntary Action (ARNOVA)

550 West North Street, Suite 301

Indianapolis, IN 46202-3272

(317) 684-2120

✐ *www.arnova.org*

Home to volumes of research on voluntary action, nonprofit organizations, and philanthropy, ARNOVA offers an annual conference, several publications, and electronic discussions and seminars.

Association of Fundraising Distributors and Suppliers

5775-G Peachtree-Dunwoody Road

Atlanta, GA 30342

(404) 252-3663

✐ *www.afrds.org*

An international association of more than 650 member companies that manufacture, supply, and distribute products that are resold by schools and other not-for-profit organizations for fundraising purposes.

Association of Fundraising Professionals

1101 King Street, Suite 700

Alexandria, VA 22314

(703) 684-0410

✐ *www.Afpnet.org*

For more than forty years, AFP has been the standard-bearer for professionalism in fundraising. A multichapter organization, AFP offers members a resource center, publications, a computerized database, plus information on policies, salaries, endowments, ethics, and much more.

Association of Small Foundations

4905 Del Ray Avenue, Suite 308
Bethesda, MD 20814
(301) 907-3337 or (888) 212-9922
www.smallfoundations.org

Featuring some 2,500 member foundations, ASF is committed to building and strengthening small foundation philanthropy by providing top quality, timely, practical, member-driven programs to all foundations with few or no staff. Benefits of membership include a newsletter, awareness program, and national and regional meetings.

BoardSource

1828 L Street NW, Suite 900
Washington, DC 20036-5114
(202) 452-6262 or (800) 883-6262
www.boardsource.org

BoardSource offers numerous resources related to nonprofit board governance. Formerly the National Center for Nonprofit Boards, BoardSource is a resource for practical information, tools, training, and leadership development for board members of nonprofit organizations.

The Campaign Finance Institute

1990 M Street NW, Suite 380
Washington, DC 20036
(202) 969-8890
www.cfinst.org

A nonpartisan, nonprofit institute affiliated with George Washington University, the Campaign Finance Institute conducts objective research and provides education.

Council on Foundations

1828 L Street NW
Washington, DC 20036
(202) 466-6512
✐ *www.cof.org*

A nonprofit membership association of foundations and corporations, the council serves the public good by promoting and enhancing effective and responsible philanthropy.

The Foundation Center

79 Fifth Avenue
New York, NY 10003
(212) 620-4230
✐ *www.fdncenter.org*

The Foundation Center's mission is to support and improve institutional philanthropy by promoting public understanding of the field and helping grant seekers succeed. They provide a wealth of information at five libraries throughout the country and various cooperating collections of foundation information. Founded in 1956, they are widely recognized as the nation's leading authority on institutional philanthropy.

GuideStar Customer Service

427 Scotland Street
Williamsburg, VA 23185
(757) 229-4631
✐ *www.guidestar.org*

The GuideStar Web site is produced by Philanthropic Research, Inc., a 501(c)(3) public charity founded in 1994. GuideStar's mission is to revolutionize philanthropy and nonprofit practice by providing information.

Pfau Englund Nonprofit Law, P.C.

1451 Juliana Place
Alexandria, VA 22304-1516
(703) 751-8203
✐ *www.nonprofitlaw.com*

Nonprofit Law provides a wealth of legal information about fundraising and starting a nonprofit plus materials for conducting nonprofit research.

Women's Philanthropy Institute

134 West University, Suite 105
Rochester, MI 48307
(248) 651-3552
✍ *www.women-philanthropy.org*

A nonprofit educational institute that brings together philanthropists, volunteers, and professional funders to educate and empower women as philanthropists, donors, and volunteers. The institute's Web site includes resources, articles, a bureau of speakers and trainers, and a schedule of upcoming presentations.

Web Sites

Charity Channel

✍ *www.charitychannel.com*

Charity Channel features reviews of nonprofit periodicals, books, and software plus a resource guide, newsletter, discussion groups, and other valuable materials for the nonprofit community.

FundRaising.com

✍ *www.fundraising.com*

Cookie dough, lollipops, smoothies, wrist bands, donation cards, plenty of successful fundraising tips, numerous products, special promotions, a newsletter, and more can be found at FundRaising.com. The site helps tens of thousands of nonprofit groups raise millions of dollars each year for worthy causes.

Fundraising Ideas and Products Center

✍ *www.fundraising-ideas.org*

A comprehensive Web site from LarMar Enterprises, Inc., includes fundraising ideas, information, news, and a product directory.

Fundsnet Online Services

✑ *www.fundsnetservices.com*

Fundsnet provides nonprofit organizations plus colleges and universities with information on financial resources available on the Internet. It also features fundraising programs, resources, grant writing information, an online foundation directory, and much more.

Give.org

✑ *www.give.org*

The Web site of the Better Business Bureau's Philanthropic Advisory Service, Give.org offers operational standards and guidelines developed by the BBB for nonprofit 501(c)(3) organizations.

Nonprofit Resource Center

✑ *www.not-for-profit.org*

A resource portal, the site offers a comprehensive list of links to Web sites of interest to nonprofits. Included is information on finance and accounting, fundraising, managing your board of directors, and more.

Nonprofits.org

✑ *www.nonprofits.org*

A program by the Evergreen State Society, Nonprofits.org provides various resources, including the uniform registration statement used by many states to allow nonprofit organizations to register so that they can fundraise in their states.

Schoolpop Inc.

✑ *www.schoolpop.com*

A major online fundraiser, Schoolpop has helped raise over $6 million for K–12 schools nationwide. It provides access to hundreds of stores, catalogs, and online merchants where shoppers purchase items and a percentage goes to the nonprofits. Various fundraising programs are offered.

Grant Information

The Grant Advisor

P.O. Box 520
Linden, VA 22642
(703) 646-1520
✍ *www.grantadvisor.com*

Grant Advisor features a newsletter that provides grant-writing tips and information on grant opportunities from agencies such as the National Science Foundation, National Endowment for the Humanities, and the United States Information Agency.

The Grantsmanship Center

1125 W. Sixth Street, Fifth Floor
P.O. Box 17220
Los Angeles, CA 90017
(213) 482-9860
✍ *www.tgci.com*

The center offers training and low-cost publications for nonprofit organizations and government agencies. It started as a local project in Los Angeles, and today it has over 100 workshops a year and more than 75,000 alumni. It teaches the grant process.

Prominent Charitable Organizations

A few of the most successful fundraising organizations in America:

American Cancer Society

1599 Clifton Road, NE
Atlanta, GA 30329
(800) ACS-2345
✍ *www.cancer.org*

American Heart Association

National Center
7272 Greenville Avenue
Dallas, TX 75231
(800) 242-8721
✎ *www.americanheart.org*

American Red Cross

American Red Cross National Headquarters
431 18th Street NW
Washington, DC 20006
(202) 639-3520
✎ *www.redcross.org*

Americares

161 Cherry Street
New Canaan, CT 06840
(800) 486-4357
✎ *www.americares.org*

Boys & Girls Clubs of America

1230 W. Peachtree Street NW
Atlanta, GA 30309
(404) 487-5700
✎ *www.bgca.org*

Catholic Charities

1731 King Street
Alexandria, VA 22314
(703) 549-1390
✎ *www.catholiccharitiesusa.org*

Family Violence Prevention Fund

383 Rhode Island Street, Suite 304
San Francisco, CA 94103-5133
(415) 252-8900
✎ *www.Endabuse.org*

Girl Scouts of the USA

420 Fifth Avenue
New York, NY 10018-2798
(800) 478-7248 or (212) 852-8000
✎ *www.girlscouts.org*

Humane Society of the United States

2100 L Street NW
Washington DC 20037
(202) 452-1100
✎ *www.Hsus.org*

National Conservancy

4245 North Fairfax Drive, Suite 100
Arlington, VA 22203-1606
(703) 841-5300
✎ *www.nature.org*

Salvation Army

615 Slaters Lane
P.O. Box 269
Alexandria, VA 22313
✎ *www.salvationarmyusa.org*

United Way of America

701 N. Fairfax Street
Alexandria, VA 22314-2045
(703) 836-7100
✎ *www.unitedway.org*

World Wildlife Fund

1250 24th Street NW
P.O. Box 97180
Washington, DC 20037
(800) CALL-WWF
✍ *www.worldwildlife.org*

YMCA of USA

101 North Wacker Drive
Chicago, IL 60606
312-977-0031
✍ *www.ymca.net*

Major Foundations

Bill & Melinda Gates Foundation

P.O. Box 23350
Seattle, WA 98102
(206) 709-3140
✍ *www.gatesfoundation.org*
Grant inquiries info@gatesfoundation.org

J. Paul Getty Trust

The Getty Center
1200 Getty Center Drive
Los Angeles, CA 90049-1679
(310) 440-7300 Grant Program: (310) 440-7320

The Ford Foundation

320 East 43rd Street
New York, NY 10017
(212) 573-5000
✍ *www.fordfound.org*

The Robert Wood Johnson Foundation

P.O. Box 2316
College Road East and Route 1
Princeton, NJ 08543-2316
(888) 631-9989
✍ *www.rwjf.org*

W. K. Kellogg Foundation

One Michigan Avenue East
Battle Creek, MI 49017-4058
(269) 968-1611
✍ *www.wkkf.org*

The David and Lucille Packard Foundation

300 Second Street, Suite 200
Los Altos, CA 94022
(650) 948-7658
✍ *www.packard.org*

The Starr Foundation

70 Pine Street, 14th Floor
New York, NY 10270
(212) 772-5202
✍ *www.fdncenter.org*

Major Fundraising Companies

American Publishers, Inc.

208 Old Lancaster Road
Devon, PA 19333

(800) 220-1247 (Ext. 3 for starter kit)
✍ *www.apifund.com*

Major magazine drive fundraiser since 1987, it provides a starter kit and offers over 800 magazine titles. API has fundraising programs, customer service, fundraising tips, and more.

Cherrydale Farms

(800) 333-4525

✑ www.cherrydale.com

Billing itself as America's School Fundraising Company, Cherrydale helps thousands of schools put together fundraising programs featuring its wide variety of products, including candy, candles, and more. The cheerful Cherrydale Web site includes fundraising ideas, promotions, features, and tracking information.

Entertainment Fundraising

(800) 933-2605

✑ www.entertainment.com

A leading player in entertainment coupon books, it has helped schools pull in over $90 million in a given year. You'll find fundraising ideas, plenty of products (including Sally Foster wrapping paper), plus travel guides and fundraising information on its Web site.

Hershey's Fundraising

100 Crystal A Drive

P.O. Box 810

Hershey, PA 17033-0810

(800) 803-6932

✑ www.hersheysfundraising.com

Plenty of Hershey favorites, including Hershey Bars and Kit Kats, offered in one-dollar and fifty-cent programs, plus incentives and prize programs, can be found from the company that is synonymous with candy.

Innsbrook Wraps

1006 Emerald Drive

Alexandria, VA 22308

(703) 360-8507

✑ www.innsbrook.com

One of the leaders in school gift-wrapping drives, Innsbrook sets the standard for thousands of schools through holiday sales.

M&M/Mars Fundraising

Hackettstown, NJ 07840

✍ *www.mmmarsfundraising.com*

Snickers, Skittles, and, of course, M&Ms are among many popular favorites offered as part of the company's fundraising programs, which have raised millions of dollars for schools and other charities. Constantly updated fundraising programs and a bright, user-friendly Web site can get you started.

Scholastic Book Fairs

1080 Greenwood Boulevard

Lake Mary, FL 32746

(800) 242-7737

✍ *www.scholastic.com/bookfairs*

The fundraising arm of the corporate giant in kids' educational books, the Book Fairs division puts together fairs utilizing each school and its PTO staff. Kids can select paperback and hardcover titles from over 150 publishers.

PBS: Thirty Years of Successful Fundraising

Public television features a wide range of programming, from the classic *Masterpiece Theater* to newfound favorites like the *Antiques Roadshow* to the many educational programs such as *Sesame Street* and *Reading Rainbow*. But how does it all work? Without commercials, public broadcasting is indeed supported by the public. It is, and has been for over thirty years, a prime example of the power of ongoing fundraising efforts.

How PBS Works

It all began in the mid-1960s when President Lyndon Johnson signed the public broadcasting act and launched public television. Today, 349 public television noncommercial stations are part of the nonprofit media enterprise known as the Public Broadcasting System. Nearly 100 million people in the fifty states, Puerto Rico, Guam, the U.S. Virgin Islands, and American Samoa watch public television every week.

Unlike many cultural institutions that receive a large portion of their funding from a few wealthy donors, PBS receives small gifts from a very large audience. In fact, an estimated 4.5 million people contribute annually to PBS, at numbers that have reached the $400 million mark in recent years.

To their advantage, PBS has the ability to reach millions of people by the fact that they are broadcasting on the premier medium, television. Viewers then donate on a local basis to the member stations in their area. Each station has its own distinctive manner of membership, and most provide incentives in the form of gifts such as umbrellas, tote bags, CDs, or other items at different contribution price points. The National PBS is able to cut deals with companies and buy items in bulk, which local stations can then utilize if they so choose. These provide added incentives for people to contribute, besides the overall knowledge that their money goes to keep quality educational, cultural, and informational programming on the air.

According to Robert Altman, senior vice president of Development and Corporate Relations at the main headquarters in Alexandria, Virginia, "since we are relying on many small donations, we are less affected by a downturn in the economy than other nonprofits that may be relying on donors to give large sums of money. People can still give their $35 or $50 even in a poor economic climate."

PBS conducts three pledge drives a year to attract new members. They acquire special programming to run on the stations during these months. Stations elect to run programming as they choose and, for that matter, may have three pledge drives or only one. The national network provides a framework including scripts, recorded breaks, taped roll-ins, and so on. There are also preproduced pledge programs called "virtuals" that can be used by local stations. Volunteers to take pledges are set up at the local level, with each station seeking out its own volunteers and orchestrating its own membership drives. The system works very well, with the smaller stations able to utilize assistance from the National PBS, whereas larger stations such as WNET in New York City and WGBH in Boston are able to operate more independently.

Pledge Practices

Recent years have seen an increase in pledge hours and a decrease in total number of pledges per hour to PBS stations. Altman stresses that while broad guidelines for stations to follow during pledge programming can be put together, the diversity of the stations and their needs makes it up to the stations to establish their own rules and practices.

PBS wants programming to remain the focus and pledge drives to continue to reflect that same high level of programming. The goal is to integrate pledge drives into the stations' overall development and not turn public television into pledge television. Additionally, pledge drives should be directed to all levels of potential donors and should not mislead or confuse viewers.

By and large, stations enact their own rules and guidelines to govern their pledge drives, and most stations continue to find them effective.

Research, Timing, and Programming

Research is key to planning pledge drives, as the station generally looks for times that contrast the programming of the commercial networks. For example, the spring drive usually lands in March so as not to coincide with the May sweeps period (ratings period), and the August drive is planned to precede the September season premieres. Timing is key to drawing viewers from more highly publicized network hits.

Programs are selected to try to appeal to the PBS market. "We're conscious of selecting programs for the different segments of our audience," says Altman. "One of our most distinctive and attractive features is our daily children's programming, which most stations run. It's a safe haven for kids to watch these shows without commercials and young parents rate the kids' programming very high on the list when we survey what people value about public television. In fact, people who don't even have kids find these programs valuable."

FACT

Between 1998 and 2002, PBS operating revenue increased 21 percent from $262 million to $318 million, mostly from private funding. The growth allowed PBS to provide more original national programming, enhanced promotion, and the Web site, ✑ www.pbs.org.

The other PBS audience for prime-time viewing is largely made up of people fifty and over. The station therefore plans accordingly when approaching these two primary audiences. Attempting to capture an under-fifty audience, PBS also looks to feature programming that will have a broader appeal so as to draw in new membership from this demographic group.

Diversity

Like most successful fundraising campaigns, PBS combines its built-in broadcasting capabilities with more traditional strategies that include direct mail and telemarketing.

Using different sets of copy, one geared at appealing to young parents and another for the prime-time older audience, the direct mail campaigns are used as a strong renewal device for existing members. Most people renew via direct mail or from a telemarketing campaign, which many stations conduct in conjunction with their pledge drives.

The popularity of auctions has also become a viable means by which numerous public television stations raise money during the spring months. Items are presented on-air, allowing for a mass audience to see the items and bid by telephone or by e-mail.

While the largest chunk of PBS funding comes from viewer

membership, state governments, Corporation for Public Broadcasting (CPB) and federal grants, businesses, colleges/universities, and foundations also account for a portion of the contributed support.

Sponsorship and In-Kind Gifts

You've probably heard the statement at the end of some PBS shows that the program was made possible by a grant from a major corporation. In every community, corporations and foundations of various sizes sponsor and support both educational and cultural programming. A separate arm of the national PBS organization, called the PBS Sponsorship Group, works independently and seeks sponsors for national programs. In addition, the cost of acquiring programs that have been produced and broadcast elsewhere, such as the BBC in Great Britain, can be underwritten by companies.

Companies may provide gifts or services to a program or to the network to help with its fundraising drive. The in-kind gifts reduce the costs of fundraising. Again, because PBS has a viewership of millions of people, the window is open to showcasing or highlighting the products or services of a company in front of a mass audience, making the donation of flowers for the pledge drive tables or other tangible items a very inviting means of contributing and receiving significant free advertising in return.

In all, the Public Broadcasting System's method of combining pledge drives to attract new viewers with other follow-up means to enhance member renewals has proven very successful. In addition, the incentives and the means of a national umbrella PBS have helped both smaller and larger stations with their individual needs, while they maintain their own distinctive identities. Ⓔ

Index

501(c)(3) nonprofits
  filing as, 236–38
  and grants, 212, 214
  and political groups, 239
  regulations for, 89, 150, 151,
    170, 238, 240, 247, 248

A

"A-thons," 20, 25, 94, 160, 181,
  239
Accounting
  "creative accounting," 107
  paperwork, 241–44, 259–60
  responsibilities, 241–42
  software for, 116–17, 242–43
  systems of, 242–43
  and taxes, 235–40
Acknowledgment, statement of,
  248
Activities to avoid, 107–9
Administration committee, 64
Advertising committee, 34
Advertising materials, 49, 70,
  71, 128–29, 131–33, 197, 247
Advertising plugs, 108
American Association of
  Fundraising Counsel, 8
American Heart Association, 3
American Institute of
  Architects (AIA), 149
American Institute of
  Philanthropy, 108
Annual campaigns, 93–94
Annual events, 54–55
Antiques Roadshow, 275
Article writing, 132

Association of Fund-Raising
  Distributors and Suppliers
  (AFRDS), 184, 186
Associations, 149, 262–65
Auctions
  adding, 40
  celebrities for, 53–54
  for children, 181
  donations for, 21–22
  planning, 19, 21
  prizes for, 203
  types of, 20–21
Audience, targeting, 4–5, 13–14
Audits, 243, 247
Awards. See Incentives

B

Babysitting, 207
Badgering, 93, 108–9
Banners, 132–33, 197
Barnes and Noble, 143
Baseline dates, 48
Bazaars, 12, 181
Beauty pageants, 36
Better Business Bureau, 108,
  186
Bike-a-thons, 20, 25, 94, 160
Bipartisan Campaign Reform
  Act, 194
Bloomberg, Michael, 199
Board manuals, 35
Board members, 34–35,
  126–27, 158–59, 251
Borough News, 164, 166
Boston Post, 135
Bowl-a-thons, 25, 160

Boy Scouts, 188
Boys Club, 149, 172
Brainstorming, 9, 40, 168–69
Bridge, The, 149
British Broadcasting
  Corporation (BBC), 279
Broadcasting yearbook, 96
Budget committee, 64
Budgets, x, 48, 70–73, 223,
  226–27, 250
Bulk mail, 88
Burnout, 18
Bush, George W., 198
Businesses locally, 159–60

C

Campaign Finance Institute,
  195
Campaign fundraising. See
  Political fundraising
Car washes, 12, 36, 179, 181
Carnivals, 12, 20, 24–25, 128,
  181, 182
Cash-based accounting system,
  242
Cash flow, 243–44
Catalog of Federal Domestic
  Assistance, 218
Celebrities, 52–54, 198
Charitable Choices, 108
Charitable organizations, 8,
  267–70
Charitable Organizations
  Society, 151
Charities, 170, 171
Child care, 207

Children
  events for, 178–83
  fundraising companies,
    184–87
  incentives for, 39, 187–88
  involving, 177–79
  school fundraisers, 2, 183–84
  teaching skills, 179–80
"Chinese Auction," 21, 181
Churches, 155, 156, 171, 173,
  174, 236, 241
Circulars, 131–32
Classified ads, 131–32, 247
Clean-up process, 258, 260
Clinton, Bill, 198
Coca-Cola, 149
Collecting money, 202–3
Commercial ventures, 107
Committees
  evaluating, 251
  forming, 63–65
  meetings, 36–38
  reports for, 65
  tasks of, 33–34
  types of, 33–34, 64, 191, 195
Communications
  among members, 111–14
  importance of, 33
  on-site communication, 113
  via e-mail, 92, 111–14, 126, 194
  via Web site, 118–19
Community businesses, 159–60
Community Chest, 151
Community events, 135
Community fundraising
  benefits of, 2

board members, 158–59
core group, 154–56
efforts, 164–66
identifying issues, 157
laws, 160–61
meetings, 156
ordinances, 160–61
planning, 157–58
publicity, 161–62
roots, 162–64
sponsors for, 159–60
Community involvement, 2–3,
  6–8, 14–15, 142–43
Community meetings, 156
Computer Use in Social
  Services Network, 117
Conduct, code of, 100–102, 107
Conflicts of interest, 103, 159
Consultants, 40–42
Contingency plans, 51–52
Contribution numbers, 8
Contribution programs, 149–50.
  See also Donations
Contributions online, 122–23
Contributors, 75–76
Corporate fundraising, 141–51
Corporate grants, 217–18. *See
  also* Grants
Corporations
  approaching, 144
  donations from, 75, 77–78,
    142
  employees, *x*, 142–43
  executives, 35, 77–78, 145–46
  incentives for, 146–47
  learning about, 147–48

partnerships, 148–49
relationship-building, *x*, 146
role of, 142–44
sponsorship from, 77–78,
  143–44
tax status, 238
Cost considerations, 16–17,
  70–72, 100–101, 185–86. *See
  also* Financial considerations
Coyote Communications, 117
"Creative accounting," 107
Credibility, 107, 173–75
Customer service, 19
CVS Pharmacy, 148

D

Dance-a-thons, 25, 40, 160, 181
Data storage software, 114–18
Databases, updating, 47, 93–94,
  114–18
Dates, selecting, 46
Dates, setting, 48, 162
Deadlines, 8, 15–16, 30, 38, 48
Deductions, 240
Democratic organizations, 192,
  195
Demographics
  determining, *x*, 89
  party demographics, 192–93,
    195
Design software, 136
Details, 127, 201–8
Dinners, 12, 20, 40, 190,
  196–97, 248
Direct mail campaigns, 12, 36,
  78–80, 86–89

Disclosure requirements,
    247–48
Display ads, 131–32, 247
Diversity, 278–79
"Do not call" lists, 85
Donations
    for auctions, 16–17, 21–22
    from corporations, 75,
        77–78, 142
    from employees, 149–51
    importance of, 209
    incentives, 81–82
    online donations, 122–23
    for political fundraisers,
        192–94
    soliciting, 70, 78–81
    and tax issues, 238–40,
        247–48
    toward expenses, 70–71
Donors, 72–75, 78
Door prizes, 71
Door-to-door solicitations, 23, 81
Downtown revitalization,
    164–66

E

E-fundraising, 120–23, 130
E-mail communications, 92,
    111–14, 126, 194
E-mail marketing, 105–6, 130
E-newsletters, 130–31
Elections, 190–91
Employee donations, 149–51
Employee pride, x, 142–43, 150
Ethics, 99–109
Etiquette, 109

Evaluation errors, 254
Evaluation process, 250–52
Evaluation standards, 252–54
Events, 12, 40, 135, 160
Expenses, 16–17, 70–72,
    100–101, 185–86, 250

F

Federal Communications
    Commission (FCC), 80, 85,
    128
Federal funding, 218
Federal grants, 218. *See also*
    Grants
Fenway Park, 136
Finance committees, 64, 191, 195
Financial accountability, 246–48
Financial Accounting Standards
    Board, 239
Financial considerations
    accountability, 246–48
    accounting systems, 242–43
    budgets, x, 48, 70–73, 223,
        226–27, 250
    collecting money, 202–3
    ethics, 100–101
    expenses, 16–17, 70–72,
        100–101, 185–86, 250
    financial statements, 245–46
    planning ahead, 244
    related income, 246–47
Financial picture, 244–46
Financial software, 116–17, 242–43
Financial statements, 245–46
Flyers, 126, 128, 132–33,
    138–39, 197

Formula grants, 218
Foundation Center, The, 76,
    160, 210, 211
Foundation Directory, 211
Foundations, 76–77, 212–13,
    270–71
Franklin Zoo, 135
Fraudulent practices, 108
Friends of Rosedale, 163–64
Funding, sources of, 24, 72–74,
    215
Fundraisers
    details of, 43–55
    evaluating, 250–57
    getting started, 27–42
    parameters for, 58–59
    peak times, 46
    selecting, 11–25
    types of, 12, 19–25
    wrapping up, 258–60
Fundraising
    basics of, 1–10
    benefits of, 2–4
    fund usage, 4
    importance of, *xi–xii*
    mission of, 7–8
    options for, 19–25
    reasons for, 2–3
    researching, 4–6, 13–14
    skills for, 83–98
    tips for, *x*
Fundraising companies
    cost considerations, 185–86
    licensing, 186
    percentage required, 185
    products offered, 187

resources, 271–73
selecting, 184–85
services provided, 185–86
Fundraising letters, 89
Funds, misuse of, 100–101
Future events, 258–59

G

Gap, The, 160
Gifts, accepting, 102–3
Girl Scouts, 12, 94, 182, 188
Girls Club, 149, 172
Giving to others, *xii*, 13–14,
81–82, 175
Giving USA, 8
Goals, 3–8
Government subsidy
assistance, 218
Grant writing
application, 228–34
budgets, 223, 226–27
classes on, 228
conclusion, 228
document attachments, 228
needs assessment, 224
objectives, 221, 222, 224–25
organization information,
222, 223–24
plan of action, 223, 225–26
problem statement, 222, 224
professionals, 217
project evaluation, 223, 226
project summary, 222, 223
proposals, *x*, 213–16, 222–34
sample of, 228–33
topics, 222–23

Grants
advisors, 267
application process, 213–16,
219, 228–34
corporate grants, 217–18
endorsements, 215
federal grants, 218
finding, 210–13
follow-up, 216–17
guidelines, 209, 211–12, 214
policies, 212
presentation of, 215–16
professionals, 217
proposal writing, *x*, 213–16,
222–34
renewal grants, 213
researching, 76–77, 210–11
support for, 215
timing, 216
types of, 213, 217, 218
writing, 217, 221–34
Grantsmart.org, 211
Graphic design software, 136
Graphic designers, 138–39
Grassroots fundraising
brainstorming, 168–69
credibility of, 167, 173–75
focus, 172–73
making connections, 87–88,
173–74
procedures for, 169
responsibilities, 170–72
Groups
involvement in, 12–13
number of, 47
organizing, 12–13, 47, 154–56

Grozier, Edwin, 135
Guerrilla marketing, 133
Guest list, 197
Guests, inviting, 52
Guide to U.S. Foundations, 211
Guidelines, setting, 58–59

H

Hamilton, Andrew, 163
Handouts, 49, 126, 128, 132–33,
138–39, 197
Harassment, 93, 108–9
Historic preservation, 146–47,
149, 163–64
Hospitals, 2, 236
Hub events, 173
Human resources, 18. *See
also* Volunteers

I

Ideas, 9, 12
Image-building, 13, 198–99
Improvements, 255–57
In-kind gifts, 279
In-kind services, 227
Inappropriate conduct, 107
Incentives
for children, 187–88
and code of conduct, 100
for contributions, 81–82
for motivation, 31, 39
for promotions, 133–35
for sponsors, 146–47
Income, and taxes, 246–47
Incorporating, 238
Individual contributors, 75–76

Information storage, 114–18
Information Technology
    Resource Center, 117
Insurance, 52
Internal publicity, 126–27
Internet fundraising
    advantages of, 121–22
    disadvantages of, 122
    potential of, 120–21, 130–31
    publicity, 130
    regulations, 121
    requirements, 122–23
    see also Web presence
Internet Service Provider
    (ISP), 123
Involvement in community,
    2–3, 6–8, 14–15, 142–43
IRS
    contacting, 236
    filing with, 212, 214, 236–37,
        240–41
    requirements of, 246–48

K

Kidney Foundation, 6
Kids. *See* Children
Kraft Foods, 148–49

L

Laws, 19, 160–61, 194–95
Leaders
    qualities of, 28–30
    responsibilities, 30
    role of, 27, 30–42
    selecting, 28–30
Leads, following up, 78

Letters, 89, 195–96
Little League, 246
Loans, 218
Lobster Pot, 134
Local businesses, 159–60
Local establishment, 162–64
Local publicity, 161–62
Locations
    cost considerations, 70
    finding, 45–46
    selecting, *x*, 16, 19, 44
    see also Site committee

M

Magazines, 132, 162, 247
Mailing lists, purchasing, 104–5
Mailing lists, selling, 103–4
Major donors, 78
Market research, 13–14
Marketing, 90, 133, 257
Masterpiece Theater, 275
Materials required, 17–18, 70
Maxwell Autos, 136
McDonald's, 142–43, 160
Media
    damage control, 97–98
    lists, 96
    personalities, 52–54
    working with, *x*, 96–97, 191
Meetings
    announcing, 36
    breaks during, 37
    committee meetings, 36–38
    community meetings, 156
    keeping minutes, 37
    length of, 38

number of, 38
preparing for, 36
sites for, 37–38
structure for, 37
time frame for, 37, 38
tips on, 36–38
Merck Pharmaceuticals, 257
Milestone, 50
Minutes, keeping, 37
Misleading public, 108
Money, collecting, 202–3
Money, handling, 100–101
Motivation, 31, 38–40
Motivators, 40
Mujeras Latinas en Accion, 149
Muscular Dystrophy Telethon,
    94

N

Necessities, 17–18, 70
Neighborhood fundraising. *See*
    Community fundraising
Neighborhood involvement.
    See Community involvement
Networking, *x*, 16
Networks, 114–15
Newsletters, 126, 128, 130–31,
    194, 259
Newspapers, 131–32, 162
Nonprofit corporation, 238
Nonprofit Matrix, 117
Nonprofit organizations
    board members, 34–35
    credibility of, 107
Nonprofit status
    applying for, 236–38

filing as, 236–38
and grants, 212, 214
and political groups, 239
regulations for, 89, 150, 151, 170, 238, 240, 247, 248
verifying, 246–48
Nonprofitabout.com, 120
NPO-NET, 117

O

O'Reilly, Samuel, 136
Old House Fair, 128–29, 146–47, 149, 207
On-site communications, 113
Online contributors, 122–23
Online newsletters, 130–31
Options, 19–25
Ordinances, 19, 160–61
Organizational software, 47
Organizations, 34–35, 149, 262–65
Orientation handbook, 35

P

Paperwork, 241–44, 259–60
Partnerships, 148–49
Party delegates, 192
Party demographics, x, 192–93, 195
PBS, 275–79. See also Public Broadcasting System
PBS Sponsorship Group, 279
People skills, 28–29
Permits, 160–61
Perot, Ross, 199
Personal conduct, 107
Personal involvement, 6, 14

Philanthropic endeavors, x, 142–43, 150
Philanthropic Research, Inc., 108
Photos, 139–40, 175
Physical Culture Hotel, 136
Planning ahead, 244, 258–59
Planning committee, 33–34, 44, 64
Plans, formulating, 8–9
Plans, presenting, 9–10
Pledge sheets, 25
Pledges, 2, 25, 123, 239–40, 277–79
Policies, establishing, 102–3, 109
Political fundraising
approaches to, 189–91
donations for, 192–94
finance committee, 191, 195
image-building, 198–99
legal issues, 194–95
letters for, 195–96
limits on, 195
parties for, 196–97
personal appearances, 197–98
plan for, 190–91
and self-funded candidates, 199–200
successes, 258
support for, 198
Polls, 130, 157
Portals, 117, 120
Positive points, 256. See also Success
Postcards, 127, 139

Posters, 128, 132–33, 139, 197
Postevent coverage, 140, 162
Postproject duties, 258–60
Postproject evaluations, 250–57
Presidential candidates, 198
Press kit, 97
Press releases, 95–97
Print media publicity, 131–32, 136–38
Printers, hiring, 137–38
Printing costs, 137
Printing schedules, 49
Privacy policy, 109
Pro bono services, 227
Procrastinators, 33, 34
Professional associations, 149
Professional consultants, 40–42
Professional motivators, 40
Professionals, hiring, 66–67, 70
Programming committee, 33–34, 64
Progress, tracking, 50
Project grants, 218
Project-planning software, 9
Promotional activities, x, 133–36
Promotional materials, 49, 70, 128, 132–33, 197
Promotions committee, 34
Promotions locally, 161–62
Prospective donors, 73–75
PSAs. See Public service announcements
PTAs/PTOs, 20, 39, 180, 183, 184, 185, 188

Public Broadcasting System (PBS)
diversity, 278–79
growth of, 278
in-kind gifts, 279
pledges, 2, 277–79
programming, 6, 275, 277–78
research, 277–78
revenues, 278
sponsorships, 279
timing, 277–78
workings of, 276–77
Public, misleading, 108
Public relations, 3, 95–98
Public service announcements
(PSAs), 97, 128–29
Public speaking, 92–93
Public television fundraising,
275–79. *See also* PBS
Publicity, 48, 126–27, 161–62,
198–99
Publicity committee, 64
Publishers Weekly, 96

R

Radio publicity, 97, 129–30
Raffles, 40, 71, 135, 240
Reading Rainbow, 275
Record keeping, 47, 259
Records, falsifying, 106
Red Cross, 5, 163
Regulations, 19
Rehearsals, 208
Relationship-building, *x*, 146, 174
Repeat performances, 54–55
Republican organizations, 192,
195

Research
for fundraising, 4–6, 13–14
for grants, 76–77, 210–11
by PBS, 277–78
Resources
for fundraising, 261–73
necessities, 17–18, 70
utilizing, 204–5
Results, reporting, 259
Results, viewing, 257–58
Retailers, 159
Risks, taking, 101–2
Robert's Rules of Order, 36
Ronald McDonald House, 142–43

S

Sales drives, 20, 22–23, 159,
161, 178, 179, 180, 182
Salvation Army, 60
Salvation Army Sidewalk
Santa, 94
Schedules, creating, 62–63
Schedules, setting, 47–49, 162
School auctions, 20, 181
School fundraisers, 2, 5–6, 20,
171, 173–74, 178–84
Schools, 2, 21, 60, 156, 212,
236, 240
Security committee, 64
Security concerns, 208
Seed money, 24, 72–74, 215
Self-evaluation, 251–52
Self-funded candidates,
199–200
Sesame Street, 275
Shipping, 205–6

Signs, 132–33, 197
Silent auctions, 21
Site committee, 34, 44–45, 64
Site coordinator, 34, 45
Sites
cost considerations, 70
finding, 45–46
selecting, *x*, 16, 19, 44
Skills
honing, 83–98
teaching, 179–80
types of, 28–30
Small-scale efforts, 168
Software, 9, 114–18, 136, 242–43
Solicitations
considerations for, 21–22
donations from, 70, 78–81
telephone solicitations, 12,
80, 84–86
Sources, tapping, 79–81
Spam, 130
Special events, 12
Sponsorship committee, 64
Sponsorships, 72–73, 77–78,
135, 143, 159–60, 246, 279
Sports events, 135, 182
Staff involvement, 126–27. *See
also* Volunteers
Standard & Poor Directory, *x*,
205
Statement of acknowledgment,
248
Stickers, 133, 197
Strong points, 256
Substantiation requirements,
247–48

Success
    audience evaluation, 13
    celebrating, 258
    errors evaluation, 254
    funds evaluation, 250–51
    improvements for, 255–57
    keys to, *xii*, 3, 73
    looking ahead, 258–59
    measuring, 249, 252–54
    member evaluations, 251
    and paperwork, 259–60
    reporting results, 76, 259
    self-evaluation, 251–52
    standards evaluation, 252–54
    thank-you notes, 260
    viewing results, 257–58
Sultan, Rebecca, 164
Support, 2–3, 6–7
Surveys, 130, 157

T
Talk shows, 128–29
Tapping sources, 79–81
Target audience, 4–5, 13–14
Task assignments, 33
Tax-exempt status, 89, 214,
    236–38. *See also* 501(c)(3)
Taxes, 235–41
Teamwork, 3, 22, 33–34, 62,
    143–44
Teenagers
    events for, 178–83
    fundraising companies,
        184–87
    incentives for, 187–88
    involving, 177–79

school fundraisers, 2, 183–84
    teaching skills, 179–80
Telemarketers, 80, 84
Telephone solicitations, 12, 80,
    84–86
Television fundraising, 275–79.
    See also PBS
Test marketing, 90, 257
Thank-you notes, 260
Tickets, selling, 71, 126–27,
    133–34, 161, 240, 248
Time frames, 8, 15–16, 30, 38, 48
Timeline, 48–49
Tracking progress, 50
Trade associations, 149
Training tips, 61–62

U
Unique promotions, 135–36
United Way, 35, 149, 151
Unity, 33–34
Urban Preservation
    Foundation, 234

V
Variety, 55
Vendors
    finding, 22–23
    ordering from, 203–4
    soliciting, 22
Visual effects, 138–40
Volunteerism
    and children, 177
    level of, 13
    reasons for, 31
    trends in, 61

Volunteers
    appreciation of, 34, 65–66
    character traits of, 33
    dedication of, 30–31, 61–62
    evaluating, 32–34, 251
    finding, 59–60
    firing, 63
    gathering, 30–31
    input from, 9, 40, 168–69
    interests of, 32
    keeping, 60–61
    participation of, 18, 31, 127
    reaching, 6–8
    recruiting, 59–60
    task assignments, 33
    teamwork, 3, 22, 33–34, 62,
        143–44
    training, 61–62

W
Walk-a-thons, 20, 25, 94, 160,
    239
Walk for the Cure, 25
Walk-throughs, 208
Weak points, 255–57
Weather considerations, 46
Web presence, 81, 90–92, 109,
    118–23, 130–31
Web sites, 265–66
Who's Who in America, x, 205
Worthwhile causes, *xii*, 13–14,
    175

Z
Zoo on Wheels, 207
Zoo publicity, 135

The EVERYTHING Series!

BUSINESS

Everything® **Business Planning Book**
Everything® **Coaching and Mentoring Book**
Everything® **Fundraising Book**
Everything® **Home-Based Business Book**
Everything® **Leadership Book**
Everything® **Managing People Book**
Everything® **Network Marketing Book**
Everything® **Online Business Book**
Everything® **Project Management Book**
Everything® **Selling Book**
Everything® **Start Your Own Business Book**
Everything® **Time Management Book**

COMPUTERS

Everything® **Build Your Own Home Page Book**
Everything® **Computer Book**
Everything® **Internet Book**
Everything® **Microsoft® Word 2000 Book**

COOKBOOKS

Everything® **Barbecue Cookbook**
Everything® **Bartender's Book, $9.95**
Everything® **Chinese Cookbook**
Everything® **Chocolate Cookbook**
Everything® **Cookbook**
Everything® **Dessert Cookbook**
Everything® **Diabetes Cookbook**
Everything® **Indian Cookbook**
Everything® **Low-Carb Cookbook**
Everything® **Low-Fat High-Flavor Cookbook**

Everything® **Low-Salt Cookbook**
Everything® **Mediterranean Cookbook**
Everything® **Mexican Cookbook**
Everything® **One-Pot Cookbook**
Everything® **Pasta Book**
Everything® **Quick Meals Cookbook**
Everything® **Slow Cooker Cookbook**
Everything® **Soup Cookbook**
Everything® **Thai Cookbook**
Everything® **Vegetarian Cookbook**
Everything® **Wine Book**

HEALTH

Everything® **Alzheimer's Book**
Everything® **Anti-Aging Book**
Everything® **Diabetes Book**
Everything® **Dieting Book**
Everything® **Herbal Remedies Book**
Everything® **Hypnosis Book**
Everything® **Massage Book**
Everything® **Menopause Book**
Everything® **Nutrition Book**
Everything® **Reflexology Book**
Everything® **Reiki Book**
Everything® **Stress Management Book**
Everything® **Vitamins, Minerals, and Nutritional Supplements Book**

HISTORY

Everything® **American Government Book**
Everything® **American History Book**
Everything® **Civil War Book**
Everything® **Irish History & Heritage Book**

Everything® **Mafia Book**
Everything® **Middle East Book**
Everything® **World War II Book**

HOBBIES & GAMES

Everything® **Bridge Book**
Everything® **Candlemaking Book**
Everything® **Casino Gambling Book**
Everything® **Chess Basics Book**
Everything® **Collectibles Book**
Everything® **Crossword and Puzzle Book**
Everything® **Digital Photography Book**
Everything® **Easy Crosswords Book**
Everything® **Family Tree Book**
Everything® **Games Book**
Everything® **Knitting Book**
Everything® **Magic Book**
Everything® **Motorcycle Book**
Everything® **Online Genealogy Book**
Everything® **Photography Book**
Everything® **Pool & Billiards Book**
Everything® **Quilting Book**
Everything® **Scrapbooking Book**
Everything® **Sewing Book**
Everything® **Soapmaking Book**

HOME IMPROVEMENT

Everything® **Feng Shui Book**
Everything® **Feng Shui Decluttering Book, $9.95 (15.95 CAN)**
Everything® **Fix-It Book**
Everything® **Gardening Book**
Everything® **Homebuilding Book**

All Everything® books are priced at $12.95 or $14.95, unless otherwise stated. Prices subject to change without notice.
Canadian prices range from $11.95–$31.95, and are subject to change without notice.

Everything® **Home Decorating Book**
Everything® **Landscaping Book**
Everything® **Lawn Care Book**
Everything® **Organize Your Home Book**

EVERYTHING® *KIDS' BOOKS*

All titles are $6.95
Everything® **Kids' Baseball Book, 3rd Ed.** ($10.95 CAN)
Everything® **Kids' Bible Trivia Book** ($10.95 CAN)
Everything® **Kids' Bugs Book** ($10.95 CAN)
Everything® **Kids' Christmas Puzzle & Activity Book** ($10.95 CAN)
Everything® **Kids' Cookbook** ($10.95 CAN)
Everything® **Kids' Halloween Puzzle & Activity Book** ($10.95 CAN)
Everything® **Kids' Joke Book** ($10.95 CAN)
Everything® **Kids' Math Puzzles Book** ($10.95 CAN)
Everything® **Kids' Mazes Book** ($10.95 CAN)
Everything® **Kids' Money Book** ($11.95 CAN)
Everything® **Kids' Monsters Book** ($10.95 CAN)
Everything® **Kids' Nature Book** ($11.95 CAN)
Everything® **Kids' Puzzle Book** ($10.95 CAN)
Everything® **Kids' Riddles & Brain Teasers Book** ($10.95 CAN)
Everything® **Kids' Science Experiments Book** ($10.95 CAN)
Everything® **Kids' Soccer Book** ($10.95 CAN)
Everything® **Kids' Travel Activity Book** ($10.95 CAN)

KIDS' STORY BOOKS

Everything® **Bedtime Story Book**
Everything® **Bible Stories Book**
Everything® **Fairy Tales Book**
Everything® **Mother Goose Book**

LANGUAGE

Everything® **Inglés Book**
Everything® **Learning French Book**
Everything® **Learning German Book**
Everything® **Learning Italian Book**
Everything® **Learning Latin Book**
Everything® **Learning Spanish Book**
Everything® **Sign Language Book**
Everything® **Spanish Phrase Book,** $9.95 ($15.95 CAN)

MUSIC

Everything® **Drums Book (with CD),** $19.95 ($31.95 CAN)
Everything® **Guitar Book**
Everything® **Playing Piano and Keyboards Book**
Everything® **Rock & Blues Guitar Book (with CD),** $19.95 ($31.95 CAN)
Everything® **Songwriting Book**

NEW AGE

Everything® **Astrology Book**
Everything® **Divining the Future Book**
Everything® **Dreams Book**
Everything® **Ghost Book**
Everything® **Love Signs Book,** $9.95 ($15.95 CAN)
Everything® **Meditation Book**
Everything® **Numerology Book**
Everything® **Palmistry Book**
Everything® **Psychic Book**
Everything® **Spells & Charms Book**
Everything® **Tarot Book**
Everything® **Wicca and Witchcraft Book**

PARENTING

Everything® **Baby Names Book**
Everything® **Baby Shower Book**
Everything® **Baby's First Food Book**
Everything® **Baby's First Year Book**
Everything® **Breastfeeding Book**

Everything® **Father-to-Be Book**
Everything® **Get Ready for Baby Book**
Everything® **Getting Pregnant Book**
Everything® **Homeschooling Book**
Everything® **Parent's Guide to Children with Autism**
Everything® **Parent's Guide to Positive Discipline**
Everything® **Parent's Guide to Raising a Successful Child**
Everything® **Parenting a Teenager Book**
Everything® **Potty Training Book,** $9.95 ($15.95 CAN)
Everything® **Pregnancy Book, 2nd Ed.**
Everything® **Pregnancy Fitness Book**
Everything® **Pregnancy Organizer,** $15.00 ($22.95 CAN)
Everything® **Toddler Book**
Everything® **Tween Book**

PERSONAL FINANCE

Everything® **Budgeting Book**
Everything® **Get Out of Debt Book**
Everything® **Get Rich Book**
Everything® **Homebuying Book, 2nd Ed.**
Everything® **Homeselling Book**
Everything® **Investing Book**
Everything® **Money Book**
Everything® **Mutual Funds Book**
Everything® **Online Investing Book**
Everything® **Personal Finance Book**
Everything® **Personal Finance in Your 20s & 30s Book**
Everything® **Wills & Estate Planning Book**

PETS

Everything® **Cat Book**
Everything® **Dog Book**
Everything® **Dog Training and Tricks Book**
Everything® **Golden Retriever Book**
Everything® **Horse Book**
Everything® **Labrador Retriever Book**
Everything® **Puppy Book**
Everything® **Tropical Fish Book**

All Everything® books are priced at $12.95 or $14.95, unless otherwise stated. Prices subject to change without notice.
Canadian prices range from $11.95–$31.95, and are subject to change without notice.

REFERENCE

Everything® **Astronomy Book**
Everything® **Car Care Book**
Everything® **Christmas Book, $15.00**
  ($21.95 CAN)
Everything® **Classical Mythology Book**
Everything® **Einstein Book**
Everything® **Etiquette Book**
Everything® **Great Thinkers Book**
Everything® **Philosophy Book**
Everything® **Psychology Book**
Everything® **Shakespeare Book**
Everything® **Tall Tales, Legends, &**
  Other Outrageous
  Lies Book
Everything® **Toasts Book**
Everything® **Trivia Book**
Everything® **Weather Book**

RELIGION

Everything® **Angels Book**
Everything® **Bible Book**
Everything® **Buddhism Book**
Everything® **Catholicism Book**
Everything® **Christianity Book**
Everything® **Jewish History &**
  Heritage Book
Everything® **Judaism Book**
Everything® **Prayer Book**
Everything® **Saints Book**
Everything® **Understanding Islam**
  Book
Everything® **World's Religions Book**
Everything® **Zen Book**

SCHOOL & CAREERS

Everything® **After College Book**
Everything® **Alternative Careers Book**
Everything® **College Survival Book**
Everything® **Cover Letter Book**
Everything® **Get-a-Job Book**
Everything® **Hot Careers Book**

Everything® **Job Interview Book**
Everything® **New Teacher Book**
Everything® **Online Job Search Book**
Everything® **Resume Book, 2nd Ed.**
Everything® **Study Book**

SELF-HELP/ RELATIONSHIPS

Everything® **Dating Book**
Everything® **Divorce Book**
Everything® **Great Marriage Book**
Everything® **Great Sex Book**
Everything® **Kama Sutra Book**
Everything® **Romance Book**
Everything® **Self-Esteem Book**
Everything® **Success Book**

SPORTS & FITNESS

Everything® **Body Shaping Book**
Everything® **Fishing Book**
Everything® **Fly-Fishing Book**
Everything® **Golf Book**
Everything® **Golf Instruction Book**
Everything® **Knots Book**
Everything® **Pilates Book**
Everything® **Running Book**
Everything® **Sailing Book, 2nd Ed.**
Everything® **T'ai Chi and QiGong Book**
Everything® **Total Fitness Book**
Everything® **Weight Training Book**
Everything® **Yoga Book**

TRAVEL

Everything® **Family Guide to Hawaii**
Everything® **Guide to Las Vegas**
Everything® **Guide to New England**
Everything® **Guide to New York City**
Everything® **Guide to Washington D.C.**
Everything® **Travel Guide to The**
  Disneyland Resort®,
  California Adventure®,

Universal Studios®, and
  the Anaheim Area
Everything® **Travel Guide to the Walt**
  Disney World Resort®,
  Universal Studios®, and
  Greater Orlando, 3rd Ed.

WEDDINGS

Everything® **Bachelorette Party Book,**
  $9.95 ($15.95 CAN)
Everything® **Bridesmaid Book, $9.95**
  ($15.95 CAN)
Everything® **Creative Wedding Ideas**
  Book
Everything® **Elopement Book, $9.95**
  ($15.95 CAN)
Everything® **Groom Book**
Everything® **Jewish Wedding Book**
Everything® **Wedding Book, 2nd Ed.**
Everything® **Wedding Checklist,**
  $7.95 ($11.95 CAN)
Everything® **Wedding Etiquette Book,**
  $7.95 ($11.95 CAN)
Everything® **Wedding Organizer,**
  $15.00 ($22.95 CAN)
Everything® **Wedding Shower Book,**
  $7.95 ($12.95 CAN)
Everything® **Wedding Vows Book,**
  $7.95 ($11.95 CAN)
Everything® **Weddings on a Budget**
  Book, $9.95 ($15.95 CAN)

WRITING

Everything® **Creative Writing Book**
Everything® **Get Published Book**
Everything® **Grammar and Style Book**
Everything® **Grant Writing Book**
Everything® **Guide to Writing**
  Children's Books
Everything® **Screenwriting Book**
Everything® **Writing Well Book**

Available wherever books are sold!
To order, call 800-872-5627, or visit us at everything.com

Everything® and everything.com® are registered trademarks of F+W Publications, Inc.